Lecture Notes in Computer Sci

T0238312

Commenced Publication in 1973
Founding and Former Series Editors:
Gerhard Goos, Juris Hartmanis, and Jan van Leeuwen

Editorial Board

Nozha Boujemaa   Marcin Detyniecki
Andreas Nürnberger (Eds.)

Adaptive
Multimedial Retrieval:
Retrieval, User,
and Semantics

5th International Workshop, AMR 2007
Paris, France, July 5-6, 2007
Revised Selected Papers

 Springer

Volume Editors

Nozha Boujemaa
INRIA Rocquencourt, 78153 Le Chesnay, France
E-mail: nozha.boujemma@inria.fr

Marcin Detyniecki
University Pierrre and Marie Curie
CNRS - LIP6
75016 Paris, France
E-mail: marcin.detyniecki@lip6.fr

Andreas Nürnberger
Otto-von-Guericke-University Magdeburg
Faculty of Computer Science
39106 Magdeburg, Germany
E-mail: andreas.nuernberger@ovgu.de

Library of Congress Control Number: 2008930128

CR Subject Classification (1998): H.3, H.5.1, H.5.5, I.4, I.2

LNCS Sublibrary: SL 3 – Information Systems and Application,
incl. Internet/Web and HCI

ISSN   0302-9743
ISBN-10   3-540-79859-5 Springer Berlin Heidelberg New York
ISBN-13   978-3-540-79859-0 Springer Berlin Heidelberg New York

Springer is a part of Springer Science+Business Media

springer.com

© Springer-Verlag Berlin Heidelberg 2008
Printed in Germany

Typesetting: Camera-ready by author, data conversion by Scientific Publishing Services, Chennai, India
Printed on acid-free paper   SPIN: 12267644   06/3180   5 4 3 2 1 0

Preface

This book is a selection of the revised contributions that were initially submitted to the International Workshop on Adaptive Multimedia Retrieval (AMR 2007). The workshop was organized at the University Pierre and Marie Curie in Paris, France, during July 5–6, 2007.

The goal of the AMR workshops is to intensify the exchange of ideas between different research communities, to provide an overview of current activities in this area and to point out connections between the diverse involved researches communities, among them the most important ones focussing on multimedia retrieval and artificial intelligence. In this spirit, the first three events where collocated with Artificial Intelligence conferences: in 2003 as a workshop of the 26th German Conference on Artificial Intelligence (KI 2003); in 2004 as part of the 16th European Conference on Artificial Intelligence (ECAI 2004) and in 2005 as part of the 19th International Joint Conference on Artificial Intelligence (IJCAI 05). Because of its success, in 2006 the University of Geneva, Switzerland, organized the workshop for the first time as a standalone event.

In 2007 the workshop revealed three main topics: retrieval, user and semantics. Retrieval, a core subject, was tackled from several perspectives. Researchers were interested not only in the efficiency of the multimedia access by looking at peer-to-peer methods, middleware and databases techniques, but also in the type of retrieved data, ranging from music to images and video. The user was also at the center of attention. Several papers investigated the different ways multimedia data can be searched, as, for instance, through navigation, summaries and interaction. Particular attention was given to methods that try to model the user and its feedback. Finally, in this set of works, it becomes clear that behind the idea of retrieval and user the notion that connects both is hidden: semantics. Most of the works try to respond, at least to a certain degree, to the inherent difficulty when retrieving multimedia data: its non-correspondence between the signal description and the conceptual meaning of the object. Researchers are developing approaches that try either to bridge this gap by, for instance, proposing cross-modal content enrichment through automatic annotation methods, or to get around the difficulty by organizing the meanings through ontologies.

This last point is today at the center of the debate and is emphasized in this book with the two invited contributions presented in the first chapter: "Learning Distance Functions for Automatic Annotation of Images" by Josip Krapac and Frédéric Jurie and "Ontology: Use and Abuse" by Simone Santini. The discussion continues in the other 18 contributions that are classified here into 7 main chapters, following rather closely the workshop's sessions: Image Annotation, Feedback and User Modelling, Music Retrieval, Fusion, P2P and Middleware, Databases and Summarization and Ontology and Semantics. We believe that this book provides a good and conclusive overview of the current research in this area.

We would like to thank all members of the Program Committee for supporting us in the reviewing process, the workshop participants for their willingness to revise and extend their papers for this book, the sponsor for their financial support and Alfred Hofmann from Springer for his support in publishing this book.

January 2008

Nozha Boujemaa
Marcin Detyniecki
Andreas Nürnberger

Organization

General Chair

Nozha Boujemaa   INRIA, Rocquencourt, France

Program Chairs

Marcin Detyniecki   CNRS, Lab. d'Informatique de Paris 6, France
Andreas Nürnberger   University of Magdeburg, Germany

Technical Chair

Christophe Marsala   Lab. d'Informatique de Paris 6 (LIP6), Paris, France

Publicity Chair

Sebastian Stober   University of Magdeburg, Germany

Local Organization

Thomas Bärecke   Lab. d'Informatique de Paris 6 (LIP6), Paris, France

Program Committee

Kobus Barnard	University of Arizona, USA
Jenny Benois-Pineau	University of Bordeaux, LABRI, France
Stefano Berretti	Università di Firenze, Italy
Susanne Boll	University of Oldenburg, Germany
Eric Bruno	University of Geneva, Switzerland
Bogdan Gabrys	Bournemouth University, UK
Ana M. García Serrano	Universidad Politécnica de Madrid, Spain
Xian-Sheng Hua	Microsoft Research, China
Philippe Joly	Université Paul Sabatier, Toulouse, France
Gareth Jones	Dublin City University, Ireland
Joemon Jose	University of Glasgow, UK
Stefanos Kollias	National Technical University of Athens, Greece
Stéphane Marchand-Maillet	University of Geneva, Switzerland

Trevor Martin	University of Bristol, UK
José María Martínez Sánchez	Universidad Autónoma de Madrid, Spain
Bernard Merialdo	Sophia Antipolis Cédex, France
Jan Nesvadba	Philips Research, The Netherlands
Gabriella Pasi	Università degli Studi di Milano Bicocca, Italy
Valery Petrushin	Accenture Technology Labs, Chicago, USA
Stefan Rüger	Imperial College London, UK
Simone Santini	Universidad Autonoma de Madrid, Spain
Raimondo Schettini	University of Milano Bicocca, Italy
Ingo Schmitt	University of Magdeburg, Germany
Nicu Sebe	Leiden University, The Netherlands
Alan F. Smeaton	Dublin City University, Ireland
Arjen De Vries	CWI, Amsterdam, The Netherlands

Supporting Institutions

INRIA, Rocquencourt, France
MUSCLE – EC Network of Excellence Multimedia Understanding
    through Semantics, Computation and Learning
Universite Pierre & Marie Curie, Paris, France
Laboratoire d'Informatique de Paris 6 (LIP6), France

Table of Contents

Fusion

P2P and Middleware

Databases and Summarization

Ontology and Semantics

Learning Distance Functions for Automatic Annotation of Images

Josip Krapac and Frédéric Jurie

INRIA Rhône-Alpes, 655, Avenue de l'Europe, 38334 Saint Ismier Cedex, France
{josip.krapac,frederic.jurie}@inrialpes.fr

Abstract. This paper gives an overview of recent approaches towards image representation and image similarity computation for content-based image retrieval and automatic image annotation (*category tagging*). Additionaly, a new similarity function between an image and an object class is proposed. This similarity function combines various aspects of object class appearance through use of representative images of the class. Similarity to a representative image is determined by weighting local image similarities, where weights are learned from training image pairs, labeled "same" and "different", using linear SVM. The proposed approach is validated on a challenging dataset where it performed favorably.

1 Introduction

In the last decade we have witnessed a rapid increase in the number of digital images. However, the access to this content is hindered by the availability of methods to search and organize it. Available systems that perform these tasks rely on textual information that describes the image's semantics and use text search algorithms to search image collections. Major drawback of this approach is that it limits search only to images for which textual labels are available and since labeling of images is usually performed by humans, it is a slow and inherently subjective process.

Methods that search and organize images by their visual content are known as *content-based image retrieval* (CBIR) methods. This way the problem of absence, incorrectness or incompleteness of textual labels is circumvented.

Applications of CBIR [7] include search of image databases by content, automatic annotation of image collections as well as user localization in real environments and building virtual worlds from real images.

Questions that need to be answered in solving these tasks are: (1) how to represent the images to allow search and organization by their content, (2) how to define similarity function between the image representations so that it reflects human perceptual similarity.

The main contribution of this paper is a new distance function between an image and a category. This distance function is used for propagation of category tags to unannotated images. The distance function to a category is obtained by combining the distance functions to typical representatives of the categories – *focal*

N. Boujemaa, M. Detyniecki, and A. Nürnberger (Eds.): AMR 2007, LNCS 4918, pp. 1–16, 2008.
© Springer-Verlag Berlin Heidelberg 2008

images. The similarity function between focal image and unannotated image combines local similarities from detected, represented and matched image *patches* to obtain global image similarity. The combination of local (patch) similarities which defines global similarity is learned from a few training image pairs labelled as "same" or "different" which labelling presents equvivalence constraints.

The paper is organized as follows: we first give in the next section an overview of recent advances in this very active field, and then describe in Section 3 the proposed approach. Finally, Section 4 gives a few experimental results obtained on a very challenging problem.

2   Related Work

2.1   Global vs. Local Approaches

The first question to ask is what features to extract that will help perform meaningful retrieval. Ideally, features should be related to image semantics, but that is very difficult to obtain because of the semantic gap. However, noticing that there is a statistical dependency between real world raw images' pixels and semantics, it is possible to show that only small amount of information contained in the raw image data is necessary for the image retrieval and classification. Therefore the first step is to choose a suitable low dimensional representation for the image in which information important for discrimination is retained.

First developed methods used global image histograms of color and shape [9] or texture [17] features. The distance between representations is generally computed using L_2 distance, or in case of normalized histograms using standard distance measures between probability distributions: χ^2 distance or KL divergence. While global representations have advantage to be easy to build and to be invariant to position of objects in the image, they provide only a very rough representation of images allowing to deal only with global contexts (like "forest" images) or with objects covering the whole image.

To overcome limitations of global approaches *relevance feedback* has been introduced. The idea is to take the results provided by an algorithm and to use information about whether or not those results are relevant before performing a new query. The feedback, given by the user, allows to weight the image representation before re-computing the distance.

Recently developed image representations overcome problems of global approaches the other way: by representing the image as collection of image parts – patches. These representations are thus called *local representation*.

Most popular way to select patches is by means of interest point detectors [28]. Interest point detector detect characteristic structures (corners [8], blobs [15] or ridges [30]) in the image. One of the main reasons for their popularity is the ability to adapt to scale variation of the characteristic structures, detecting characteristic structure at their *intrinsic scale*. In this case patches are defined as local neighborhoods of detected interest points at detected intrinsic scale of characteristic structure.

Patches can also be sampled randomly [24] or even densely [32] from the image.

Selected patches are described by signatures or *patch descriptor*. Important condition on design of patch descriptor is their robustness to various photomotric and geometric transformations in the sense that patches that belong to *same* object parts should have *same* descriptions. To achieve invariance to these changes, patch descriptors either model the distribution or characterize the properties of distribution of patch's color [31], grayscale values [25,12] or response of filter banks which describe local texture (SIFT [16], textons [14], geometric blur [2], PCA-SIFT [13]). In the case when patches are obtained by segmentation they can be described by the shape of segment boundary [1].

2.2   Query-by-Example Image Search

Local image representation maps image into a set of patches described by visual descriptors. This image representation scheme can be used for building image search algorithms because images can be compared by comparing two sets of visual descriptors. Schmid and Mohr [28] propose to match the visual descriptors extracted from the query image with those extracted from the images in the image database and to vote for the image from database that accumulates the largest number of matched keypoints.

This very efficient yet powerful approach have been used by many authors for different tasks such as the localization of the camera [5,10], the reconstruction of 3D scenes by assembling images searched over the Internet [5,10] or the navigation of autonomous robots [22].

2.3   Category Tagging

These approaches allow to search images by presenting an example image as query. To broaden the application of image search methods beyond these *query-by-example* approaches, a small set of images is semantically annotated by humans with category tags that semanticaly describe image's content, so that images can be searched both by content *and* semantics. The problem is then how to propagate category tags from annotated to unannotated images.

This enriching images with tags related to their content, termed here as *category tagging*, can be casted as a binary classification problem: if the image belongs to the category – the corresponding tag is added. Generally, *recognition algorithms* which assign an object identifier to an image possibly containing the object, are used for tagging images.

One strong limitation of these early patch based approaches for category tagging is their restriction to the recognition of images that are strictly identical to the query. This is because the comparison is based on the matching of local structures, which are assumed to be strictly identical.

We are here more interested in methods working at the *category level* instead of the *instance level*. The difference between *object instance recognition* and *object class recognition* is in the definition of the visual class denoted by object identifier. In the former case all images that contain the exactly same object instance (eg. same car) are tagged as belonging to same visual category, so images containing different object instances belong to different visual categories (eg. different car models). In later case all images that contain the same object class are tagged as belonging to the same visual category (eg. cars are one visual category, cats are other visual category...).

In object instance recognition only variability between the images of same object is due to changes in object pose (changes of observer's viewpoint with respect to the object), object configuration (changes between parts of the object with respect to each other) and scene illumination. Object surface can locally be approximated by a plane so local pose changes can be approximated as rigid, and hence majority of research efforts are concentrated on capturing the variation due to object pose [19] in local descriptions. In object class recognition there is additional variability due to intra-class (or within-class) differences between objects of the same visual class. This variability is complex and hard to characterize as it stems from assigment of semantic category tags, and thus makes the problem of object class recognition significantly harder then problem of object instance recognition.

2.4   Visual Vocabularies

Because of large intra class variation of object appearances and because of the small number of training data generally available, building geometric models of classes is difficult, not to say impossible. Similar problem occurs in texture classification, which can be considered as a source of inspiration for object class recognition problems. Interestingly, Malik et al. [14], in their work on texture classification, suggest to vector quantize local descriptors of images (called *textons*) and then to compute texton statistics.

This idea of building a distance between images based on the comparison of texton statistics have then been widely used for image classification. Indeed, instead of comparing the two sets directly (each patch with each patch) an indirection step in introduced – description of patch by *visual word*. Visual words are quantized patch description vectors, where quantization bins can be obtained by clustering (K-means [29], hierarchical k-means [18], mean shift [11]) of training description vectors. Visual word is representative of the bin (cluster), and set of all visual words is called *visual vocabulary*. Analogously to descriptions of text documents, here an image is described by occurrences of visual words. This representation relies on local descriptions and is invariant geometrical structure (layout) of detected patches and hence is termed *bag-of-(visual) words representation*. Each image is described by histogram of occurrences of visual words that are present in the image, so that each object class is characterized by a distribution of visual words.

Visual vocabulary influences the classification performance, so creation of visual vocabulary is an important step. Majority of clustering techniques used for creation of visual vocabulary are computationally expensive, and more importantly, don't use the information about patch class so created vocabularies are not discriminative.

In [20] extremely randomized forests were used for vocabulary creation. Creation of random forest is computationally much less complex then other methods of vocabulary creation, while attaining comparable results. Also, patch class labels are used to guide the cluster splitting towards creation of discriminative clusters.

The very recent Pascal VOC2007 image categorization challenge[1] has demonstrated the superiority of these vocabulary based approaches over all other competitive ones.

2.5   Similarity Functions and Focal Images

In [23] similar approach was used to learn the similarity function between images from train image pairs labeled "same" or "different". Image pair is represented by the set of patch pairs, which are formed in process of *patch matching*. Instead of quantization of patch descriptions, *pairs* of patch descriptions were quantized discriminatively using extremely randomized forests. Each visual word in this case represents the characteristic local (patch) (dis)similarity. The patch pairs are weighted towards "same" or "different" prediction by linear classifier, so global similarity is obtained by weighting and integrating over local (patch) similarities. We use this algorithm to build the visual vocabularies and measure image distance to focal images.

Regarding the class models, our work is inspired by the recent work of Frome *et al.* In [6] classification of query image is performed by combining the similarities to representative images of the object class – *focal images*, and choosing the class for the query image with biggest combined similarity. Similarity is learned from training image pairs, for each focal image separately. This is an example of divide-and-conquer approach, since calculating the similarity to an image is easier task then calculating the similarity to a class, because class has more complex feature distribution then an image.

Our work is inspired by both approaches: we use focal images to divide problem into simpler problems, but we learn similarity measure as in [23].

3   Method

As mentioned before, we cast the *category tagging* problem as the problem of object class recognition, i.e. we determine the classes a *query image* belongs to.

In general, the decision of object class membership is brought by calculating a measure of similarity to each learned object class for given query image and comparing that similarity measure with a threshold. If the similarity is high enough, the tag is added.

Here, inspired by [6], we experiment with a different approach. We calculate similarity between query image and an object class by combining similarity measures calculated between query image and representative images of an object class. Representative images of an object class are called *focal images*.

---

[1] http://www.pascal-network.org/challenges/VOC/voc2007/

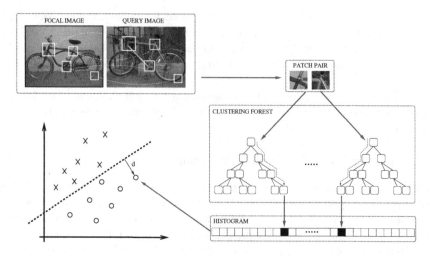

Fig. 1. Similarity between focal image and query image: 1) Matching patch pairs 2) Clustering patch pairs by clustering forest 3) Representation of image pair by histogram of cluster occurrences 4) Weighting clusters to calculate similarity d between focal image and query image

The overview of similarity the measure calculation for an image is outlined in the Fig. 1, while in Fig. 2 we show how we bring the final decision by combining the results of similarities to focal images.

3.1 Similarity to the Focal Image

For each focal image we construct a classifier that gives the measure of similarity between the selected focal image and the query image. Training image pairs (focal,query) are formed and labelled "same" and "different" by choosing the query images of a known class from training set. The calculation of similarity measure between the focal image and the query image, as illustrated Fig. 1, can be divided in 4 steps.

Step 1: Selection, Description and Matching of Patches. We represent the image as a collection of patches and use an interest point detector to select the patches.

Using interest point detector ensures that local image structures detected in one image will be also detected in other images, an important requirement for creating patch pairs by matching of selected patches. Although one could question if the patches selected this way are discriminative enough to be used in challenging task of object class recognition, we believe that by selecting a large number of patches we will be able to form patch pairs which are discriminative for an object class.

Motivated by results of a recent comparative study [18] of interest point detectors and descriptors for object class recognition we use scale-invariant Hessian point detector, which enables the patch description to be invariant to structure's scale, and consequently makes our methods invariant to the scale of the object.

We choose SIFT [16] descriptor to describe patches, because it has been shown to be sufficiently robust to capture the intra-class variance of patches [18]. Patch pairs are formed by selecting similar patches in two images, where similarity between patches relates inversely to L_2 distance between patches' SIFT descriptors.

Step 2: Clustering Patch Pairs. Once we have formed patch pairs that describe local similarities between focal and query image we can combine these local similarities to form global similarity. Instead of using only the distance between visual descriptors to describe local similarities (as in [6]) we introduce clustering step to additionally characterize the similarity between patches. We choose to cluster patch pairs using EXTRA trees, motivated by their good performance in the similar task of learning of the distance between images [23]. Each cluster describes characteristic patch (dis)similarity.

EXTRA trees are binary trees constructed by recursively splitting the nodes on the basis of labelled data in the node. The process starts from the root node, which contains all training patch pairs from focal image to query images. At each node, we randomly generate a number of splitting criteria and select the optimal splitting criterion for the node.

Splitting criterion $c(\cdot, \cdot | i, s, t)$ is binary predicate that as input has a pair of patches, represented as pair of vectors $\mathbf{f}^{\text{focal}}$ and $\mathbf{f}^{\text{query}}$ and is determined by parameters i,s and t. Parameter i selects the dimension of vector which represents the patches in the pair, t is threshold and $s \in \{-1, 1\}$ determines sign of comparison:

$$c(\mathbf{f}^{\text{focal}}, \mathbf{f}^{\text{query}} | i, s, t) = (s \cdot (\mathbf{f}_i^{\text{focal}} - t) \geq 0) \wedge (s \cdot (\mathbf{f}_i^{\text{query}} - t) \geq 0) \qquad (1)$$

We can interpret the above equation as: "If i^{th} dimension of *both* focal image patch vector and query image patch vector are above (or below, depending on s) threshold t then splitting criterion is true." Random splitting criterion is created by selecting parameters i, s and t at random.

When splitting criterion is applied to all patch pairs in the current node of the tree it splits the patch pairs into two disjunctive sets: a set of patch pairs for which the splitting criterion is true, and a set of patch pairs for which the splitting criterion is false. These sets correspond to two child nodes. The optimality of splitting criterion is evaluated by its information gain IG which is calculated from the two sets obtained by applying the splitting criterion: $IG = H - \frac{n_0 H_0 + n_1 H_1}{n}$, where H,H_0 and H_1 denote, respectively, the entropy of patch pairs in current (parent) node, entropy of patch pairs for which splitting criterion is false (entropy of first child) and entropy of patch pairs for which splitting criterion is true (entropy of second child node). Similarly n,n_0 and n_1 denote, respectively, numbers of patch pairs in the parent node, first and second child. The criterion with highest information gain is selected for the node.

By selecting this optimality measure of splitting criteria we supervise the clustering process to create discriminative clusters. Each leaf of the tree is a cluster which defines similarity between patches of the match: patch similarity is determined by the path the patch pair took from root to leaf node.

The main advantage of random trees is computational simplicity of construction because, in contrast to methods that search the optimal values of splitting criterion parameters, we just select them at random and keep the one with highest information gain. On the other hand, randomness responsible for computational simplicity of construction increases variance of resulting clusterer.

To reduce the variance introduced by random sampling of parameters of splitting criteria we use a number of independently grown trees – a clustering forest [23]. Since every tree defines a different clustering of patch pair feature space, every pair of patches reaches several clusters (leaves of the trees in the forest) – one cluster per tree in the forest.

The number of patch pairs to create the clusterer is question of bias/variance trade-off. If we construct a tree from too small number of patch pairs the variance will be large and if we use all available matches we will over-fit the training data so clusters will be specific to training data and will not generalize to test data. On the other hand,as always in vision, the available data is scarce and we want to use information from all available patch pairs. Intermediate solution is to create tree using all available matches, but stop the splitting of the node if number of patch pairs remaining in the node is too small, to prevent over-fitting. This procedure is known as *pruning*.

Step 3: Representing a Pair of Images by Histogram. Global similarity between focal image and query image is represented by a set of patch pairs. Using the clusterer we represent global similarity between focal and query image by a histogram of occurrences of clusters that describe local (patch) (dis)similarities.

Having constructed clusterer we can represent every pair of images (focal, query) by a histogram of occurrences of clusters – leaves in the forest which are reached by patch pairs from this pair of images.

The histogram of pair of images is interpreted as a vector in a high dimensional space where each dimension of a vector (each histogram bin) corresponds to a cluster (leaf of the forest).

We choose to binarize histograms, as in [20], to avoid the problem of non-binary normalized histograms where the influence of small (relative) number of discriminative patch pairs can be reduced by a large (relative) number of non-discriminative ones.

Step 4: Weighing the Clusters. We believe that clusters are specific to an object class and that some clusters are more significant for the similarities of objects within the class (and dissimilarities of objects between the classes) then the others. This relative relevance of clusters for classification is acknowledged by assigning weights to clusters.

Since for every query image in the training set we know the true class we use this information to learn the linear classifier to find a hyper-plane that separates pairs of images of the same class as focal image from pairs of images which have different class from focal image. The normal to the obtained hyper-plane is a

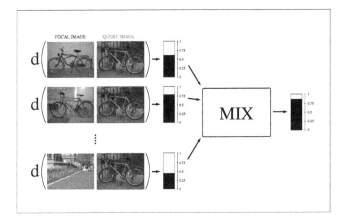

Fig. 2. Combining distances from focal images to query image by mixture of experts

vector of weights that reflect relative importance of clusters (local similarities) for classification (global similarity).

We use linear support vector machine as a classifier because for a large number of applications it has shown good generalization performance when using high dimensional data and small training set, as it is our case.

3.2 Similarity to an Object Category

Focal images represent the different aspects of object class appearance. To obtain similarity of a query image to an object category we need to combine all learned similarities to focal images. We call the classifiers that give similarity measures to the focal images *base classifiers*, and their scores *similarities*.

In general, to combine base classifiers their decisions must be comparable. Standard way is to convert similarities to probabilities, so for each query image classifier reports probability that query image belongs to the same categories as focal image.

To this end we use Platt's scaling [27], a procedure that finds the parameters of the sigmoid function that performs mapping of base classifier's scores (similarities) to probabilities by maximum likelihood fit to the data. It has been shown that this procedure outperforms others in case of small learning sets [21]. To find these parameters we have used the validation set. In the rest of the paper we will assume that similarities are mapped to probabilities and will use terms *similarities* and *probability estimates* interchangeably.

To combine the probability estimates of base classifiers, in absence of any additional information about the data that would guide the combination process, fixed rules are usually used. The most common fixed rules are: sum, product, median, maximum and minimum of all scores of base classifiers [4].

Most commonly used fixed rule is the "sum of scores" rule, also used by [6] to combine the similarities from focal images. This rule assumes that all classifiers have the same influence on the combined decision.

Each of these fixed rules will perform well if some assumptions are satisfied [4], but since these assumptions are never fully satisfied we can always find a better way to combine classifiers if we use specific information about the data we want to combine.

This is why we train linear SVM to learn the classifier relative weights on the validation data. Since category tags are available for the images in the validation set we can use probability estimates of base classifiers on validation data as training data for *mixture-of-experts* classifier that learns classifier weights. Learned weight vector can have negative components, which means that we reverse decisions of some classifiers. To avoid this anomaly, we map negative components of weight vector $\mathbf{w}^c$ by taking their absolute value and dividing it by L_1 norm of the weight vector:

$$w_i^{c'} = \frac{|w_i^c|}{\sum_{i=1}^{N_c} |w_i^c|}$$

The decision is then brought by *weighted sum* rule, where weights are learned by combining linear classifier and mapped to be positive.

4   Experimental Results

4.1   Dataset

We have tested the proposed method on Graz-02 database [26]. This database has been designed for object recognition or object categorization, containing images with objects of high complexity, high intra-class variability and highly cluttered backgrounds.

We used only two classes: bicycles and background. Bicycles are selected to have same orientation which leaves 102 images of bicycles and 300 images of background.

The data-set is divided in 4 subsets: set of focal images, training set, validation set and testing set. Half of randomly selected images are selected for testing, and another half is divided between testing and validation set. Images in the training set are used to learn the clusterer (EXTRA trees) and classifier (SVM), and images in the validation set are used to find the parameters of sigmoid function that performs mapping of similarities to probabilities and to find the mixture-of-experts classifier weights.

We have selected 8 focal images from the class of bicycles: in first four focal images different types of bicycles (corresponding to different aspects of bicycle class distribution) are prominent object in the image; in the remaining focal images bicycles are not prominent due to various degradations (small scale of the object, occlusions, overlapping and low contrast).

4.2   Experimental Setup

We use scale-invariant Hessian point detector to select the patches from imagesm and set low detection threshold to get enough patches for construction of patch pairs. The scaling factor between neighboring scales of image pyramid, used in the process of scale selection, is set to 1.2. We discard the patches detected at small scales.

For patch description we use SIFT descriptor. SIFT descriptors are calculated at scale detected by scale-invariant Hessian interest point detector. For SIFT descriptor we use 4 bins for spatial distribution of gradients (both in x and y direction) and 8 bins to describe gradient orientation distribution, giving a 128-dimensional patch descriptor. Descriptors are normalized to have L_2 norm equal to 1 so they are invariant to affine illumination changes.

We use 5 trees in the forest, motivated by results of [23]. The dimension of histogram that represents the pair of images is approximately 20000. Average depth of the trees is 39 ± 4.

For weighting the clusters we use C-SVM, with parameter $C = 1$.

We have used Platt's scaling implementation from LIBSVM library [3] to perform mapping of similarities to probabilities.

Performance is expressed as equal error rate (EER) of precision and recall. For each focal image, due to random nature of classifier construction, we construct 5 classifiers and report mean and standard deviation.

4.3   Matching Patch Pairs

We constrain matching procedure by forming matches for each patch in the focal with just the most similar patch in query image. We call this kind of matching *unidirectional matching*.

Bidirectional matching is the matching procedure which additionally constrains unidirectional matches to keep only the patch pairs which are most similar in other direction also (from query image to focal image).

Using the unidirectional matching the number of patch pairs is equal to number of patches in focal image, while with bidirectional matching limits the number of patch pairs to $\min(N_{\text{focal}}, N_{\text{query}})$, where N denotes the number of patches detected in the image. This is why in case of unidirectional matching we use binary histograms, while in case of bidirectional matching the use of binary histograms would introduce bias due to different number of patch pairs per query image. In latter case we therefore use non-binary histograms and normalize them (to have L_1 norm 1) to make the description vector of image pair invariant to number of formed patch pairs.

We conducted experiments to test the effectiveness of described matching strategies. The results are presented in Table 1.

Table 1. Influence of matching patch pairs strategy to classification results

Focal image ID	1	2	3	4	5	6	7	8	all
unidirectional matching	0.88	0.85	0.88	0.87	0.89	0.87	0.90	0.86	**0.87 ± 0.02**
bidirectional matching	0.82	0.83	0.82	0.82	0.83	0.75	0.80	0.82	**0.81 ± 0.03**

This results show that unidirectional matching performs better. This results can be explained by several reasons:

- Number of matches to describe the image is smaller in case of bidirectional matching, which means that clusters will be formed on the basis of smaller amount of data and hence may not be representative characterization of local (dis)similarities.
- Representation of image pair by non-binary histogram causes the suppression of small, but important discriminative clusters
- Bidirectional matching limits the patch matching to patches from region of feature space where feature distributions of both images overlap. If in this region most patches belong to background we will not be able to learn from patches that belong to object.

4.4   Creation of the Clustering Forest

We have performed the experiments to determine what is the best way to create the clusterer with given number of matches. We have created the clusterer using only 5% and 20% of available training patch pairs, selected randomly from all available training patch pairs. In this case we do not need to prune the trees. When we use all training patch pairs we prune the trees, when node contains less then 20 patch pairs, by turning the node into leaf. Table 2. summarizes the experiment's results.

Results of experiments show that our assumption was correct: the trees created from only 5% of patch pairs perform worse than the ones created with 20%. Although the results of experiments in last two columns of Table 2. are the same, we choose to use the trees created from all available patch pairs because we do not introduce randomness due to nature of patch pairs selection to create the clustering forest.

4.5   Influence of Context

To investigate the influence of background patches we have cropped images of the bicycles to contain only the bicycles (object). We have lowered the detection threshold of interest point detector to 0 to get approximately same number of patch detections in cropped image as in original, uncropped one.

The results in Table 3. show that for some focal images context (background) shows important role, especially in focal image 5 where bicycle is not prominent object in the image due to small scale. For focal image 7 results are also significantly worse when using cropped images. In this image bicycles are overlapping (stacked one behind another), and therefore, because of the overlap, parts of the bicycles locally do not look like bicycles. The good result of the method on these focal images in uncropped case can be explained by influence of patch pairs

Table 2. Influence of percentage of matches to create the clusterer

% matches to create clusterer	5%	20%	100%
Pruned	no	no	yes
EER of PR	0.80 ± 0.03	0.83 ± 0.03	0.83 ± 0.03

Table 3. Influence of background of matches to classification results

Focal image ID	1	2	3	4	5	6	7	8	all
object + background	0.88	0.84	0.88	0.87	0.88	0.86	0.90	0.86	0.87 ± 0.02
object		0.87	0.83	0.85	0.86	0.76	0.85	0.83	0.86	0.84 ± 0.03

formed from background patches in focal image. Nevertheless, for majority of focal images results are not significantly influenced by patch pairs formed from background patches, so we can conclude that method learns to discriminate the object dominantly from object part of image.

4.6 Combination of Classifiers

We have performed experiment with use of fixed rules to combine the probability estimates of base classifiers and compared with results of a linear support vector machine (weighted sum). The results are presented in Table 4.

4.7 Advantages and Limitations

The results are presented for one focal image, because the results for other focal images are similar, so advantages and limitations of the method can be empathized on one example. From results of classification for first focal image presented in the Fig. 3 we can conclude that similarity is correctly determined as high for images where object (bicycle) is dominant in the image. Since the bicycles are not compact objects there is large amount of background present even in the patches which contain parts of the bicycle. For bicycles which have simple, almost uniform background the performance is good. Majority of misclassified bicycles (detected as background) displays has complex, textured background or/and object of the small size compared to size of the background. The low performance in this case can be explained by the small fraction of detected patches that belong to the object.

Background images misclassified as object all display parts that are locally similar to bicycle parts due to significant texture whose rich structure ensures existence of these local similarities. The misclassification can be explained by observing the patches that contribute to misclassification (patches that are weighted towards prediction "same as object class"). Our matching procedure is not constrained to one-to-one matches and hence it is possible to have *popular patches* in query image – patches that are matched to many patches in focal image (e.g. in the case of misclassifier motorbike brake handle is matched to parts of bycicle's frame). If this patch pair is similar in the way the object patch pairs are then it will be assigned to cluster that is weighted for object class

Table 4. Results of classifier combination

Combination rule	max	min	median	sum	product	weighted sum (linear SVM)
EER of PR	0.84	0.88	0.86	0.86	0.86	0.88

Fig. 3. Results for first focal image. First row: focal image, second row: first 3 most similar images, third row: two false positive followed by two false negative images, fourth row: last 3 most similar images.

prediction and wrong decision will be brought. To solve this problem a better matching procedure has to be employed, perhaps also including simple geometric constraints.

As expected, images which are misclassified for all focal images are misclassified in combination, which means that we could get better results using combination of classifiers only if we improve the performance of base classifiers.

5   Conclusion

We have given an on overview of approaches for image description and image similarity measures used for content-based image retrieval.

The matching in the case of object classes is not well defined problem since definition of "corresponding part" is ambiguous. It has been shown that matching strategy, which determines "corresponding parts", severely influences the results, and we believe that better matching strategy could improve the results.

We employed divide-and-conquer strategy through use of focal images, and we have shown that in the case of complex problem of object class recognition (used here for category tagging) it has shown to be beneficial.

Additional work is required to fully validate these preliminary results. First, it would be interesting to experiment the approach with more categories and evaluate the performance on large scale problems. Second, as the question of finding best correspondences between categories is the most critical part of the proposed algorithm, it would be interesting to try to learn to find these correspondences using labeled sets of corresponding parts.

References

1. Belongie, S., Malik, J., Puzicha, J.: Shape matching and object recognition using shape contexts. IEEE Trans. Pattern Anal. Mach. Intell. 24(4), 509–522 (2002)
2. Berg, A.C., Malik, J.: Geometric blur for template matching. In: CVPR, vol. 1, pp. 607–614 (2001)
3. Chang, C., Lin, C.: LIBSVM: A library for support vector machines (2001), http://www.csie.ntu.edu.tw/~cjlin/libsvm
4. Duin, R.P.W.: The combining classifier: To train or not to train? In: ICPR (2002)
5. Fritz, G., Seifert, C., Paletta, L.: A mobile vision system for urban detection with informative local descriptors. In: Computer Vision Systems (2006)
6. Frome, A., Singer, Y., Malik, J.: Image retrieval and classification using local distance functions. In: NIPS, pp. 417–424. MIT Press, Cambridge, MA (2007)
7. Gudivada, V.N., Raghavan, V.V.: Content-based image retrieval-systems. Computer 28(9), 18–22 (1995)
8. Harris, C., Stephens, M.: A combined corner and edge detector. In: Proc. of Fourth Alvey Vision Conf., pp. 147–151 (1988)
9. Jain, A.K., Vailaya, A.: Image retrieval using color and shape. Pattern Recognition (1996)
10. Johansson, B., Cipolla, R.: A system for automatic pose-estimation from a single image in a city scene. In: Int. Conf. Signal Proc. Pattern Rec. and Analysis (2002)
11. Jurie, F., Triggs, B.: Creating efficient codebooks for visual recognition. In: International Conference on Computer Vision (2005)
12. Kadir, T., Brady, M.: Saliency, scale and image description. International Journal of Computer Vision V45(2), 83–105 (2001)
13. Ke, Y., Sukthankar, R.: Pca-sift: a more distinctive representation for local image descriptors. In: CVPR 2004, pp. II: 506–513 (2004)
14. Leung, T., Malik, J.: Recognizing surfaces using three-dimensional textons. In: ICCV, vol. 2, pp. 1010–1017. IEEE, Los Alamitos, CA (1999)
15. Lindeberg, T.: Feature detection with automatic scale selection. Int. J. Comput. Vision 30(2), 79–116 (1998)
16. Lowe, D.G.: Distinctive image features from scale-invariant keypoints. Int. J. Comput. Vision 60(2), 91–110 (2004)
17. Manjunath, B.S., Ma, W.Y.: Texture features for browsing and retrieval of image data. IEEE Trans. Pattern Anal. Mach. Intell. 18(8), 837–842 (1996)
18. Mikolajczyk, K., Leibe, B., Schiele, B.: Local features for object class recognition. In: ICCV, vol. 2, pp. 1792–1799. IEEE, Los Alamitos, CA (2005)
19. Mikolajczyk, K., Schmid, C.: Scale and affine invariant interest point detectors. International Journal of Computer Vision 60(1), 63–86 (2004)
20. Moosmann, F., Triggs, B., Jurie, F.: Fast discriminative visual codebooks using randomized clustering forests. In: NIPS, pp. 985–992 (2007)
21. Niculescu-Mizil, A., Caruana, R.: Predicting good probabilities with supervised learning. In: ICML, pp. 625–632. ACM, New York, NY, USA (2005)
22. Nistér, D., Naroditsky, O., Bergen, J.: Visual odometry for ground vehicle applications. Journal of Field Robotics 23(1), 3–20 (2006)
23. Nowak, E., Jurie, F.: Learning visual similarity measures for comparing never seen objects. In: CVPR. IEEE, Los Alamitos, CA (2007)
24. Nowak, E., Jurie, F., Triggs, B.: Sampling strategies for bag-of-features image classification. In: European Conference on Computer Vision. Springer, Heidelberg (2006)

25. Obdrzalek, S., Matas, J.: Object recognition using local affine frames on distinguished regions. In: BMVA 2002, vol. 1, pp. 113–122 (2002)
26. Opelt, A., Pinz, A., Fussenegger, M., Auer, P.: Generic object recognition with boosting. IEEE Trans. Pattern Anal. Mach. Intell. 28(3), 416–431 (2006)
27. Platt, J.: Probabilistic outputs for support vector machines and comparison to regularized likelihood methods. Technical report, Microsoft Research (1999)
28. Schmid, C., Mohr, R.: Local grayvalue invariants for image retrieval. IEEE Transactions on Pattern Analysis and Machine Intelligence 19(5), 530–535 (1997)
29. Sivic, J., Zisserman, A.: Video google: A text retrieval approach to object matching in videos. In: ICCV 2003, pp. 1470–1477 (2003)
30. Steger, C.: An unbiased detector of curvilinear structures. IEEE Trans. Pattern Anal. Mach. Intell. 20(2), 113–125 (1998)
31. van de Weijer, J., Schmid, C., Verbeek, J.: Learning color names from real-world images. In: CVPR (June 2007)
32. Winn, J., Criminisi, A., Minka, T.: Object categorization by learned universal visual dictionary. In: Computer Vision, 2005. ICCV 2005. Tenth IEEE International Conference, vol. 2, pp. 1800–1807 (2005)

Ontology: Use and Abuse

Simone Santini

Escuela Politécnica Superior, Universidad Autónoma de Madrid, Spain

Abstract. This paper is a critical analysis of the use of ontology as an instrument to specify the semantics of a document. The paper argue that not only is a logic of the type used in ontology insufficient for such a purpose, but that the very idea that meaning is a property of a document that can be expressed and stored independently of the interpretation activity is misguided.

The paper proposes, in very general lines, a possible alternative view of meaning as modification of context and shows that many current approaches to meaning, from ontology to emergent semantics, can be seen as spacial cases of this approach, and can be analyzed from a very general theoretical framework.

In his book *What do you care what other people think?* the physicist Richard Feynmann remembers the way his father used to teach him about birds on their hiking trips together:

> "See that bird?" he says "It's a Spencer's warbler." (I knew he didn't know the real name.) "Well, in Italian, it's a *Chutto lapittida*. In Portugese is a *Bom da Peida*. In Chinese is a *Chung-long-ta*, and in Japanese it's a *Katano Tekeda*. You can know the name of that bird in all the languages of the world, but when you are finished, you'll know absolutely nothing whatever about the bird. You'll only know about humans in different places, and what they call the bird."[1]

I am often reminded of this story when I think of ontology. The feeling I have is that one can encode a document in whatever formalism one can think of, as many times as one wants but, in the end, one will know nothing about the document, only something about the person who encoded it.

Generally speaking, computational ontology, which I will simply call *ontology*, is an attempt to encode the semantics of a text or of a document in a formal structure that can be manipulated following logical (syntactic) rules. A formula, really. In this paper, I will use the word *text* in the very extended sense in which semioticians use it: to me, for the purposes of this paper, a written document, an image, a video, fashion, a series of moves in a chess games, the etiquette on how to behave in a given circumstances, and many, many other things, are examples of texts.

Some of the texts for which one might want to formalize a meaning are themselves highly formalized, programming languages, for example. I am not interested in them here, although they will make a fleeting appearance later on. I am interested in the texts that people use to communicate with each other, of which one can ask with some

---

[1] (Feynman, 1988), p. 13-14.

N. Boujemaa, M. Detyniecki, and A. Nürnberger (Eds.): AMR 2007, LNCS 4918, pp. 17–31, 2008.

interest "What do they mean?". Ontology tries to answer this question by creating a logic theory meant to give the possibility to *process* the meaning of texts in an automatic fashion. Using an algorithm, as it is. The adjective "syntactic", in parentheses in the previous paragraph, is in this sense very important: logic systems manipulate data based on their *form*, not on their meaning; in this sense ontology can be seen as an attempt to reduce semantics to syntax. Note that ontology makes weaker (viz. less assailable) epistemological claims than artificial intelligence[2]: it never assumes that meaning can be extracted from a text and encoded in an automatic fashion. Ontologists are quite content with the idea that a person might have to be there to make the encoding. What they *do* assume is that a formal code exists in which meaning can be translated and that, once the translation is done, meaning can be accessed through an algorithm, that is, through syntactic means. They do not assume that the semantics of a document can be interpreted in the document itself, but they do assume that there is a code in which semantics reduces to syntax.

My purpose in this paper is to analyze the plausibility of these assumptions. I will present several reasons to believe that the theoretical assumptions of ontology, although weaker than those of "strong" artificial intelligence, are no more tenable than those. I will argue this point based on what we now about the semantics of natural language. It is worth noticing that the objections I will make do not cover the whole field of application of ontology. In Section 3 I will make a distinction between eminently *syntactic* applications, such as schema integration (Hakimpour & Geppert, 2001), and those that claim to be doing *semantics*. The prototype of the latter class of application are the rather extravagant claims of the *semantic web* (Berners-Lee, Hendler & Lassila, 2001). What the web semanticians are after is nothing less than the codification of the meaning of web sites, with their multimedia expressivity and cultural variability.

The first class of applications is, *mutatis mutandis* a slight variation of what was once known as *deductive databases*. While I don't see any major breakthrough coming from the renewed interest and the new terminology that are being used these days, there are certainly problems in this general area that can benefit from the "ontological" methods. The second class of problems is the focus of this paper and, I will argue, the area where the claims are more doubtful and less supported.

1   What Is an Ontology?

A good answer to this question is surprisingly difficult to find. The definition that is usually quoted comes from (Uschold & Gruninger, 1996) and sounds something like this:

> [an ontology is] an explicit account of a *shared understanding*[3]

This definition is bizarre for at least three reasons. The first is the presence of the word *shared*. Now, it is true that in general one creates an ontology in order to share

---

[2] Weaker in this context means that it stands on a smaller number of hypotheses, that is, that it doesn't assume as much. In this sense of the term, a weaker assumption is harder to disprove.

[3] Emphasis in the original.

it but why on God's green earth shouldn't I be allowed to create an ontology only for myself? Looking at the definition it seems that, if I create a certain artifact (we'll see which) for myself it is not an ontology but, at the moment when I share it with my friend Bob from down the street, it becomes, *ipso facto*, one. I am not quite sure this is what Uschold had in mind but, as they say, *scripta manent*, and this is a logical consequence of his definition.

The second is the presence of the word *understanding*. The word sounds suspiciously related to the "offer he cannot refuse" from the *Godfather* but, apart from this, such a crucial point of the definition is no clearer than the thing that one is trying to define. If we don't know what an understanding is, this definition will tell us nothing about the substance of an ontology. So, what is an understanding? The ontologists don't tell us.

But the main problem of this definition is that it is not *structural* but *functional*: it doesn't tell us what an ontology *is* but, simply, what it is used *for*. Allow me to make a parallel. Take a well known computing concept, that of formal grammar. Had the same style of definition been used in that case, a formal grammar would be defined as:

a formal grammar is the specification of a programming language.

Any computing scientist worth her salary knows that this is not a proper way to define a formal grammar, because the definition doesn't tell what a grammar is, but merely what one of its possible uses is. Rather, we define it as a quadruple N, T, P, s, where N is a set of non-terminals, T a set of terminals disjoint from N, P a set of pairs called productions (whose precise definition depends on the type of grammar), and $s \in N$ the initial non-terminal.

Can one find a similar definition of ontology? There doesn't seem to be a widespread agreement on any precise definition, but one can try to unify the common usages of the term. One relatively uncontroversial aspect of the matter is that an ontology is a system of axioms that spell out the rules that allow reasoning on the terms of a certain domain. Terms in the axioms are usually interpreted as universals in an extensional interpretation of meaning. In other words, they are interpreted as sets of individuals.

Also, an ontology contains more than just axioms: it also contains the definition of the terms in the domain of discourse and the relations that, subject to the axioms, hold between these terms: more than a set of axioms, it looks like a logical *theory*. We can therefore give a first, quite informal, definition of ontology:

An ontology is a theory that admits a model that associates a set to each term defined in the theory.

We still haven't specified what kind of logic system should be used to express the theory. To see what this entails, consider a simple system that defines three terms: *person*, *employee*, and *retiree*. Ontologists are fond of taxonomies, so the first thing an ontologist would do is to say that *retiree* and *employee* are *subsorts* of *person*. This entails defining, in our theory, a subsort relation $\preceq$, introducing axioms for it, and then declaring which terms are in that relation:

$$\forall X, Y, x \ \ X \preceq Y \ \wedge \ X(x) \ \Rightarrow \ Y(x) \tag{1}$$

(here I have used the convention that upper-case letters denote sets, and lower-case letter denote elements of the set. Also $X(x)$ is the unary predicate "x is an X".)

$$\text{employee} \preceq \text{person} \tag{2}$$
$$\text{retiree} \preceq \text{person}$$

and similarly for the disjunction relation $\neq$:

$$\forall X, Y, x \ \ X \neq Y \wedge X(x) \Rightarrow \neg Y(x) \tag{3}$$

$$\text{employee} \neq \text{retiree} \tag{4}$$

These axioms are expressed using set variables and the unary predicates X and Y, which is a rather obvious thing to do if we deal with models in which the variables can be interpreted as set. Alas, this means that the logic that we are using to express them is *monadic second order logic*, which, containing first order logic, has the unpleasant characteristic of being undecidable.

There is no immediately obvious reason why undecidability should be a negative thing. On the one hand, it doesn't seem to generate any problem that, on a pragmatic plane, can't be solved by a good heuristics and common sense. On the other hand, at least for semantic web applications, undecidability seems to resonate with the general web attitude (a very positive one) of seeing imprecision and messiness as a positive fact of life: something to be welcomed as a source of expressive richness, not to be avoided as a source of potential problems[4]. In spite of this, ontologists are in general wary of undecidability, so they take great care to restrict the logic system in which they work, so as to make it decidable. With these considerations in mind, one can work, at least in the first approximation, with the following definition, which is not by all means above all suspicions but around which, I believe, the consent of the majority of the people involved could be gathered.

Definition 1. *Given a set V (of elements called terms) and a collection R of relations on V, an ontology for V and R (or (V, R)-ontology) is a decidable logical theory O on V and R that admits a model M such that $M \models O$ and, for each $v \in V$, $M(v)$ is a set.*

Consider again the *subclass* relation $X \prec Y$. In an extensional semantics the basis for this relation is subset-hood, so we might want to include two statements in the theory:

i) every X is also an Y;
ii) every statement about the properties of the term Y applies, *ipso facto* to X.

We can formulate these points with the following expressions, the first of which we have already encountered in (1):

i) $\forall x, X, Y \ \ X(x) \wedge X \prec Y \Rightarrow Y(x)$;
ii) $\forall X, Y, P \ \ P(Y) \wedge X \prec Y \Rightarrow P(X)$.

---

[4] This attitude notwithstanding, ontology doesn't seem to prepare for the task of dealing with this messiness. For example, all the current ontological approaches use some form of monotonic logic, which is not the best model to use in an environment in which contradicting facts are to be expected with a certain frequency.

As I have already mentioned, in so doing, we have introduced enough machinery from monadic second order logic that the logic is no longer decidable.

The problem in this case is that the machinery that we have introduced is very expressive—it can express much more than we need—and this expressivity generates undecidability. If we insist on decidability, we must find a way to limit the expressive power of monadic second order logic so that it will express the properties that one needs but, at the same time, it won't express too much, so to speak. One way in which this reduction can be achieved is by restricting the use of quantifiers to pre-specified patterns through the use of *operators* with defined semantics[5]. There seems to be two major classes of logics that ontologists use for this purpose: the first is the family of *description logics* in its various flavors, the second is *Horn logic* and its various extensions. Neither description logics nor Horn logic allow the unrestricted use of quantifiers but, for instance, in standard description logic an expression such as $X \sqsubseteq Y$ is equivalent to (1), with the quantification used therein, while in Horn logic the expression

$$A(x,z), B(z,y) \implies C(x,y) \tag{5}$$

is implicitly quantified as

$$\forall x, y \, \exists z \, A(x,z) \wedge B(z,y) \implies C(x,y) \tag{6}$$

All these syntactic restrictions entail, of course, corresponding restrictions in the modeling possibilities of the logic. Description logic, for instance, can't offer a model for the proposition "a resident student is a student who lives in the same city where he studies", while Horn logic (which can model the previous statement) can't model "a person is either a man or a woman, and no person is at the same time a man and a woman" (a statement that can be modeled in description logic).

In this paper, I am not quite interested in the technicalities of these logic systems, since they are irrelevant for the arguments that will follow: the point of contention here is not whether this or that specific logic system is expressive enough to encode the meaning of a document, but whether meaning is something that can be encoded at all, let alone encoded in a logic system, whatever its expressive power. So, from the point of view of the issue at hand, we don't need to be too specific on the type of logic that is being used: we may even assume the use of the full monadic second order logic: it won't make any difference.

For our purposes, it will suffice to know that an ontological approach to meaning consists of two parts:

i) a set of terms and relations specific to a document which contains the meaning of *that* document;
ii) an ontology, which may be divided in several chunks more or less coherently connected, which defines the classes from which these terms are drawn, and the general relations among these classes, and a number of axioms, in a suitable logic system.

---

[5] In this context, when I speak of semantics, I mean the formal (e.g. denotational) semantics of the operators, nothing to do with the semantics of text, which is the subject of this paper. I have observed this confusion to happen, a fact that contributes greatly to muddle the ontological waters.

2   Ontology and Meaning

Is ontology a viable way of representing meaning? Let us begin by noting that, by posing the problem in these terms we are already begging the question of whether meaning can be represented at all, that is, if it can be reified as a property of a document. Ontology says that it can, and that it can be represented as a collection of axioms on terms and relations.

Since relations and their axioms are an important part of any ontology, one obvious way to start our analysis is to ask is whether they are constitutive of meaning or not, that is, once we have represented a text by referring its elements to an ontology, whether the meaning resides in the terms themselves or in the relations. We shall see that none of the two alternative is ultimately satisfactory.

Let us consider the first option first. This point of view is expressed quite well in Jerry Fodor's *informational semantics*:

> Informational semantics denies that "dog" means *dog* because of the way it is related to other linguistic expressions [...]. Correspondingly, informational semantics denies that the concept DOG has its content in virtue of its position in a network of conceptual relations

The "correspondingly" here does a lot of work, and requires a fairly important metaphysical investment since it maps conceptual structures to linguistic ones. This, *passim,* is the same investment that ontology requires when it takes a linguistic structure (composed of words and relations) and calls it a conceptual model.

Let us get rid immediately of the idea that "dog" means DOG because of the three letters of which it is composed. There is absolutely nothing in the sequence /d/, /o/, and /g/ that is in any way connected to dogness. The fact that I can read it and understand that we are talking about a dog tells something about me and the linguistic community in which I function, but absolutely nothing about dogs or dogness. If you don's speak Italian, to you the sequence /c/, /a/, /n/, and /e/ doesn't mean anything, but to me it means the same thing (with some important distinguos that I will consider shortly). As a matter of fact, the sequence

$$0\ 1\ 0\ 0\ 0\ 1\ 0\ 0\ 0\ 1\ 0\ 0\ 1\ 1\ 1\ 1\ 0\ 1\ 0\ 0\ 0\ 1\ 1\ 1$$

will probably appear obscure to most people but, if one assumes an 8 bit ASCII code, it means exactly the same thing.

The idea that the three symbols /d/, /o/, and /g/ are somehow related to the *concept* dog is, indeed, quite naïve, and the fact that in ontology not only it is never openly denied but, many times, it appears to be tacitly assumed as obvious, doesn't increase our confidence in the soundness of the approach.

But if the letters themselves do not create any connection between the symbol "dog" and the meaning of the word, where does this connection come from? What is left of the symbol once you take away the elements that constitute it? Where does its identity lie? The only way one can save the symbol is to say that its identity derives from its relations of opposition with the other symbols of the system. Dog is dog not because of the letters that make it up, but because they allow us to distinguish it from *dot*, from *hog*, from *god*. We are led, in other words, to a position that might oscillate between some form of cognitive functionalism (Stich, 1983) and structural semantics (Greimas, 1966), depending on the degree to which we want to rely on logic formulas in order to define meaning. Both these positions, in spite of their fundamental differences, will agree that the meaning of a symbol is not in the symbol itself, but in the whole system, and in the relation of the symbols with the other symbols.

In mathematical terms, one could say that a system of signification must be invariant to any isomorphic transformation of its terms: if we change dog in hog, hog in bog, and so on, in such a way that the differences between symbols are maintained, the ontology that we get must be exactly equivalent to the original one. Of course, we, as English speaking people, will be completely unable to read it, but here we are talking about algorithms, and they do not care if we write dog or bog, as long as they can distinguish one name from the other.

An isomorphism of this type will leave the relations between symbols unchanged so, if we take the second position outlined above—namely that the relations are constitutive of meaning—we obtain the necessary invariance. This position also entails that, whenever this relational invariance is not in force, meaning is not preserved. In other words: any transformations that is not an isomorphism of the terms of an ontology will not preserve meaning. A good way to test the plausibility of this assumption is to look at the relations between different languages. Different languages break the semantic field in different ways, and concepts arise at the fissures of these divisions. Consider, for example, the way in which adjectives of old age are constituted in Italian, Spanish and French[6]. The basic adjective, *vecchio/viejo/vieux* is applied both to things and to persons. There are specific forms, however: in Spanish, *añejo* is an appreciative form used mainly for liquors *(un ron añejo)*. The Italian adjective *anziano* is applied mainly to people, and the correspondence is roughly *anziano/anciano/âgé*, but *anziano* has a broader meaning than the other two adjectives, being used in expressions such as "il sergente anziano" to denote seniority in a function, a situation in which the Spanish would use *antiguo* and the French *ancien*. Note that Spanish also has the possibility of using the word *mayor* as a softer and more respectful form of denoting a person of old age, while the corresponding Italian and French words are never used in this sense. The correspondence is, in other words, according to the schema that follows. The differences are not just in the way different languages divide the same semantic axes, but also in the choice of semantic axes along which concepts are divided. In English, for instance, the two most widely used words that indicate moving bodies of sweet water are *river* and *stream*, while in Italian they are *fiume* and *affluente*.

Italian	Spanish	French
	añejo	
vecchio	viejo	vieux
anziano	anciano	âgé
	mayor	
	antiguo	ancien
antico		antique

---

[6] This example is an extension of a similar one in (Geckeler, 1976).

The semantic field in English is organized by size: streams are smaller than rivers and have a more irregular course. In Italian the semantic field is organized by destination: fiumi end up in the sea, while affluenti end up in other rivers.

One could build many examples of this, and even better ones if one considers languages that are culturally very different, such as Chinese and French, or Urdu and Italian. European languages are all (with notable exceptions: Welsh, Euskera, Hungarian, etc.), Indo-European languages, and have the same basic structure. Moreover, Europeans have been trading with each other and killing each other for centuries, activities that, of course, tend to mix up the language and to have them influence one another. People whose first language is not Indo-European, or who are proficient speakers of a non Indo-European language are in a better position to determine the extent to which different languages differ in their organization of the semantic field.

To the extent to which a functional translation from Chinese to English, or from Hungarian to Quechua are possible, then, we must admit that a meaning-preserving morphism is not required to be an isomorphism of terms that preserves relations[7]. Meaning, in other words, is a more abstract entity than a mere structural correspondence: depending on the global organization of the semantic field operated by a language, one can introduce considerable structural distortion and still end up with documents that "mean the same thing". Of course, this doesn't mean that all transformations are admissible; to make a trivial example, our previous consideration on the constitutive nature of relations tell us that, since a symbol is identified only by differentiation with other symbols, one can't have a signification system composed of a single symbol: a morphism that maps all the terms of a document or an ontology to a single one would not only destroy the meaning of that document, it would destroy the very idea of meaning even though, mathematically, we are in the presence of a homomorphism.

These example show or, at least, hint that terms and relations are simply not enough to determine meaning. Both the nature of the terms and of the relations can change quite dramatically, and we still have signification systems that can be considered roughly equivalent, at least to the extent that it is possible to translate an Milorad Pavic novel, written in Serbian, into English.

But is translation simply a linguistic problem? Language differences are very relevant to the problem of signification, and I believe that focusing on a single language one will not be able to place the problem of encoding meaning in its proper light. So, it might be useful to look at translation in a little more depth. All modern theories of translation deny that translation is simply, or even mainly, a linguistic fact. If this were so, automatic translation would be relatively easy while we know that, declarations of success notwithstanding, it is an unsolved problem.

Eugene Nida, an American theorist considers translation as an act of cultural replacement (Nida, 1964). The work of a translator consists in studying the effect of a text in its original culture and translate it into a text that will achieve the same effect in the *target* culture. The emphasis for the translation of meaning here is not much on the content of the original linguistic expression, as much as on the *effect* that this expression has

---

[7] As a matter of fact, it is not required to be a function at all: the idea of *one* correct translation has since long disappeared from translation theory (Moya, 2004). Rather, different translations are possible depending on the rôle that the translation will play in the receiving culture.

on the culture to which it is directed. In other words, the meaning of a text can't be separated from the act of interpretation, an act that is always cultural and contextual.

This orientation is even more pronounced in the successive developments of the theory of translation. The *skopos* theory (Vermeer, 1983) emphasizes that the primary force behind translation is the function assigned to the translated text by the translator, as an independent reader and interpreter of the text. This theory incorporates the opinions of reception theory of reading as a contextualized act in which meaning is created. The translator, as a reader of the original text, translates not the text itself, but his own specific reading of the text.

How is this relevant for ontology? Well, the transformation of a document into a formal text is a form of translation and, if we follow the finding of translation theorists, it has much less to do with a phantomatic inherent meaning of the text than with the contextualized reading of whoever did the encoding.

3   The Ontology View of Meaning

The perspective on meaning given by ontology is very different from the contextual, interpretative process that emerges from the previous considerations, and here lies, I believe, its main limitation. This limitation goes beyond the use of a specific logic system, and even beyond the limitations of any conceivable logic system: it derives from the disregard of interpretation as a creator of meaning and, consequently, to the idea that meaning is a *thing* rather than a process. In order for ontology to work, it is necessary that meaning be a *property* of a document, something that can be reified, formalized, and attached as a property to a document.

I have already argued that I see the idea of formalizing meaning in a set of symbols and relations between them as highly problematic, but I want to make you notice how the observations that we are about to make will lead us even further: the very idea that the meaning of a document is *in* the document, that it can somehow be attached to the document in such a way that it can be revealed to a un-contextualized reading, is quite wrong. But let us proceed in an orderly fashion.

An ontology encodes an absolute and immutable meaning of a text[8]. Where does it come from? For such an hypothesis to work, meaning must exist prior to text and independently of the language in which it is expressed. The scheme is pretty much that of a communication channel.

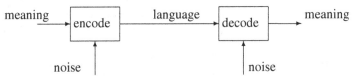

The origin of the communicative act is a *meaning* that resides with the author, and that the author wishes to express in a permanent text. This meaning is a-historical,

---

[8] This doesn't exclude the possibility that different encodings may give different, possibly conflicting, accounts of the meaning of a document, among which it may be necessary to negotiate. But every encoding will give one account of meaning, in absolute terms, that is, independently of the circumstances of interpretation.

immutable, and pre-linguistic. In order to communicate meaning, the author translates it into the shared code of language, and sends it to the receiver. This translation may be imperfect, as indicated by the "noise" arrow entering the translation box; a contingency due to the accidental imperfections of human languages. A perfect language (ontology acknowledges that this might be an unattainable theoretical limit) would be the perfect mirror of the *essential* meaning as it appears in the mind of the author and would allow a perfect translation. Once meaning is translated into language, it can be delivered to the reader, who can then proceed to decode it (possibly with the insertion of some more noise) obtaining a reasonable approximation of the original meaning as *intended* by the author.

This model of signification is necessary for the ontological enterprise because it is the only one that allows meaning to be *assigned* to a text, and recorded in a formal language other than the natural language, from which it can be extracted through automatic means following a schema like this (I have omitted the noise for the sake of simplicity):

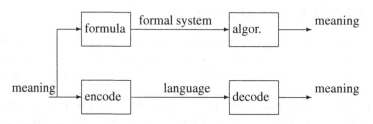

The conclusions of much of the linguistics and philosophy of language of the XX century, however, point in a different direction. There can be no meaning before language and independent of it: meaning can only exist within the categories and the strictures of language (Jameson, 1972). Not only meaning, but the signifying subject as well are a product of language (Lacan, 1982). There can be no pre-linguistic signification experience that belongs only to the author, because meaning can only be expressed in language, and language is a social instrument.

It is the act of reading, contextual and situated, that gives a text its meaning. The reader plays an active rôle in this meaning-creating activity: reading is not a one-directional activity in which a reader is imbued with meaning; it is a dynamic two-way process. It is an infinite process through which a frame of reference is created in which part of the text is interpreted, a text that changes the frame of reference and leads to a different interpretation of the text, which changes the frame of reference and so on... This process of framing and interpretation is what reception theorists call the *hermeneutic circle* (Gadamer, 1975, Eco, 1979).

Mathematically, one could say that, according to this point of view, the meaning of a text is created by a complex interpretation act of which the text is only a boundary condition. And not even the only one, for that matter. Consider the following text, from (Eagleton, 1996):

Dogs must be carried at all time on the escalator.

Quite a puzzling bit of text and, if one were to see it out of any possible context one might have a hard time understanding what it means. What escalator? What dogs? Does it mean that you can't use this particular escalator unless you are carrying a dog? Does it mean that you can only carry dogs on an escalator, but not on a regular stairway?

Now let me give you some context: this sentence is printed on a plastic sign placed near an escalator on the London subway. I imagine that the sign now will be clearer. The sign is not a piece of reading material, but a warning directed to you, the average traveller. It tells you that, if you have a dog, you must carry it in your arms while you ride the escalator. It doesn't specify that you are allowed to ride the escalator even if you don't have a dog with you: the sign relies for that on your general knowledge about what you can and can't do while being on an escalator.

The sign doesn't tell you what will happen to you if you don't follow the directive, but you can well imagine that you will be punished in some way by some appointed authority and, given your general knowledge of these things, you can imagine that the punishment will not be harsh: you will not be sentenced to years in jail because of this, although you might receive a fine.

Notice that nothing of this rich context is implied in the text itself, simply because the text has to function in different ways in different context. You could use the same text, for instance, in a paper on semantics, where it would absolve a completely different function—that of an example. For, let's face it, is it really important for my example whether this text was ever really placed near an escalator in the London subway (although, as a matter of fact, it was)? In the context of clarifying a point this text would work, and its meaning would be quite clear, even if I were lying to you regarding the placement of the text.

But if the meaning of a text depends so crucially on the context in which it is read, then the general plan of ontology, to attach meaning to a text so that a simple algorithm can decode is in quite a bit of trouble. It should be stressed again that the limitations of ontology that we have highlighted are not a limitation of the particular logic that one might use to implement an ontology, nor of logic *per se*: the limitations are at a much more fundamental level. The discussion in this section problematizes the very possibility of representing meaning as an attribute of a text. According to this view, meaning is not *in* the text: a text is merely the boundary condition of a process that depends on the interpreter, his context, the linguistic community of which the interpreter is part, its discursive practices, etc. This doesn't necessarily imply that, for the purpose of meaning formation, the text can't be usefully represented using alternative means, including formal ones. As computing scientists, we are interested, pragmatically, in situations in which reading and interpretation are somehow mediated by a computer, and alternative representations of the text may favor this mediation. What can't in any case be assumed is that representation is a representation of the meaning of the text, a representation from which meaning can be extracted in an a-contextual way by an algorithm.

4   Beyond Ontology

Is there a way we can use these observations to deal with the semantics of documents, images, videos, and whatnot? I think there is, and doing so will give us a valuable alternative to the normative staticism of ontology.

Let us start with a fairly general theoretical model. We have said that the context in which a document is interpreted is essential to determine its meaning, that is, that the context changes the meaning of a text. We can also see things going in the opposite direction: the function of the semantics of a text is to change the context of the reader. If you are interested in novel, the context in which you look at American literature will not be the same after reading *Moby Dick*; if you travel on the London subway, your context will no longer be the same after you read that "dogs must be carried at all times". A document that doesn't change the context in which you act is, by definition, meaningless. We can express this situation with the following expression:

$$C_1 \xrightarrow{\mu(t)} C_2$$

where C_1 and C_2 are the contexts of the reader before and after interpreting the text, t is the text, and $\mu(t)$ is its meaning.

This is, as I have said, a very generic model, but we can use to start answering some questions. For one thing, *is it possible to formalize meaning?* The answer of our model is that it is possible only to the extent that it is possible to formalize context. If C_1 and C_2 are formally defined in mathematical terms, then, and only then, it will be possible to give a formal definition of the function $\mu(t)$.

At one extremum, we have the situation in which the context can be completely formalized. This is the case, for instance, in programming languages: here the context can be reduced to the *state* of a computer on which the program is run. The meaning of a program, from our point of view, is a function that transforms an initial state of the computer to a final one. In other words, if the text is a program and the context of its interpretation is a computer system, meaning reduces to the usual denotational semantics of a program.

At the other extremum we have the general semiotic context, which we know can't be formalized completely in symbols, that is, given that a computer is a symbol manipulation machine, it can't be formalized in a computer. Again, this doesn't entail that any attempt to use a computer (which, because of the characteristics of the device, requires a formalization of the context) is useless, but it does imply that no computing system can be semantically complete, so to speak, and that each computer system will require user interaction to contextualize access and allow signification to happen.

The properties of the "space of contexts" depend crucially on the properties of the representation of the context that we have chosen, and it is therefore difficult to say something more about meaning is we don't impose some additional restriction. A reasonable one seems to be that we be capable of measuring the degree by which two contexts differ by means of an operation $\Delta(C_1, C_2) \geq 0$ such that, for each context C, it is $\Delta(C, C) = 0$. We don't require, for the time being, that Δ be a distance. Now the meaning of a document d in a context C can be defined as the difference that d causes to C:

$$\mu_C(d) = \Delta(\mu(d)(C), C) \tag{7}$$

Within this theoretical framework we can analyze, at least in the first approximation, various existing approaches, and devise ways to extend them. In this general scheme, the ontological approach to meaning can be synthesized as a constant function:

$$\perp \xrightarrow{\mu(d)} C \tag{8}$$

that is, ontology assigns a meaning to a document independently of the context in which the document is interpreted. This fact results, in our model, in the creation of a constant context, which depends only on the document and not on what was there before.

A very different point of view is that of *emergent semantics* (Santini & Jain, 1999, Santini, Gupta & Jain, 2001): in this approach, a highly interactive system allows the user and the system to organize the data in a way that highlights their contextual relations. The meaning of the data emerges as an epiphenomenon of this interaction. Emergent semantics does not work with one document at the time, but always with set of documents, since meaning always emerges from relations. Therefore, the meaning function μ will take as argument a suitable configuration D of documents. The user action is represented as an operator u, and the schema is the following:

$$C \underset{u}{\overset{\mu(D)}{\rightleftharpoons}} C' \tag{9}$$

The context oscillates between C, which is the new contextual situation in which the user wants to end, and C', which is the context proposed by the computer with the access to the new documents. The semantic function is, in this case, the equilibrium of that cycle or, in other terms, the fix-point of the function $\mu(D) \circ u$.

These examples show how a pair of current—and very different—approaches to signification can be placed in this general theoretical framework. The full use of it, however, entails the use of some prior context that can specify, through the specification of the desired final context, the sought meaning, or that can be used as the starting point of a emergent semantic cycle.

Where can we obtain such a context? The interactions in which we are interested take place through a computer, but the computer is much more than just the computing instrument of this interaction: it is a repository of documents, pictures, videos, and in general of all those elements that are the support and the product of the activity in which the interaction with the data is placed. Most interactions with a data repository take place as part of an activity that was developed on a computer, and whose witnesses are the files that are stored and organized in the computer. The contents of the files related to the current activity, any additional information about such activity, and the organization of these files are an ideal place to look for the context that we need.

Note that, consistently with our theoretical framework, we can no longer talk of "the meaning" of a document: independently of the way in which the context and the document are represented, the formation of meaning only takes place through the interaction between the two (mediated, always, by the user); it is the change in the context operated by the document that constitutes meaning. If the representation chosen for the document and the context is a logic formalization, the result is not too different from Jain's "personal ontology" (Scherp & Jain, 2007).

4.1 A Demise of Search?

In the previous pages, I made an effort to avoid the use of terms like "query" or "search", preferring more neutral locutions such as "interaction with the data". The reason for this is that the use of context to define semantics problematizes the notion of a generic "search" operation. The context in which the data assume a meaning is always given by a human activity, not only because of the collateral data that are the support and the product of the activity but also (an aspect that I haven't considered in this paper) because of the discursive practices of that activity, an aspect that Jain and Scherp called *expressive semantics* (Scherp & Jain, 2007).

The context, and especially the discursive practices in it, is so important that one can't quite pin down a single generic activity called "search" that can be applied to all human activities: looking for a text to elucidate a point to ourselves while writing a scientific paper is not the same activity as looking for something to read before going to bed. Looking for a picture to reinforce a point in one's presentation is not the same thing as arranging one's vacation photographs. The activity of "search", which in data bases is unique and well defined, breaks down here in a constellation of different modalities of interaction with data structures. The techniques that one uses in these different activities are largely the same, but the dynamics of the search, the type of interactions that takes place, the notion of what counts as an acceptable result, are specific of the human activity that surrounds the access to the data.

5   Conclusions

My purpose in this paper was unapologetically polemic. Ontologies are being hailed as the cornerstone of the constituenda *semantic web* and as the only viable solution to the "semantic gap" (Santini & Jain, 1998) based on justification that—when they are offered at all—are, in my opinion, mislead and insufficient. Most of the solutions of the semantic web come from the area of knowledge engineering, whose success in the representation of meaning in unrestricted domains has been questionable, but there is the unspoken assumption that, simply by replicating these techniques on a larger scale, one can make them successful. I believe that this is an illusion.

I have argued in this paper that meaning is not "in" a document, nor is it a property of a document, but that it comes from an interpretative act, contextually and culturally situated. If these arguments are valid, then there are serious doubts on the feasibility of the ontological programme, at least in its semantic incarnations. This, as I have shown, doesn't imply that the instruments and the techniques of ontology can't have a place in a system that deals with semantics, but it does mean that an ontology can't in any way be considered as the repository of the meaning of a document or of the semantics of a community.

References

[Berners-Lee, Hendler & Lassila, 2001]Berners-Lee, T., Hendler, J., Lassila, O.: The semantic web. Scientific American 284 (2001)

[Eagleton, 1996]Eagleton, T.: Literary theory, an introduction. Minnesota University Press, Minneapolis (1996)

[Eco, 1979]Eco, U.: The role of the reader. University of Indiana Press, Bloomington (1979)

[Feynman, 1988]Feynman, R.: What do you care what other people think? Norton, New York (1988)

[Gadamer, 1975]Gadamer, H.-G.: Truth and method, London (1975)

[Geckeler, 1976]Geckeler, H.: Semántica estructural y teoría del campo léxico. In: Hernández, M.M. (ed.) Spanish translation of Strukturelle Semantik und Wortfeldtheorie, Gredos, Madrid (1976)

[Greimas, 1966]Greimas, A.J.: Sémantique structurale. larousse, Paris (1966)

[Hakimpour & Geppert, 2001]Hakimpour, F., Geppert, A.: Resolving semantic heterogeneity in schema integration: An ontology based approach. In: Proceedings of the International Conference on Formal Ontologies in Information systems (2001)

[Jameson, 1972]Jameson, F.: The prison-house of language. Princeton, NJ (1972)

[Lacan, 1982]Lacan, J.: Escrits: A selection. Norton, New York (1982)

[Moya, 2004]Moya, V.: La selva de la traducción. Cátedra, Madrid (2004)

[Nida, 1964]Nida, E.: Towards a science of translating. E.J. Brill, Leiden (1964)

[Santini, Gupta & Jain, 2001]Santini, S., Gupta, A., Jain, R.: Emergent semantics through interaction in image databases. IEEE Transaction on Knowledge and Data Engineering (2001)

[Santini & Jain, 1998]Santini, S., Jain, R.: Beyond query by example. In: Proceedings of ACM multimedia (1998)

[Santini & Jain, 1999]Santini, S., Jain, R.: The "el niño" image database system. In: Proceedings of the IEEE International Conference on Multimedia Computing and Systems, pp. 524–529 (1999)

[Scherp & Jain, 2007]Scherp, A., Jain, R.: Towards an ecosystem for semantics. In: Proceedings of ACM Multimedia systems (2007)

[Stich, 1983]Stich, S.: From folk psychology to cognitive science. MIT Press, Cambridge, MA (1983)

[Uschold & Gruninger, 1996]Uschold, M., Gruninger, M.: Ontologies: Principles, methods and applications. Knowledge engineering review 11(2) (1996)

[Vermeer, 1983]Vermeer, H.J.: Ein rahmen eür eine allgemeine translatontheorie. Aufsätze zur Translationtheorie, 48–61 (1983)

Imagination: Exploiting Link Analysis for Accurate Image Annotation*

Ilaria Bartolini and Paolo Ciaccia

DEIS, University of Bologna, Italy
{i.bartolini,paolo.ciaccia}@unibo.it

Abstract. The advent of digital photography calls for effective techniques for managing growing amounts of color images. Systems that only rely on low-level image features are nowadays limited by the semantic gap problem, which leads to a mismatch between the user subjective notion of similarity and the one adopted by a system. A possible way to reduce the semantic gap is to (semi-)automatically assign meaningful terms to images, so as to enable a high-level, concept-based, retrieval. In this paper we explore the opportunities offered by graph-based link analysis techniques in the development of a semi-automatic image captioning system. The approach we propose is appealing since the predicted terms for an image are in variable number, depending on the image content, represent correlated terms, and can also describe abstract concepts. We present preliminary results on our prototype system and discuss possible extensions.

1 Introduction

The use of digital cameras and camera phones has become widespread in recent years. As a main consequence, individuals make frequent use of home computers with the aim of building sizeable personal digital photo collections. Photo sharing through Internet has also become a common practice at present time. There are many examples of on-line photo-sharing communities, such as flickr[1], photo.net[2], and airliners.net[3], just to name a few. These archives of personal photo collections are growing at phenomenal rate, so that the need for effective and efficient techniques for managing color images becomes more and more pressing. Even if content-based image retrieval (CBIR) systems represent a completely automatic solution to image retrieval [15], low level features, such as color and texture, are hardly able to properly characterize the actual image content. This is due to the semantic gap existing between the user subjective notion of similarity and the one according to which a low level feature-based retrieval system evaluates two images to be similar. Just to give an intuitive example, let us consider the

---

* This work is partially supported by a Telecom Italia grant.
[1] flickr: http://www.flickr.com/
[2] photo.net: http://photo.net/
[3] airliners.net: http://www.airliners.net/

N. Boujemaa, M. Detyniecki, and A. Nürnberger (Eds.): AMR 2007, LNCS 4918, pp. 32–44, 2008.

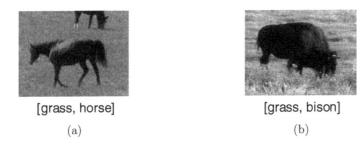

[grass, horse]   [grass, bison]

(a)   (b)

Fig. 1. Two images with associated terms

two images depicted in Figure 1. Even if they could be considered "similar" by a CBIR system, they indeed represent different animals (namely a horse and a bison). On the other hand, if the user is just looking for some "mammals on the grass", the two images could be considered similar even at a semantic level.

Note that, although user feedback [14,3] and context-based techniques [1] can indeed be helpful in improving the precision of results, i.e., the percentage of returned images which are actually relevant to the query, they stay well below the optimal 100% precision value, in particular when the user is looking for images matching some high-level concept (e.g., landscape).

A possible way to fill the semantic gap is to (semi-)automatically assign meaningful terms to images, so as to indeed allow a high-level, concept-based, retrieval. For instance, assuming that the two images in Figure 1 are annotated as shown in the figure, it would be possible to discriminate among them if, say, one is looking for horses and, at the same time, to consider both relevant if one is looking for mammals on grass.

Several techniques [9,7,13,6,10,12,11] have been proposed in recent years and the first image annotation prototypes are now available on Internet (e.g., ALIPR.com[4] and Behold[5]). We can group state-of-the-art solutions into two main classes, namely *semantic propagation* and *statistical inference*. In both cases, the problem to be solved remains the same: *Given a* training *set of annotated color images, discover* affinities *between low-level image features and terms that describe the image content, with the aim of predicting "good" terms to annotate a new image.* With propagation models [9,7,11], a supervised learning technique that compares image similarity at a low-level and then annotates images by propagating terms over the most similar images is adopted. Working with statistical inference models [12,6,10,13], an unsupervised learning approach tries to capture correspondences between low-level features and terms by estimating their joint probability distribution. Both approaches improve the annotation process and the retrieval on large image databases. However, among the predicted terms for unlabelled images, still too many irrelevant ones are present.

---

[4] ALIPR.com: http://www.alipr.com/
[5] Behold: http://go.beholdsearch.com/searchvis.jsp

In this paper we explore the opportunities offered by graph-based link analysis techniques in the development of an effective semi-automatic image captioning system - namely *Imagination* (IMAGe (semI-)automatic anNotATION). In our approach each image is characterized as a set of *regions* from which low-level features are extracted. The training set is built by associating a variable number of terms to each image. In this way, not only terms related to a particular region of the image, but even abstract concepts associated to the whole image (e.g., "landscape" and "pasture") are possible.

We turn the annotation problem into a set of *graph-based* problems. First, we try to discover *affinities* between terms and an unlabelled image, which is done using a *Random Walk with Restart* (RWR) algorithm on a graph that models current annotations as well as regions' similarities. Then, since the RWR step might predict unrelated, or even contradictory, terms, we compute pairwise *term correlations*. Again, this relies on the analysis of links in a (second-order) graph. Finally, we combine the results of the two steps to derive a set of terms which are both *semantically correlated* each other and affine to the new image. This final step amounts to solve an instance of the Maximum Weight Clique Problem (MWCP) on a small graph. Doing this way, the number of terms we predict for each new image is variable, and dependent on the actual image content.

The paper is organized as follows: In Section 2 we define the problem. Section 3 shows how to compute affinities between an image and the terms of the training set and Section 4 analyzes correlations of terms. In Section 5 we show how we derive the most correlated affine terms and in Section 6 we provide some preliminary results obtained from *Imagination*. Section 7 concludes and discusses possible extensions.

2   Problem Definition

Before presenting our image annotation technique, we need to precisely define the problem. We are given a dataset of N manually annotated images that constitute the image *training set* $\mathcal{I}$. Each image $I_i \in \mathcal{I}$ is characterized as a set of *regions* R_j, for each of which a D-dimensional feature vector is automatically extracted. For instance, features could represent the color and the texture of R_j [2]. Moreover, each image $I_i \in \mathcal{I}$ is manually annotated with m_i *terms* $\{T_{i_1}, \ldots, T_{i_{m_i}}\}$. Thus, each image I_i is represented as $I_i = (\{R_{i_1}, \ldots, R_{i_{n_i}}\}, \{T_{i_1}, \ldots, T_{i_{m_i}}\})$.

Problem 1. *Given an unlabelled (or* query*) image* I_q, *with regions* $\{R_{q_1}, \ldots, R_{q_{n_q}}\}$, *exploit the knowledge of images in* $\mathcal{I}$ *to predict a "good" set of terms* $\{T_{q_1}, \ldots, T_{q_{m_q}}\}$ *able to effectively characterize the content of* I_q.

We turn the annotation problem, an instance of which is depicted in Figure 2, into a *graph*-based problem that is split into three main steps:

1. **Affinities of terms and query image:** Starting from the training images $\mathcal{I}$, we build a graph G_{MMG} and "navigate" it so as to establish possible *affinities* between the query image I_q and the terms associated to images in $\mathcal{I}$.

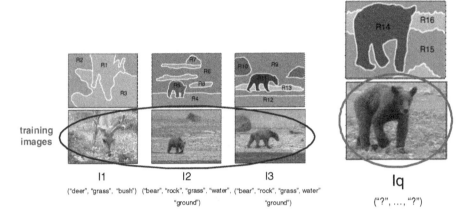

Fig. 2. Visual example of the image annotation problem

2. **Correlation of terms:** Starting from G_{MMG}, we derive a *second-order* graph G_T^2 from which to compute the *similarity* among terms.
3. **Correlated affine terms:** In this step we combine the results of the first two steps and derive the set of most *semantically correlated* terms to label the query image I_q.

3   Affinities of Terms and Query Image

As for the implementation of the 1st step, we follow the Mixed Media Graph approach [13].

3.1   Graph Construction

The Mixed Media Graph (MMG) $G_{MMG} = (V, E)$ is a 3-level undirected graph, where each node represents an image (identifier), a region, or a term, in the training set. More precisely, if $\mathcal{T}$ is the set of terms and $\mathcal{R}$ is the set of regions, then $V = \mathcal{I} \cup \mathcal{T} \cup \mathcal{R}$. Edges in E are of two types. An *object-attribute-value* (OAV) edge connects an image node with either a region or a term node. Therefore for each image $I_i \in \mathcal{I}$, there are edges (I_i, R_j) for all regions R_j in I_i, and similarly for terms. *Nearest neighbor* (NN) edges connect a region to its k ($k \geq 1$) nearest neighbors regions in $\mathcal{R}$, where the similarity between two regions is computed based on the regions' feature vectors. The graph G_{MMG} can be extended, so as to account for a new unlabelled image I_q, into the graph $G_q = (V_q, E_q)$ by adding nodes for I_q and its regions, and NN edges for the regions of I_q. Figure 3 shows the G_q graph for the example in Figure 2.

3.2   Graph Navigation

As we turn the annotation problem into a graph problem, methods for determining how related a node X is to a "start" node S are needed to establish the

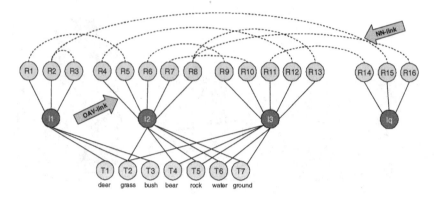

Fig. 3. The G_q graph for the example depicted in Figure 2, assuming $k = 1$

affinity between the query image I_q and the terms in G_{MMG}. For this task we find appropriate to adopt the *random walk with restart* (RWR) technique [13]. The basic idea of RWR is to consider a random walker that starts from node S and at each step chooses to follow an edge, randomly chosen from the available ones. Further, at each step, with probability p the walker can go back to node S (i.e., it *restarts*). The *steady state probability* that the random walker will find itself at node X, denoted $u_S(X)$, can be interpreted as a measure of affinity between X and S. In our case it is $S = I_q$ and relevant steady state probabilities are only those of term nodes (i.e., $X \in \mathcal{T}$). Intuitively, if $u_{I_q}(T_j)$ is high, this is an evidence that T_j is a good candidate for annotating I_q. Details on how the steady state probabilities can be efficiently computed even for large graphs can be found in [16].

In Figure 4 an example of RWR navigation is shown. In particular, the G_q graph displayed in Figure 3 is navigated (with $k = 1$) by starting from the query image I_q and crossing nodes R_{16}, R_8, R_{13}, I_3, T_2, I_1, R_3, respectively.

3.3   Limits of MMG

Even if MMG with RWR is usually able to find some relevant terms for annotating a query image, it suffers some limits. First of all, the predicted terms are those that have been crossed most frequently during the graph navigation. It can be argued that using only frequency to evaluate the relevance of each term for annotating a new image is rather imprecise. For instance, when using MMG, querying *Imagination* with an image representing a "horse" often returned as result the term "cow". Indeed, one should bear in mind that the MMG + RWR method heavily relies on the NN edges involving the regions of I_q, thus on low-level similarities. If a region R_{q_i} of I_q is (highly) similar to a region R_j of an image I, which however has some terms unrelated to I_q, this might easily lead to have such terms highly scored by RWR (consider the example in Figure 1).

Another shortcoming of MMG regards the number of terms, PT, with the highest steady state probabilities that are to be used for annotation. There are two alternatives here. If one insists to take only the best PT terms, then each

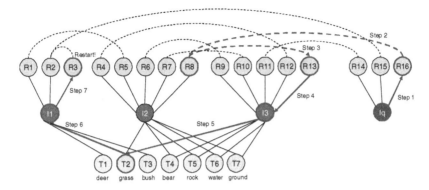

Fig. 4. RWR navigation example ($k = 1$)

image will be annotated with a same number of terms, thus independently of the actual image content. Note that setting PT to a high value might easily lead to wrong annotations, whereas a low value might easily miss relevant terms. The same problem would occur should the predicted terms be all those whose steady state probability exceeds a given threshold value.

4   Analyzing Correlations of Terms

The approach we take to overcome MMG limitations is to perform a link analysis on a sub-graph of G_{MMG} so as to find highly-correlated terms. In turn, this is evidence that such terms are also semantically related, thus good candidates to annotate a new image.

4.1   Link Analysis

From the graph $G_{MMG} = (V, E)$, we derive the sub-graph $G_T = (V_T, E_T)$, where $V_T = \mathcal{I} \cup \mathcal{T}$, i.e., G_T is derived from G_{MMG} by deleting region nodes. With the aim of estimating the similarity between couples of terms, we derive from G_T a *second-order* (bipartite) graph $G_T^2 = (V_T^2, E_T^2)$. A node in V_T^2 is either a pair of images (I_i, I_j), $I_i, I_j \in \mathcal{I}$, or a pair of terms (T_r, T_s), $T_r, T_s \in \mathcal{T}$. An edge between nodes (I_i, I_j) and (T_r, T_s) is added to E_T^2 iff the two edges (I_i, T_r) and (I_j, T_s) (equivalently, (I_i, T_s) and (I_j, T_r)) are both in E_T. This is to say that each image I_i and I_j contains (at least) one of the two terms, and the two images, when taken together, contain both terms. Notice that when $I_i = I_j$, then terms T_r and T_s appear together in image I_i. An intuitive example of G_T and of the derived G_T^2 graph are depicted in Figures 5 (a) and (b), respectively.

Given the second-order graph G_T^2, the problem of estimating the correlation of two terms transforms into the problem of assigning a score to nodes corresponding to pairs of terms. For this one can use any link-based algorithm, such as those adopted for ranking Web pages [8]. We denote with $corr(T_r, T_s)$ the

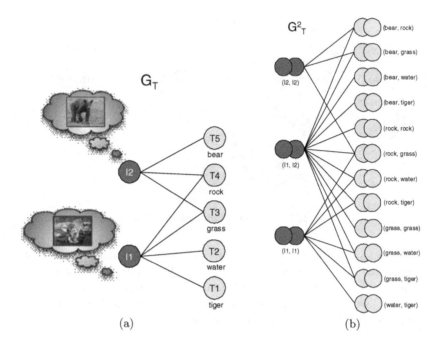

Fig. 5. Example of G_T graph (a) and the derived second-order graph G_T^2 (b)

(correlation) score computed by such an algorithm for the node in V_T^2 corresponding to the pair of terms (T_r, T_s). Note that this step can be performed off-line, since it is independent of the query image.[6]

5 Putting It All Together

In this last step we combine the results of the previous phases. As to the output of the MMG + RWR step, we always take the set of PT terms with the highest steady state probabilities, $T_{MMG} = \{T_1, \ldots, T_{PT}\}$. This will be possibly reduced considering terms correlations, $corr(T_r, T_s)$, so as to obtain a set of terms to annotate the query image I_q that: 1) are affine to I_q, and, at the same time, 2) are all tightly correlated each other.

We solve the problem by modelling it as an instance of the Maximum Weight Clique Problem (MWCP) [5]:

Definition 1 (MWCP). *Let* $G = (V, E, w)$ *be an undirected and weighted graph, where the j-th component of the weight vector* w *is the weight of the j-th node in* V. *A clique* $G' = (V', E')$ *is a complete sub-graph of* G, *i.e.,* $V' \subseteq V$, *and there is an edge in* E' *between every pair of nodes in* V'. *The weight of clique*

---

[6] We are currently studying how correlations can be efficiently updated in front of insertions in the training set.

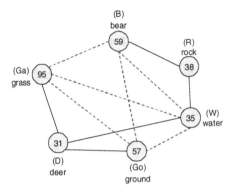

Fig. 6. Dashed edges define the clique with the maximum weight

G' is the sum of weights of the nodes in V', $W(G') = \sum_{j \in V'} w_j$. The Maximum Weight Clique Problem (MWCP) is to find the clique, G'_{max}, with the maximum weight.

The correspondence with our problem is almost immediate. The set of nodes in the graph consists of the terms in $\mathcal{T}_{MMG}$ (i.e., $V = \mathcal{T}_{MMG}$), and each node T_j is weighted by its steady state probability $u_{I_q}(T_j)$ (i.e., $w_j = u_{I_q}(T_j)$). As to edges, we only add to E those between nodes (terms) whose correlation exceeds a given threshold value c, i.e., $(T_r, T_s) \in E$ iff $corr(T_r, T_s) > c$. Doing this way, solving the MWCP amounts to find the subset $\mathcal{T}_{OPT}$ of *optimal terms* in $\mathcal{T}_{MMG}$ such that: 1) all terms in $\mathcal{T}_{OPT}$ are highly correlated, and 2) there is no other set of terms satisfying the same condition whose global affinity is higher.[7]

To give an example, Figure 6 shows a sample graph G in which $PT = 6$. Numbers within each node represent unnormalized steady state probabilities (normalizing would not change the net effect). Solving MWCP, the optimal terms (maximum weight clique) turn to be $\mathcal{T}_{OPT} = \{grass, bear, ground, water\}$, as it can be seen from Table 1 in which we report all cliques in G together with their weights. Notice that, without taking into account terms correlations, the affinity of *rock* is higher than that of *water*. However, *rock* is loosely correlated with almost all other terms in $\mathcal{T}_{MMG}$, thus it does not enter into the solution.

6   Preliminary Results

We have implemented all above-described algorithms within our prototype system *Imagination*. In particular, *Imagination* runs on top of the Windsurf system, which provides functionalities for image segmentation and support for k-NN queries [2]. Each image is automatically segmented into a set of homogeneous regions which convey information about color and texture features. Each region

---

[7] Although the MWCP problem is NP-hard, the graphs we deal with are rather small (e.g., tens of nodes), so the computational overhead is negligible.

Table 1. All the (weighted) cliques in the graph G of Figure 6. For the sake of conciseness, terms are represented in abbreviated form. In particular, the correspondence is Ga for *grass*, B for *bear*, Go for *ground*, R for *rock*, W for *water*, and D for *deer*.

1	Ga (95)	B (59)	Go (57)	R (38)	W (35)	D (31)
2	Ga,B (154)	B,Go (116)	Go,W (92)	R,W (73)	W,D (66)	
	Ga,Go (152)	B,R (97)	Go,D (88)			
	Ga,W (130)	B,W (94)				
	Ga,D (126)					
3	Ga,B,Go (211)	B,Go,W (151)	Go,W,D (123)			
	Ga,B,W (189)	B,R,W (132)				
	Ga,Go,W (187)					
	Ga,Go,D (183)					
	Ga,W,D (161)					
4	**Ga,B,Go,W (246)**					
	Ga,Go,W,D (218)					

corresponds to a cluster of pixels and is represented through a 37-dimensional feature vector. With respect to regions comparison (thus, to define the NN edges of G_{MMG}) the Bhattacharyya metric is used [4]. The dataset we used was extracted form the IMSI collection.[8]

We trained *Imagination* by manually annotating about 50 images with one, two, or three terms. The query workload consists of other about 50 randomly chosen images. Each query image was assigned a set of terms by a set of volunteers so as to obtain a ground truth to evaluate the effectiveness of our system. We computed the annotation accuracy in terms of *precision* (i.e., the percentage of relevant terms predicted) and *recall* (i.e., the percentage of relevant predicted terms with respect to those assigned by our volunteers), averaged over the 50 query images. Table 2 summarizes the parameters used by *Imagination*, together with their default values which we used in our preliminary experiments.

6.1 Effectiveness

Figure 7 shows the annotation accuracy in term of precision and recall. In particular, we compare our results with those obtained when using only MMG (i.e., without considering term correlations). As we can observe from the figure,

Table 2. Parameters used by *Imagination* together with their default values

parameter	default value
Average number of regions per image	4.4
Number of NN edges per region	$k = 5$
Maximum number of terms per image	$PT = 6$
RWR restart probability	$p = 0.8$
Correlation threshold	$c = 0.3$

---

[8] IMSI MasterPhotos 50,000: http://www.imsisoft.com/

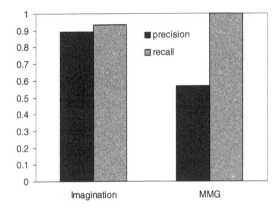

Fig. 7. Precision and recall levels of *Imagination* and *MMG* ($PT = 6$, $c = 0.3$)

Imagination is able to guarantee an improvement in average precision of about 32.66% with respect to *MMG*, even if maintaining an average recall level that is comparable to that of *MMG*. Although it happened that for some queries predicted terms also included irrelevant ones, the precision of *Imagination* was better than that of MMG alone on each query image, thus validating the effectiveness of correlation analysis.

In Figure 8 an example of *Imagination* in action is reported. In this case, the optimal terms that *Imagination* returns are *sheep* and *grass*, which are indeed the only appropriate ones among the $PT = 6$ predicted by MMG. Finally, Table 3

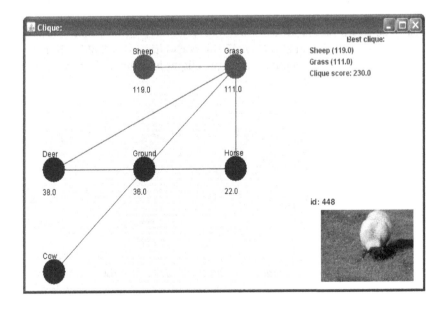

Fig. 8. The maximum weight clique for the image on the right

Table 3. Sample terms predicted by *Imagination*

Query image	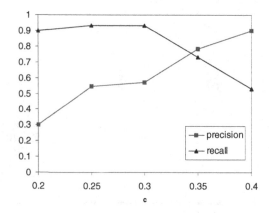		
Ground truth	*bear, grass, water, ground*	*deer, water, grass, rock*	*horse, sky*
Imagination	*grass, bear, ground, water*	*deer, tree, water, rock*	*horse, sky*

gives some examples of annotation given by *Imagination*. For the first and third images, *Imagination* annotates them correctly, whereas for the middle image *Imagination* predicts the term "grass" instead of the term "tree".

6.2   Influence of Parameters

We conclude the experimental section by discussing the role of parameters shown in Table 2. With respect to k (number of NN links per region) and p (RWR restart probability), which influence the MMG+RWR step, we used the values suggested in [13]. In particular, in [13] the authors prove that the effectiveness of RWR is almost insensitive to the k value, as long as $k \in [3, 10]$. As for the RWR restart probability p, it is demonstrated in [13] that good results are obtained for $p \in [0.8, 0.9]$.

Concerning the PT parameter (number of terms with the highest affinities with the query), in our experiments we observed that values of $PT > 6$ (for $c = 0.3$) often resulted in lowering the precision. A possible explanation, consistent with the results we observed, is as follows. When PT grows, more terms are candidate to be used for annotation. If the correlation threshold c is not too high, the chance that the maximum weight clique is composed of many nodes

Fig. 9. Precision and recall levels varying the correlation threshold c ($PT = 10$)

(terms) with not-so-high affinity with the query grows as well. In turn, this suggests that PT and c are tightly related. To justify this claim, we considered a high PT value, $PT = 10$, and changed the correlation threshold. Figure 9 shows precision and recall curves we obtained. As it can be observed from the figure, the precision at $PT = 10$, $c = 0.3$ is quite lower than that observed in Figure 7, in which $PT = 6$. On the other hand, if c is increased, *Imagination* is still able to reach a remarkable 90% precision level. However, in this case the recall drops to about 50%. Summarizing, if PT grows, c should grow as well to stay at a given precision level. On the other hand, not all (PT, c) combinations are equally good if one also considers recall.

7 Conclusions

In this paper we have presented *Imagination*, an effective approach for semi-automatic image annotation based on link-analysis techniques. Our approach is able to predict terms that are highly correlated each other, which improves the accuracy of the annotation. At present, we are working on a more accurate, large-scale, evaluation. Further, we plan to extend our term analysis by means of ontologies, so as to exploit, besides term correlations, also their semantic relationships (e.g., "the horse is a mammal"). This will likely lead to further improve the precision of our approach.

References

1. Bartolini, I.: Context-Based Image Similarity Queries. In: Detyniecki, M., Jose, J.M., Nürnberger, A., van Rijsbergen, C.J.K. (eds.) AMR 2005. LNCS, vol. 3877, pp. 222–235. Springer, Heidelberg (2006)
2. Bartolini, I., Ciaccia, P., Patella, M.: A Sound Algorithm for Region-Based Image Retrieval Using an Index. In: Proceedings of the 4th International Workshop on Query Processing and Multimedia Issue in Distributed Systems (QPMIDS 2000), Greenwich, London, UK, September 2000, pp. 930–934 (2000)
3. Bartolini, I., Ciaccia, P., Waas, F.: FeedbackBypass: A New Approach to Interactive Similarity Query Processing. In: Proceedings of the 27th International Conference on Very Large Data Bases (VLDB 2001), Rome, Italy, September 2001, pp. 201–210 (2001)
4. Basseville, M.: Distance Measures for Signal Processing and Pattern Recognition. European Journal of Signal Processing 18(4), 349–369 (1989)
5. Bomze, I., Budinich, M., Pardalos, P., Pelillo, M.: The Maximum Clique Problem, vol. 4. Kluwer Academic Publishers, Boston, MA (1999)
6. Duygulu, P., Barnard, K., de Freitas, J.F.G., Forsyth, D.A.: Object Recognition as Machine Translation: Learning a Lexicon for a Fixed Image Vocabulary. In: Heyden, A., Sparr, G., Nielsen, M., Johansen, P. (eds.) ECCV 2002. LNCS, vol. 2353, pp. 97–112. Springer, Heidelberg (2002)
7. Escalante, H.J., Montes, M., Sucar, L.E.: Improving Automatic Image Annotation Based on Word Co-occurrence. In: Proceedings of the 5th International Workshop on Adaptive Multimedia Retrieval (AMR 2007), Paris, France (2007)

44   I. Bartolini and P. Ciaccia

8. Fogaras, D., Rácz, B.: Scaling Link-based Similarity Search. In: Proceedings of the 14th International Conference on World Wide Web (WWW 2005), Chiba, Japan, May 2005, pp. 641–650 (2005)
9. Hentschel, C., Stober, S., Nrnberger, A., Detyniecki, M.: Automatic Image Annotation using a Visual Dictionary based on Reliable Image Segmentation. In: Proceedings of the 5th International Workshop on Adaptive Multimedia Retrieval (AMR 2007), Paris, France (2007)
10. Jeon, J., Lavrenko, V., Manmatha, R.: Automatic Image Annotation and Retrieval Using Cross-media Relevance Models. In: Proceedings of the 26th Annual International ACM SIGIR Conference on Research and Development in Information Retrieval, Toronto, Canada, August 2003, pp. 119–126 (2003)
11. Maron, O., Ratan, A.L.: Multiple-instance Learning for Natural Scene Classification. In: Proceedings of the 15th International Conference on Machine Learning (ICML 1998), San Francisco, CA, USA, July 1998, pp. 341–349 (1998)
12. Mori, Y., Takahashi, H., Oka, R.: Image-to-word Transformation Based on Dividing and Vector Quantizing Images with Words. In: Proceedings of the 1st International Workshop on Multimedia Intelligent Storage and Retrieval Management (MISRM 1999) (1999)
13. Pan, J.-Y., Yang, H.-J., Faloutsos, C., Duygulu, P.: Automatic Multimedia Cross-modal Correlation Discovery. In: Proceedings of the 10th ACM SIGKDD International Conference on Knowledge Discovery and Data Mining, Seattle, USA, August 2004, pp. 653–658 (2004)
14. Rui, Y., Huang, T.S., Ortega, M., Mehrotra, S.: Relevance Feedback: A Power Tool for Interactive Content-Based Image Retrieval. IEEE Transactions on Circuits and Systems for Video Technology 8(5), 644–655 (1998)
15. Smeulders, A.W.M., Worring, M., Santini, S., Gupta, A., Jain, R.: Content-Based Image Retrieval at the End of the Early Years. IEEE Trans. Pattern Anal. Mach. Intell. 22(12), 1349–1380 (2000)
16. Tong, H., Faloutsos, C., Pan, J.-Y.: Fast Random Walk with Restart and Its Applications. In: Proceedings of the 6th IEEE International Conference on Data Mining (ICDM 2006), December 2006, Hong Kong, China, pp. 613–622 (2006)

Automatic Image Annotation Using a Visual Dictionary Based on Reliable Image Segmentation

Christian Hentschel[1], Sebastian Stober[1], Andreas Nürnberger[1],
and Marcin Detyniecki[2]

[1] Otto-von-Guericke-University, Magdeburg
[2] Laboratoire d'Informatique de Paris 6
chentsch@student.uni-magdeburg.de,
{nuernb,stober}@iws.cs.uni-magdeburg.de,
marcin.detyniecki@lip6.fr

Abstract. Recent approaches in Automatic Image Annotation (AIA) try to combine the expressiveness of natural language queries with approaches to minimize the manual effort for image annotation. The main idea is to infer the annotations of unseen images using a small set of manually annotated training examples. However, typically these approaches suffer from low correlation between the globally assigned annotations and the local features used to obtain annotations automatically. In this paper we propose a framework to support image annotations based on a visual dictionary that is created automatically using a set of locally annotated training images. We designed a segmentation and annotation interface to allow for easy annotation of the traing data. In order to provide a framework that is easily extendable and reusable we make broad use of the MPEG-7 standard.

1 Introduction

The increased use of digital technologies for production, processing and distribution of digital images within the last decade has led to a sudden rise of valuable information now stored within pictorial data. In order to be able to efficiently retrieve sought information from large-scale image collections two major approaches have been meanwhile established. They mainly differ in the way a query is formulated. *Content-based Image Retrieval* approaches try to find images semantically similar to a given query image example by comparing them on a low-level basis. The requirement of an initial query image, however, disqualifies these approaches in any retrieval scenario, since the availability of such an image would most likely already solve the retrieval task. Therefore, in *Annotation-based Image Retrieval* an image collection is searched based on a textual description of the depicted content. While this approach is best-suited in scenarios where the desired pictorial information can be efficiently described by means of keywords, it demands for translation of the depicted contents into a textual representation (*annotation*). Manual image annotation is a tedious and time-consuming task. Hence, *Automatic Image Annotation* attempts to automatically infer the textual description of an image based on a small set of manually annotated training images.

N. Boujemaa, M. Detyniecki, and A. Nürnberger (Eds.): AMR 2007, LNCS 4918, pp. 45–56, 2008.
© Springer-Verlag Berlin Heidelberg 2008

Automatic Image Annotation (AIA) describes a supervised classification of pictorial data. Each image class contains images, which are semantically similar and thus have at least one annotation in common. Typically these annotations are simple keywords such as "tree" or "sky". Since an image usually can be provided with more than one annotation most images belong to more than one image class at the same time. A classifier trained on a small set of manually annotated images tries to assign an image to one or more classes. A training set should preferably provide a unique mapping between a textual annotation and the described semantic entities within the image. The mapping is represented by a *visual dictionary* (also: *visual codebook*) [3, 11, 25, 30]. A classifier compares the entries or visual words with an unknown image. A successfully rediscovered visual word leads to a corresponding image classification (and thus annotation).

In [9] we introduced SAFIRE – an annotation framework to integrate semantic and feature based information about the content of images that is based on the MPEG-7 Multimedia Content Description Interface[1]. SAFIRE enables the combined use of low-level features and annotations to be assigned to arbitrary hierarchically organized image segments. In this paper we exploit this framework in the field of AIA: Based on the extraction of MPEG-7-compliant low-level features and manually assigned textual descriptions a visual dictionary is assembled, which is later used for automatic image annotation. The extensive use of the MPEG-7 standard allows for a straightforward capability of extending of the visual dictionary, even by using external tools. Moreover, the annotated images can be easily sought by other MPEG-7-compliant applications.

In the following sections, we first offer a brief overview on the field of Automatic Image Annotation and present to what extent our approach is different from these. The subsequent section will present the AIA extension of SAFIRE. Section 4 will present some results we were able to achieve with our prototypical implementation. Section 5 finally summarizes this work and gives some ideas for future research.

2   Related Work

According to [10], Automatic Image Annotation can be regarded as a type of multi-class image classification. The major characteristics are a large number of classes (as large as the annotation vocabulary size) and a possibly small number of example images per class. Recent research concentrates on applying machine learning techniques to identify correlations of low-level image features (typically color and texture) and annotations used for training. Classification of new images is later based on the visual dictionary that we obtain at this learning stage.

Learning a correlation between global low-level image features computed on a per-image level and annotation data has been successfully applied in general scene classification (see e.g. [6, 27, 28, 29]). These approaches provide good results for classifying images when applied to image classes whose discriminative visual

---

[1] The Moving Picture Experts Group (MPEG),
http://www.chiariglione.org/mpeg/standards/mpeg-7/mpeg-7.htm

properties are spread equally over the whole image surface. The classification of "city" and "landscape" images for instance provides good classification results since city scenes typically show strong vertical and horizontal edges, whereas landscape scenes tend to have edges randomly distributed in various directions.

When applied to visual object detection, however, global visual features often insufficiently represent the prominent objects that have been used to annotate the images. Hence, more recent approaches (e.g. [7, 26] propose an automatic segmentation step before the actual learning stage to identify real-world objects within the images. The general assumption is that feature computation based on a potentially strong segmentation better describes the visual objects, depicted in the image, than global features. However, since up to today no general and robust automatic segmentation algorithm has been presented, these approaches suffer from the typically low segmentation accuracy current algorithms provide on low-level images.

Partition-based approaches try to overcome this obstacle by decomposing the images into multiple regions of equal shape (patches). This can be seen as a weak segmentation, which tries not to capture the shape of a visual object, but to produce multiple regions per image each corresponding to a single depicted object. This will result in more redundancy (depending on the patch size), which will help to statistically detect a correlation between global labels and local patches. Lipson et al. [16] applied this concept to general scene classification by modelling templates of spatially aligned colored patches, to describe a specific scene. Each template is assigned a descriptive label and automatic image annotation is done by matching these templates with unclassified images.

Other approaches [13, 14, 18] apply probabilistic methods to capture the relationship between images and globally assigned labels. In their approach, images are divided into a grid of patches. Color and texture features are computed for each patch. A patch inherits all labels from the original image. Using data clustering, groups within the set of all patches are computed. Then, for each cluster center, the probability for the occurrence of all labels assigned to a patch in this cluster is derived. Labeling of an unknown image is performed on patch level. For each patch, color and texture features are computed. The probabilities for the words in the nearest cluster of each patch are combined. The most plausible words for the global image annotation are those with the highest overall probability.

A problem of all the presented approaches is a typically high correlation between different annotations. Various labels that often appear together within the training images can not be distinguished. For example, if the training images always depict sky- and tree-regions within an image together, those objects are hardly distinguishable using the presented statistical methods. Furthermore, in [29] it is argued that global annotations are more general than a pure region labeling and thus a semantic correspondence between labels and image regions does not necessarily exist (e.g. an image globally labeled "wild life" might depict regions for elephants as well as regions for tigers – deducing from both regions to a global label "wild life" is impossible with approaches that are based on color and texture computation only).

Among the first approaches of AIA was the FourEyes system presented in [21] and [17]. It divides all images in the database into patches of equal quadratic shape. By selecting a label name from a limited set of annotations the user indicates a patch to be a positive example for the chosen label, from which the system immediately infers annotations for other patches in the database. In contrast to the aforementioned approaches, learning an association between low-level features and global annotation data is not necessary here since the training images are annotated *locally*. This concept avoids the aforementioned problems that arise from label correlation and implies a strong correlation between annotations and image regions, however, at the expense of frequent user interactions.

A major drawback of all the presented approaches is that all of them apply different low-level descriptors as well as different segmentation and annotation schemes, which makes it inherently difficult to extend the applied visual dictionaries as well as reuse the (manually or automatically) annotated image data. Moreover, the presented approaches do not respect the subjectivity of human perception. Two different beholders of an image may come to different image descriptions and may identify different prominent visual objects.

The system we present here is designed to allow for multiple image segmentations and annotations depending on the beholder. Moreover, the application of the MPEG-7 standard that was initially limited in [9] to region and annotation description has been extended and now covers all aspects of image description including the applied low-level image features. We therefore gain a high degree of extensibility and reusability

Moreover, in order to avoid a possible correlation between various annotations, we follow an approach similar the one briefly discussed above (for details see [21]). However, instead of designing an highly interactive system, we introduce a separate *manual* image segmentation step to construct a reliable visual dictionary while at the same time reducing the amount of user interactions required, once the dictionary has been created.

3   Automatic Image Annotation in SAFIRE

As mentioned in the introduction, the prototypical implementation of the SAFIRE framework as presented in [9] was extended by a component to support AIA and an Annotation-based Image Retrieval component to search digital color pictures based on textual descriptions. A general overview of the framework is given in Figure 1(a).

Generation of the visual dictionary in SAFIRE is based on a locally annotated training set. An interface has been designed, to support manual, sloppy segmentation of a training image into regions of interest. These regions can be later assigned descriptive keywords by the user. Thus, each pixel in a training image can be unambiguously associated with a specific annotation. Segmentation and annotation data is stored in MPEG-7 compliant documents. These documents are used as training data for creating the visual dictionary.

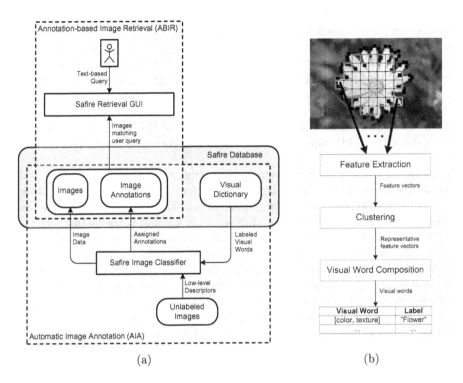

(a)   (b)

Fig. 1. Automatic Image Annotation in SAFIRE: 1(a) shows the general system overview of the proposed framework. 1(b) depicts the process of creating the visual dictionary.

In order to respect the subjectivity of the human perception the annotation interface supports different "views" for the same image. Each user can create a specific image segmentation, with specific region annotations. The training dataset and thus the visual dictionary and the annotation vocabulary can be tailored to a specific user group.

As manual image segmentation is a tedious task it should be performed only once to create a reliable dictionary. For labeling new images by matching visual words with image regions, manual segmentation should not be necessary. It was therefore decided to partition the manually derived segments into patches of equal size based on which the visual dictionary shall be created. Each patch is assigned directly the label of the surrounding image segment. The achieved local annotation can therefore be considered as highly reliable.

Image content is represented in a feature space that assembles the computed color and texture features of the derived patches. Color and texture are commonly applied characteristics of pictorial data in image retrieval [1]. Their strong advantage is a relatively low computational effort and full automatic extractability. The MPEG-7 standard comprises a number of different color and texture descriptors – each tailored to a specific application scenario. For a detailed overview see [19] and [2]. Among the color descriptors the Scalable Color Descriptor (SCD) was chosen. The SCD is a histogram-based descriptor and is recommended for retrieval of color pictures. The Homogeneous Texture Descriptor (HTD) was chosen as it has shown superior retrieval results in empirical evaluations for texture based image retrieval (see [20]). Both descriptors are computed in HSV space. While the SCD quantizes the HSV space for histogram computation, the HTD applies a Gabor filtering on the value component of the images.

Each derived feature vector describes a specific patch within the image and could be used directly for classifying unseen images. However, following [31], in order to reduce the amount of comparisons necessary for classification and to render the dictionary more robust to minor visual variances, the feature vectors of each annotation class are clustered using a simple k-means approach. The result of the clustering step can be seen as a reduction of all extracted feature vectors to a set of discriminative representatives for a specific annotation class. The computed cluster centers determine the visual words (see Fig. 1(b)). For each annotation entry in the visual dictionary a list of k describing representatives are assembled. The currently implemented classifier assumes a consistent number of visual words per annotation class. However, a varying parameter k is likewise imaginable. For example, for very homogenous classes a smaller set of representatives (a smaller values for k) might be sufficient, while very diverse classes where groups of similar objects are scattered in data space might require a bigger value for k.

New images to be labeled are statically decomposed into a regular grid of patches of the same size as the patches used in the dictionary. The automatic classification of new images in SAFIRE follows the k-nearest-neighbor approach. For each patch of the image to be classified, SCD and HTD feature vectors are computed and compared to the visual dictionary. Those k visual words are chosen, whose distance (Euclidean) is smallest to the patch to be classified. The class to which the new patch is to be assigned is derived based on a majority vote. The most frequent class is chosen. In order to avoid misclassification through visual objects that are not yet covered by the dictionary the classifier computes a confidence value for the proposed annotation. Annotation is performed only if more than 50% of the retrieved visual words agree on the same annotation class. Figure 2 shows the resulting sparse grid of patches that have been successfully labeled by the classifier. Please note that successfully here does not refer to a correct annotation in terms of human evaluation but rather to the fact that the computed confidence was above the threshold ($c(l) > 50\%$).

SAFIRE provides a simple user interface for retrieving images based on the automatically (and manually) assigned annotations. Fig. 2 shows the results of a request using the keywords "bicycle". Please note the small black squares representing the regions that have been successfully (s.a.) annotated by the classifier.

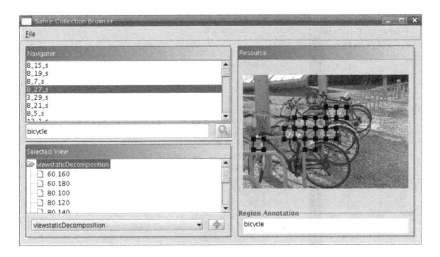

Fig. 2. Results of a request in SAFIRE for images annotated by the keyword "bicycle". Black squares indicate credibly annotated region.

4   Results and Discussion

In order to minimize the effort required to create a dataset of locally annotated training data, we selected the Microsoft Research Cambridge (MSRC) dataset[2] to create the visual dictionary. The images in this collection have been manually segmented into visual objects and background and locally (that is objectwise) annotated. When compared to the typically used Corel or PASCAL datasets[3], the MSRC dataset content is rather small in size: it comprises 591 images depicting 23 different annotation classes. As a result, for some classes only very few example images were available (see Fig. 3). Two classes even had to be neglected due to the lack of sufficient example images. However, compared to the Corel or even the PASCAL dataset, the MSRC dataset provides a precise correlation between annotations and local visual features.

For each image a MPEG-7 compliant document containing region information, annotations and low-level image features was created. The documents were split into 60% training and 40% testing data used to estimate the annotation accuracy of the proposed system. The number of visual words per annotation class was restricted to 30 representatives in the clustering process. This decision is mainly due to the rather small dataset size and in order to reduce the computation effort required for image classification. The clustering was repeated to reduce the impact of the initial choice of cluster centers.

---

[2] Computer Vision at Microsoft Research Cambridge – Object class recognition, `http://research.microsoft.com/vision/cambridge/recognition/`
[3] The PASCAL Object Recognition Database Collection, `http://www.pascal-network.org/challenges/VOC/databases.html`

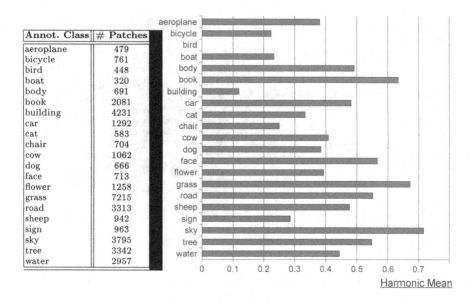

Annot. Class	# Patches
aeroplane	479
bicycle	761
bird	448
boat	320
body	691
book	2081
building	4231
car	1292
cat	583
chair	704
cow	1062
dog	666
face	713
flower	1258
grass	7215
road	3313
sheep	942
sign	963
sky	3795
tree	3342
water	2957

Fig. 3. Training Data Density and classification accuracy indicated by harmonic mean

Feng et al. [5] propose to measure the performance of an AIA system by computing the precision and recall values for each supported label. In image retrieval one typically seeks to optimize precision and recall at the same time. A measure that combines precision and recall into a single value is the weighted harmonic mean (or F-measure) [23], which averages the values of precision and recall with respect to a specific query q:

$$HM_q = \frac{2}{\frac{1}{R_q} + \frac{1}{P_q}} = \frac{2P_qR_q}{P_q + R_q} \qquad (1)$$

The annotation-based retrieval process in SAFIRE is predominantly based on the *global* annotations (that is the image-level annotations rather than the patch-level annotations). Global annotations determine whether an image appears in the result set or not. Fig. 3 lists the harmonic mean achieved for each of the 21 annotation classes. As can be seen, for several classes such as "sky", "grass" and "tree" a rather high classification performance has been be achieved. For others, the classification performance is rather low ("bird", "building").

When analyzing the results we identified three major reasons for the low annotation accuracy of some classes. First of all, due to the chosen "careful classification" based on the described confidence computation, the system generates a large number of not classified patches (false dismissals). The high redundancy of the patch-based approach, however, slightly alleviates this effect at the global annotation level.

Second, when analyzing the training data density, we identified a strong correlation between the size of the annotation classes[4] and the classification result. On the one hand "Tree", "sky" and "grass" are among the four largest classes and show high class-wise accuracy. On the other hand, "bird", "dog", "body" and "chair" are rather small classes and also show a small classification accuracy. The fact that it seems more difficult to classify patches based on underrepresented classes is plausible when making aware that the number of patches available affects the representatives in the visual dictionary. A smaller number of patches results from fewer images representing a specific label class. Consequently, the computation of the most frequent representatives for each class to create the dictionary is based on fewer examples. Thus, the impact of outliers is much stronger whereas other, more prominent examples might not even be included in the training data.

Finally, the large visual variance of some classes also affects the classification accuracy. A larger in-class variance results in a more widespread instance space as the feature vectors computed for each training patch are much more different. As a result, the visual words, which have been computed using k-means clustering, are likewise much more widespread. The dictionary entries for different classes will tend to "overlap". An unclassified patch, which falls into an overlapping region is much more difficult to be classified with a high confidence. In compact classes, the computed visual words are densely populated, which makes classification more unambiguous. A class with a high in-class variance is, for example, the "building" class. This explains the rather low classification accuracy of the "building" class despite the large number of training examples.

The more annotation classes are represented in the dictionary, the more the computed visual words will tend to overlap in the described manner. This makes classification based on a majority vote as in the presented k-NN approach more and more difficult.

An important conclusion can be drawn from the classification results despite the discussed low accuracy for some classes. When reconsidering the label classes for whom a high accuracy has been achieved, it can be remarked, that all these classes can be considered as non-shaped structures. Clearly, "grass" and "sky" have no spatial dilation or shape. They rather exhibit a textured region with a specific color. The same holds to some extent for the "tree" class. Considering the training images for "flower" and "bicycle", one will notice that instead of showing a single representative for each class, most of the images actually depict a *bunch* of bicycles as well as flower*beds*. Multiple bicycles and flowers again possess no clear shape.

In other words, when exhibiting a low in-class variance, non-shaped regions can be efficiently described using solely color and texture descriptors as has been done within this work. On the other hand, the animal classes ("cow", "dog", "sheep", "cat", "bird") for instance cannot be distinguished based on color and texture only as suggested by the results. Shape seems to be an important discriminative characteristic to capture the visual appearance.

---

[4] In terms of patches used for dictionary creation, see Fig. 3.

5   Conclusion

In this paper we have proposed an extension to the SAFIRE framework presented in [9] to support the user of an Annotation-based Image Retrieval system during the annotation process. Based on a small set of manually segmented and locally annotated training images a highly reliable, correlation-free visual dictionary is created, which is later used to infer the annotations of newly added images. The presented system fully relies on the MPEG-7 Multimedia Content Description Interface standard, which facilitates largely the extensibility and reusability of the presented solution. Our approach has shown good results in classifying non-shaped visual objects that can be sufficiently described by color and texture.

Our current research efforts concentrate on three main areas. First of all we intend to increase the classification accuracy by applying a more sophisticated classifier. Support-Vector-Machines [4,8] and Self-organizing Maps (SOM) [12,15,24] have been successfully applied in the domain of image retrieval and we intend to integrate these approaches in to SAFIRE as well. Second, we are analyzing approaches to sample the patches on the image more sparsely based on so-called keypoints or salience measures as presented e.g. in [11]. This will allow the reduction of the sample space for dictionary creation to more discriminative examples. Likewise, integrating the spatial relation between sparsely computed patches might help to introduce shape as a characteristic in the classification process. Finally, we seek to increase the training data density for the currently sparsely populated classes. The *LableMe* project at the MIT [22] intends to build a large collection of images with a manually segmented and locally annotated ground truth to be used for object detection and recognition. The current size of the *LabelMe* database (183 annotation classes in 30369 images) outperforms the MSRC dataset by large and we are evaluating means to merge the two datasets into a single one within SAFIRE, based on the standardized MPEG-7 description interface.

References

1. Bimbo, A.D.: Visual Information Retrieval. Morgan Kaufmann Publishers, Inc., San Francisco, CA (1999)
2. Choi, Y., Won, C.S., Ro, Y.M., Manjunath, B.S.: Texture Descriptors, Introduction to MPEG-7: Multimedia Content Description Interface, pp. 213–229. John Wiley & Sons, Ltd., Chichester (2002)
3. Csurka, G., Dance, C.R., Fan, L., Willamowski, J., Bray, C.: Visual categorization with bags of keypoints. In: Pajdla, T., Matas, J(G.) (eds.) ECCV 2004. LNCS, vol. 3024. Springer, Heidelberg (2004)
4. Cusano, C., Ciocca, G., Schettini, R.: Image annotation using svm. In: Santini, S., Schettini, R. (eds.) Internet Imaging V, Proceedings of the SPIE, the Society of Photo-Optical Instrumentation Engineers (SPIE) Conference, December 2003, vol. 5304, pp. 330–338 (2003)
5. Feng, S., Manmatha, R., Lavrenko, V.: Multiple bernoulli relevance models for image and video annotation. In: Computer Vision and Pattern Recognition, 2004.

CVPR 2004. Proceedings of the 2004 IEEE Computer Society Conference, 27 June–2 July 2004, vol. 2, pp. II–1002–II–1009 (2004)

6. Feng, X., Fang, J., Qiu, G.: Color photo categorization using compressed histograms and support vector machines. In: Image Processing, 2003. ICIP 2003. Proceedings. 2003 International Conference, 14-17 September, vol. 3, pp. III–753–6 (2003)

7. Frigui, H., Caudill, J.: Unsupervised image segmentation and annotation for content-based image retrieval. In: Fuzzy Systems, 2006 IEEE International Conference, July 16-21, pp. 72–77 (2006)

8. Goh, K.-S., Chang, E., Cheng, K.-T.: Support vector machine pairwise classifiers with error reduction for image classification. In: MULTIMEDIA 2001: Proceedings of the 2001 ACM workshops on Multimedia, pp. 32–37. ACM Press, New York, NY, USA (2001)

9. Hentschel, C., Nürnberger, A., Schmitt, I., Stober, S.: Safire: Towards standardized semantic rich image annotation. In: Marchand-Maillet, S., Bruno, E., Nürnberger, A., Detyniecki, M. (eds.) AMR 2006. LNCS, vol. 4398. Springer, Heidelberg (2007)

10. Inoue, M.: On the need for annotation-based image retrieval. In: Workshop on Information Retrieval in Context (IRiX), pp. 44–46 (2004)

11. Jurie, F., Triggs, B.: Creating efficient codebooks for visual recognition. In: Computer Vision, 2005. ICCV 2005. Tenth IEEE International Conference, 17-21 October, vol. 1, pp. 604–610 (2005)

12. Laaksonen, J., Koskela, M., Oja, E.: PicSOM: Self-organizing maps for content-based image retrieval. In: Proc. of International Joint Conference on Neural Networks (IJCNN 1999), Washington, D.C., USA, July 10–16 (1999)

13. Lavrenko, V., Feng, S., Manmatha, R.: Statistical models for automatic video annotation and retrieval. In: Acoustics, Speech, and Signal Processing, 2004. Proceedings (ICASSP 2004). IEEE International Conference, 17-21 May, vol. 3, pp. iii–1044–7 (2004)

14. Lavrenko, V., Manmatha, R., Jeon, J.: A model for learning the semantics of pictures. In: Proceedings of the 16th Conference on Advances in Neural Information Processing Systems NIPS (2003)

15. Lefebvre, G., Laurent, C., Ros, J., Garcia, C.: Supervised image classification by som activity map comparison. icpr 2, 728–731 (2006)

16. Lipson, P., Grimson, E., Sinha, P.: Configuration based scene classification and image indexing. In: Computer Vision and Pattern Recognition, 1997. Proceedings, 1997 IEEE Computer Society Conference, 17-19 June, pp. 1007–1013 (1997)

17. Minka, T.: An image database browser that learns from user interaction. Master's thesis, MIT Media Laboratory, Cambridge, MA (1996)

18. Mori, Y., Takahashi, H., Oka, R.: Image-to-word transformation based on dividing and vector quantizing images with words (1999)

19. Ohm, J.-R., Cieplinski, L., Kim, H.J., Krishnamachari, S., Manjunath, B.S., Messing, D.S., Yamada, A.: Color Descriptors, Introduction to MPEG-7: Multimedia Content Description Interface, pp. 187–212. John Wiley & Sons, Ltd., Chichester (2002)

20. Ojala, T., Mäenpää, T., Viertola, J., Kyllönen, J., Pietikäinen, M.: Empirical evaluation of mpeg-7 texture descriptors with a large-scale experiment. In: Proc. 2nd International Workshop on Texture Analysis and Synthesis, pp. 99–102 (2002)

21. Picard, R.W., Minka, T.P.: Vision texture for annotation. Multimedia Systems 3(1), 3–14 (1995)

22. Russell, B.C., Torralba, A., Murphy, K.P., Freeman, W.T.: LabelMe: A database and web-based tool for image annotation. MIT AI Lab Memo AIM-2005-025 (2005)

23. Schmitt, I.: Ähnlichkeitssuche in Multimedia-Datenbanken. Retrieval, Suchalgo-rithmen und Anfragebehandlung. Oldenbourg (2005)
24. Oh, K.s., Kaneko, K., Makinouchi, A.: Image classification and retrieval based on wavelet-som. dante 00, 164 (1999)
25. Sivic, J., Zisserman, A.: Video google: A text retrieval approach to object match-ing in videos. In: Computer Vision, 2003. Proceedings. Ninth IEEE International Conference, 13-16 October, vol. 2, pp. 1470–1477 (2003)
26. Town, C., Sinclair, D.: Content based image retrieval using semantic visual cate-gories (2000)
27. Vailaya, A., Figueiredo, M., Jain, A., Zhang, H.-J.: Image classification for content-based indexing. Image Processing, IEEE Transactions 10(1), 117–130 (2001)
28. Vailaya, A., Jain, A., Zhang, H.J.: On image classification: City vs. landscape. In: Content-Based Access of Image and Video Libraries, 1998. Proceedings. IEEE Workshop, 21 June, pp. 3–8 (1998)
29. Vogel, J.: Semantic Scene Modeling and Retrieval. In: Selected Readings in Vision and Graphics, vol. 33. Hartung-Gorre Verlag, Konstanz (2004)
30. Winn, J., Criminisi, A., Minka, T.: Object categorization by learned universal visual dictionary. In: Computer Vision, 2005. ICCV 2005. Tenth IEEE International Conference, 17-21 October, vol. 2, pp. 1800–1807 (2005)
31. Zhang, R., Zhang, Z.: Hidden semantic concept discovery in region based image retrieval. In: Computer Vision and Pattern Recognition, 2004. CVPR 2004. Pro-ceedings of the 2004 IEEE Computer Society Conference, 27 June–2 July, vol. 2, pp. II–996–II–1001 (2004)

Improving Automatic Image Annotation Based on Word Co-occurrence

H. Jair Escalante, Manuel Montes, and L. Enrique Sucar

National Institute of Astrophysics, Optics and Electronics,
Computer Science Department
Puebla, 72840, México
{hugojair,mmontesg,esucar}@ccc.inaoep.mx

Abstract. Accuracy of current automatic image labeling methods is under the requirements of annotation-based image retrieval systems. The performance of most of these labeling methods is poor if we just consider the most relevant label for a given region. However, if we look within the set of the $top-k$ candidate labels for a given region, accuracy of most of these systems is improved. In this paper we take advantage of this fact and propose a method (NBI) based on word co-occurrences that uses the naïve Bayes formulation for improving automatic image annotation methods. Our approach utilizes co-occurrence information of the candidate labels for a region with those candidate labels for the other surrounding regions, within the same image, for selecting the correct label. Co-occurrence information is obtained from an external collection of manually annotated images: the $IAPR\text{-}TC12$ benchmark. Experimental results using a $k-$nearest neighbors method as our annotation system, give evidence of significant improvements after applying the NBI method. NBI is efficient since the co-occurrence information was obtained off-line. Furthermore, our method can be applied to any other annotation system that ranks labels by their relevance.

1 Introduction

Content based image retrieval (*CBIR*), the task of recovering images using visual features, has became an active research field since the early nineties [18,24,15,9]. Typically, a query for a *CBIR* system consist of a visual example similar to the desired image and the task is to find, within the collection, images similar to such a visual example. However, this sort of querying is unnatural, since most of the time we would like to retrieve images by specifying queries in natural language (*images of a tiger, grass and water*), or even combining a sample image and natural language statements (*images of brown cows like in this photograph*). In consequence, it was recognized that in order to improve *CBIR* systems we would need to incorporate semantic information into the *CBIR* task. This semantic information generally consist of textual keywords (semantic descriptors, words, labels) indicating some semantic properties of the image.

Manually incorporating semantic information into images is both: expensive (in terms of human-hour costs) and subjective (due to the annotator criteria).

N. Boujemaa, M. Detyniecki, and A. Nürnberger (Eds.): AMR 2007, LNCS 4918, pp. 57–70, 2008.

Therefore, recently there is an increasing interest on automatically assigning semantic information to images. The task of assigning semantic descriptors to images is known as image annotation or image labeling. There are two ways of approaching this problem: at image level or at region level. In the first case, often called weakly labeling, keywords are assigned to the entire image as an unit, not specifying which words are related to which objects within the image. In the second approach, which can be conceived as an object recognition task, the assignment of annotations is at region level within each image, providing a one-to-one correspondence between words and regions. This later approach is the one we considered in this work, since we believe that region-level semantics are more useful for discovering relationships between semantic concepts and visual objects within an image collection.

We say a region is correctly annotated if the more likely annotation, according to our annotation method, is the same as the true (manual) annotation. Most of the annotation methods that rank words according to their relevance to belong to a determined region fail in assigning the correct label just by taking the most confident word [17,4,5,11,16]. Accuracy improves if we search for the true label within the set of the top$-k$ ranked labels for a given region. However, assigning a set of $k-$labels to an unique region is confusing and unpractical. In this work we propose a method for improving automatic image annotation by taking advantage of word co-occurrence information. The problem we approach is the following: given a set of ranked candidate labels for a given image region, selecting the *(unique) correct label* for such region. The solution we propose takes advantage of word co-occurrence information of the candidate labels for the region we are analyzing and the corresponding candidate labels for other regions within the same image. We formulate this problem as a classification task using the naïve Bayes algorithm. Candidate labels are considered classes and measures of association between labels (based on word co-occurrences) are considered as attributes/features.

Our intuitive idea is that co-occurrence information between labels assigned to regions in the same image can help us to improve annotation accuracy; since annotations for regions appearing in the same image are very likely to be related. Given that word co-occurrences are obtained from the captions of a collection of manually-annotated images we can trust in that this information can give us an indicator of words association. Since words that tend to co-occur in the captions are very likely to be visually related, as they are used to describe the same image. We performed experiments on three subsets of the benchmark Corel data set ([18,15,6,11,14]), using a $k-$nearest neighbors (knn) [19] method as our annotation strategy. Experimental results show that knn combined with our approach can result in significant improvements over knn alone and over other *soft-annotation* methods as well. An advantage of the proposed approach is that it is simple and efficient as it is based on a naïve Bayesian classifier and the co-occurrence information is obtained off-line; also the approach can be applied to other annotation methods, provided they rank words for their relevance (soft-annotation).

The rest of this paper is organized as follows. In the next Section we briefly review related work on automatic annotation. In Section 3 we describe how the *knn* classifier was used for annotation. Next in Section 4, our proposal: *Naïve Bayesian Improver based on Co-occurrences* is described. In Section 5 we describe how we obtained the word co-occurrence matrix. Then in Section 6 we report experimental results on subsets of the Corel Collection. Finally, in Section 7 we present some conclusions and outline future work directions.

2   Automatic Image Annotation

A wide variety of methods for image labeling have been proposed since the late nineties. Maybe the first attempt was the work by Mori et al, in which each word assigned globally to the image is inherited by each (square) region within the segmented image [20]; regions are visually clustered and probabilities of the clusters given each word are calculated by measuring word co-occurrence among the clusters. In this work, however, word co-occurrence was measured among clusters of regions. A reference work for this task is the one proposed by Duygulu et al, on which image annotation is seen as a problem of machine translation [11]. The task consist of finding the one-to-one correspondence between vector-quantized regions and words (that is learning a lexicon) starting from weakly annotated images. This method received much attention and since its introduction several modifications and extensions have been proposed [22,12,4,5]; furthermore, the data used by Duygulu et al have become a benchmark for comparing image annotation methods [18,15,14]. Several successful semi-supervised methods have been proposed[1] [6,1,2,4,11,16,5], some of which outperform the previous work [11]. The intuitive idea in most of these methods is to introduce latent variables for modeling the joint (or conditional) probability of words and regions. Then, when a new region needs to be labeled, these methods select the word that maximizes the joint probability between such a region and the words in the vocabulary; words are ranked according to the joint estimate. Hidden Markov models and Markov random fields have been introduced for consideration of dependencies between regions [4,13]. From the supervised learning community some approaches have been proposed for image labeling [17,6,7]. A work close in spirit to ours is that due to Li et al [17], where a probabilistic support vector machine classifier is used for ranking labels for each region. Then, co-occurrences between candidate labels within the image are calculated in order to re-rank the possible labels. Our approach is different to the works by Mori et al and Li et al because we obtained the co-occurrence information from an external corpus, instead of considering co-occurrence of labels within the same image [17] or clusters of regions [20]. Furthermore, in such works co-occurrence information is used ad-hoc for their annotation method; while in this work we propose a

---

[1] Carneiro et al refer to such methods as unsupervised, though a more convenient term would be semi-supervised; since these methods start from weakly annotated images [6], therefore there exist some supervision.

method that can be used with other annotation methods, provided they rank labels for its relevance, just as those proposed in [1,2,4,11,16,5,3,17].

3   knn as Annotation System

The *knn* classifier is an instance based learning algorithm widely used in machine learning tasks [19]. The zero training time of this algorithm makes it suitable for middle size data sets. Furthermore, it is adequate for domains in which new instances are continuously added to the data set. In this work we used this method as our automatic annotation system, due to the fact that it returns a set of ranked candidate labels for a given object; also, it does not require a training phase resulting in a fast method; and, further, this method outperforms other annotation systems, as we will show in Section 6.

knn needs a training data set $\{X,Y\}$ composed of N pairs of the type $\{(x_1, y_1), \ldots, (x_N, y_N)\}$, with the $x_i's$ being $d-$dimensional feature vectors and the $y_i's$ being the class of $x_i's$; for two class problems $y \in [0, 1]$. The training phase of *knn* consist of storing all available training instances. When a new instance, x_t, needs to be classified *knn* searches, in the training set, for $\{x_1^t, \ldots x_k^t\}$, the top $k-$objects more similar to x_t, then it assigns to x_t a weighted combination of the labels belonging to $\{x_1^t, \ldots x_k^t\}$. We used the Euclidean distance as similarity function. For automatic image annotation at region level, we use *knn* in a multiclass learning setting, in which we have as many classes as words has the vocabulary. Instead of having two classes $[0, 1]$, we have $|V|$ classes $[1, \ldots, |V|]$, with $|V|$ being the number of different words in the collection. Since we would like to annotate regions, we need to extract features for each region, the features we considered for this work were color and shape statistics as described in Section 6. We decided to assign to a new instance the class of the most similar neighbor in our training set[2].

3.1   *knn* as a Soft-Annotation System

In order to apply the proposed approach with *knn* as annotation method, we need to turn *knn* into a soft-annotation method. That is, candidate words for a given region should be ranked and weighted according the relevance of the labels to being the correct annotation for such a region. A natural way of ranking labels is by using the ordering of labels that *knn* returns. However, within the set of the top$-k$ candidate labels, according to *knn*, these can be repeated; therefore, more confidence should be given to these repeated labels. Another problem with the *knn* ordering is that labels have not a relevance weight attached. This relevance weight, (which would be the equivalent of the posterior of the words given the region for probabilistic soft-annotation systems [1,2,4,11,16,5,3,17]) should reflect the confidence we have on each candidate label. The relevance weight is an important component of our method since we take this weight (or posterior)

---

[2] We do this when *knn* should return a single label for the region, this way of annotation is referred as *1-NN* through this document.

as prior probabilities for the labels. Prior probabilities for the proposed method, should met the following: 1) they should reflect the confidence of the annotation method in the candidate labels and 2) the weight for the top$-k$ candidate labels should sum one, in order to be considered as prior probabilities.

We realized two intuitive ways of obtaining prior probabilities from the relevance ranking of knn. First we used the inverse of the distance of the test instance to the top$-k$ nearest neighbors; in this way we can infer prior probabilities directly related to the proximity of each neighbor to the test instance, as described in Equation (1).

$$Pr_d(y_j^t) = \frac{d_j(x^t)}{\sum_i^k d_i(x^t)} \qquad (1)$$

where $d_j(x^t)$ is the inverse of the distance of instance x_j^t, within the $k-$nearest neighbors, to x^t, the test instance. This prior probability is accumulative, that is, labels appearing more than once will accumulate its priors according to the times they appear and their distance in each apparition. Note that we are implicitly counting for repetitions with this formulation.

The second intuitive way of obtaining prior probabilities is by considering the repetition of labels within the set of the top $k-$nearest neighbors of x^t, as described in Equation (2)

$$Pr_r(y_j^t) = \frac{rep(y_j^t)}{k} \qquad (2)$$

with $rep(y)$ being a function that tells us the number of times label y is repeated within the $k-$nearest neighbors of x^t, note that this formulation is also normalized.

4   Naïve Bayesian Improver Based on Co-Occurrences

There are several automatic image annotation systems than rank labels in the vocabulary according to their relevance for a given region [17,4,5,3,11,16,1]. If we take the (top-one) most relevant label for a region it results on a poor performance of the annotation system. On the other hand, considering the top$-k$ possible labels for each region will result in an improvement on the system's accuracy. Unfortunately assigning a set of labels to a region is not straightforward; since this may cause confusion, adding uncertainty to the annotation and retrieval processes. However, if we measure the degree of association of each candidate label for a region with the candidate labels assigned to surrounding regions within the same image, we can determine which of the candidate labels is the most appropriate for the given region. We propose a naïve Bayes approach, abbreviated *NBI*, for the selection of the best candidate label by using co-occurrence information between candidate words of regions within the same image. We approach this problem as a learning task considering the candidate labels for a given region as classes and the (association with) candidate labels of surrounding regions as attributes.

A Bayesian classifier aims to estimate $P(H_{1,...,M}|E)$, that is the probability of each of the hypotheses (or classes) given some evidence (attributes). Then, according to decision theory [10], the H_i that maximizes $P(H_{1,...,M}|E)$ is selected as the most probable class. In our case we would like to select the label C^l, from a set of M candidate labels ($C^l_{1,...,M}$), that maximizes $P(C^l_{1,...,M}|A^k_{1,...,N})$. Taking as our evidence the top$-N$ candidate labels for the surrounding regions ($A^k_{1,...,N}$). Therefore, applying Bayes theorem for inverting the conditional probability, dropping the denominator and assuming conditional independence among attributes given the class, we have a naïve Bayesian classifier:

$$P(C^l_{1,...,M}|A^k_{1,...,N}) = P(C^l_{1,...,M}) * \prod_{i=1}^{N} P(A^k_i|C^l_{1,...,M}) \qquad (3)$$

Where $P(C^l_{1,...,M})$ are the prior probabilities for each of the M candidate labels and $P(A^k_{1,...,N}|C^l_{1,...,M})$ are the conditionals of the candidate labels of other regions given the candidate labels for the region being analyzed. Therefore, we should calculate $P(C^l_{1,...,M}|A^k_{1,...,N})$ for each of the M candidate labels for a region and select the C^l that maximizes Equation (3) as the correct label for the region. The prior probability for each candidate label is the relevance ranking returned by the annotation method (see Equations (1) and (2)). The conditional probabilities $P(A^k_{1,...,N}|C^l_{1,...,M})$ are obtained from a co-occurrence matrix, as explained in the next Section. As we can see, in order to select a label for a given region, namely X, NBI considers the rank assigned to each candidate label of X by the annotation system; as well as the *semantic cohesion* between each candidate label of X and the set of candidate labels for regions surrounding X.

5   Obtaining Co-occurrence Information

The co-occurrence information matrix M_c consist of a $|V|_X|V|$ square matrix in which each entry $M_c(w_i, w_j)$ indicates the number of documents (on an external corpus) in which words w_i and w_j appeared together, where V is the set of words in the vocabulary[3]. That is, we considered each pair of words $(w_i, w_j) \in V_X V$ and searched for occurrences, at document level, of words (w_i, w_j). Then we count one co-occurrence if (w_i, w_j) appear together in a document. We did this for each of the $|V|.|V|$ pairs of words and for each document in our textual corpus. The documents we considered on this work were the captions of a new image retrieval collection: the *IAPR-TC12* [14] benchmark. This collection consists of about $20,000$ images that were manually annotated, at image level; therefore, if two words appear together in the captions of such collection, they are very likely to be visually related. Captions consist of a few text lines indicating visual and semantic content. Our matrix M_c then contains the co-occurrence information for each pair of words within the vocabulary on such corpus. From the entries of the M_c matrix we can obtain conditional probabilities if we take: $P(w_i|w_j) = \frac{P(w_i,w_j)}{P(w_j)} \approx \frac{c(w_i,w_j)}{c(w_j)}$, where $c(x)$ indicates the number of times x appears in the

---

[3] Co-occurrence matrix and code with implementations of the methods used in this paper can be obtained at *http://ccc.inaoep.mx/~hugojair/code/*

corpus, which can be obtained from M_c. If we do this for each pair of words in the vocabulary we obtain our conditional probabilities matrix P_M.

A problem with this P_M matrix is the sparseness of data, that is, many entries of the matrix have zero values, this is a very common problem in natural language processing [8]. This problem is particularly damaging to naïve Bayes, because a zero value in Equation (3) will result on a zero confidence value for the class in consideration. In order to alleviate this problem we applied two widely used smoothing techniques: Laplace and Interpolation smoothing [8]. Laplace, also known as sum-one smoothing, is based on in Equation (4), while interpolation smoothing[4] is based on Equation (5).

$$P(w_i|w_j) \approx \frac{c(w_i, w_j) + 1}{c(w_j) + |V|} \qquad (4)$$

$$P(w_i|w_j) \approx \lambda * \frac{c(w_i, w_j)}{c(w_j)} + (1 - \lambda) * c(w_j) \qquad (5)$$

Where $|V|$ is the vocabulary size and λ is a parameter that weights the contribution of the original conditional probabilities and the counts of the conditioned term. These two smoothing techniques are the simplest ones [8], though more elaborated smoothing techniques could be applied to the M_c matrix. Laplace smoothing dramatically affects highly occurrence terms while increasing probabilities for low frequency terms. On the other hand, interpolation smoothing acts as a scaling of the original P_M matrix. In none of the smoothed matrices we have zero-valued entries now. As we will see on Section 6, the selection of smoothing technique affects the performance of our *NBI* approach. Therefore, an enhancement on the co-occurrence matrix will directly improve the performance of our method.

6   Experimental Results

In order to evaluate our method we performed several experiments on three subsets of the benchmark Corel collection, which were also used in [11,4]. First we evaluated the performance of *knn* as annotation method and we compared *knn* to other state of the art annotation methods [4,5,3,11]. Then we evaluated how much accuracy improvement can we gain by applying *NBI* to *knn*. The subsets we used were made publicly available by Peter Carbonetto[5]. We used them due to the fact that the data sets are completely annotated at region level, which facilitates the evaluation of our method. The images of each subset were segmented with normalized cuts [23]. A sample segmented image is shown in Figure 1.

As features, we used color statistics and shape information from each region, resulting in 16 visual features. These features are described in detail in [4,3]. The Corel subsets we used are described in Table 1. All of the results reported in this paper are obtained by applying our methods to the test sets of each data set.

---

[4] We used $\lambda = 0.5$ for the experiments reported here.
[5] http://www.cs.ubc.ca/~pcarbo/

Fig. 1. Sample image with manual annotations from the Corel data set. Left: original image, right: image segmented with normalized cuts [23].

Table 1. Subsets of the Corel image collection we used in the experimentation with *knn-NBI*

Data set	# Images	Words	Training blobs	Testing blobs
A-NCUTS	205	22	1280	728
B-NCUTS	299	38	2070	998
C-NCUTS	504	55	3328	1748

6.1 *knn* as Automatic Image Annotation Method

In the first experiment we evaluated the performance of *knn* as an automatic image annotation method. We measured accuracy as the percentage of correctly annotated regions, where a region is say to be correctly annotated if the label assigned to the region corresponds to its true label. Results of this experiment for different values of k, in the three Corel subsets we considered, are shown in Table 2. As we may expect, accuracy of the *knn* method increases as we consider more neighbors. Furthermore, *knn* is not much sensible to the number of classes being considered; for subset C with 55 classes, accuracy was higher than that of subset B with 38 classes.

We also compared the *knn* method against several semi-supervised annotation methods, proposed in [4,5,3,11]. These methods are extensions and modifications

Table 2. Percentage of correctly annotated regions, considering a region is correctly annotated if the true label is found within the top$-k$ neighbors

K	A-NCUTS	B-NCUTS	C-NCUTS	Average
1	36.8%	28.22%	29.11%	**34.99%**
5	61.5%	49.15%	54.57%	**59.29%**
10	72.8%	57.65%	63.95%	**68.42%**
15	77.1%	62.21%	69.73%	**73.05%**
20	81.5%	65.67%	72.76%	**76.27%**

to the work proposed in [11]. A description of these methods is over the scope of this paper, for a detailed description of the methods we encourage the reader to follow the references. In order to provide an objective comparison, we used the code provided by Peter Carbonetto. This code includes implementations of the above mentioned methods and it is designed to work with the same Corel subsets we used. The error calculation and the plotting functions are also provided, which guarantee a fair comparison. In Figure 2 a comparison between the *knn* approach and the methods proposed in [11,4,5,3], for the *A-NCUTS* data set, is presented[6]. In this plot, error is computed using the following equation:

$$e = \frac{1}{N} \sum_{n=1}^{N} \frac{1}{M_n} \left(1 - \delta(\bar{a}_{nu} = a_{nu}^{max})\right) \tag{6}$$

Where M_n is the number of regions on image n, N is the number or images in the collection; and δ is an error function which is 1 if the predicted annotation a_{nu}^{max} is the same as the true label $\bar{a}_{nu}$. We ran 10 trials for each method, note that for *knn* a single trial could suffices since for every run the results are the same.

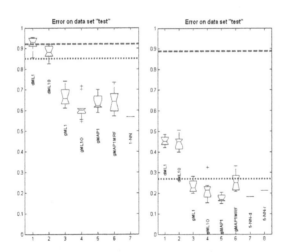

Fig. 2. Comparison of *knn* against semi-supervised methods proposed on [4,5,3,11], using a Box-and-Whisker plot. The central box represents the values from the 25 to 75 percentile, outliers are shown as separate points. Left: accuracy at the first label. Right: accuracy considering the top−5 labels as candidate ones. Suffixes *d* and *r* stand for the way we ranked labels for *knn*. The upper dotted line represents a random bound, while the bottom dotted line represents a naïve method that always assigns the same label to all regions.

---

[6] We only used the *A-NCUTS* data set, since we later report results with *NBI* on this data set, and the labels of the *A-NCUTS* set are the only ones that are fully contained in our P_M matrix.

The left plot in Figure 2 shows error at the first label. Error is high for all of the methods we considered, however *knn* outperforms in average to all of the semi-supervised approaches; in the plot this is clear for most of the considered methods. The *gMl0* method [3] is the closer in accuracy to *knn*, although *gMl0* obtains a superior average error of 4.5%. In the right plot of Figure 2 we consider a label is correctly annotated if the true label is within the top−5 candidate labels. As we can see, error for all methods is reduced, this clearly illustrates the fact that accuracy of annotation methods is high considering a set of candidate labels instead of the first one. In this case the *gMAP* method [5] outperforms *5-NN-d* in average by 0.9% which is not a significant improvement. The other approaches obtain higher average error than that of *knn-d*. The ranking by distance (Equation (1)) is a better ranking strategy, this can be due to the fact that with this formula we are implicitly taking into account repetition information as well as the relevance based on distance.

Results from Figure 2 and those from Table 2 give evidence that the *knn* approach is an accurate method for image annotation, besides the simplicity of the method. However, we have to say that while the *knn* method needs of a training data set composed of pairs of feature regions and label, the semi-supervised methods start from a data set of weakly annotated image. It is surprising that, to best of our knowledge, *knn* has not been widely used as a method for image annotation given its simplicity and accuracy. Probably, the main reason is the need of a representative training data set. However, it can be possible to take advantage of semi-supervised learning algorithms and unlabeled data for obtaining good training data sets, as in [21].

6.2   *knn* + NBI: Improving Annotation Accuracy

We conducted several experiments with *knn* followed by *NBI* in order to measure the annotation improvement based on word co-occurrence. We have several parameters to consider when running *knn + NBI*: *1)* we varied the way we calculated the priors for *NBI* from *knn*, using the distance approach (Equation (1)) or using the repetition of labels (Equation (2)); *2)* the number of neighbors to consider for each region $k \in [3, \ldots, 7]$ in *knn*, *3)* the number of top candidate labels for surrounding images that we considered, $k_{img} \in [1, \ldots, 5]$; *4)* a binary valued variable, indicating if we should take the intersection of labels occurring on the surrounding regions, or if we should count for each label[7]. Due to the efficiency of *knn* and *NBI* for the data sets we considered, we could ran experiments with all of the data subsets, though results in global accuracy are shown for the *A-NCUTS* only; since all of the words in this data set are present in our co-occurrence matrix P_M; while for the *B-NCUTS* and *C-NCUTS*, only a portion of the labels are present in P_M, therefore, accuracy improvement in these data sets should be measured differently, as we did in Figure 4.

Due to space limitations and the number of parameters considered, we report results of the best parameter configuration we obtained with *knn+NBI* over 100

---

[7] Where, if a label is repeated *t*-times we weight the conditional by a factor of *t*.

Table 3. Best configuration for each smoothing technique, we show the number of candidate labels for the region being analyzed (column 2), the number of candidate labels for the surrounding regions (column 3), if we used the intersection of candidate labels for surrounding images (column 4) and the way we obtained priors from *knn* to *NBI* (column 5)

Smoothing	#-C's	#-A's	Intersection	Prior-type
Interpolation	6	1	Yes	Distance
Laplace	6	1	Yes	Repetition

runs, varying the parameters as described at the beginning of this section. The best configuration for each of the smoothing techniques is presented in Table 3.

We can appreciate consistency in the parameters for both configurations. The only difference is in the way that priors where calculated; with Laplace smoothing Equation (2) worked well, while for the Interpolation smoothing, Equation (1) worked best. Something not showed here is that in every run (different parameters) of the interpolation smoothing there was always an improvement over *knn* alone. Although with the Laplace smoothing, only half of the times (approximately) there was an improvement.

In Figure 3 we show the error as in Equation (6), this time we compared the methods proposed in [4,5,3,11] with *knn* and *knn+NBI* with the Laplace

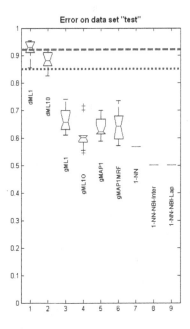

Fig. 3. Comparison of *knn* and *knn+NBI* against semi-supervised methods in [4,5,3,11]; error is measured at the first label. We used the parameter configurations described in Table 3.

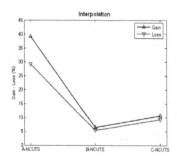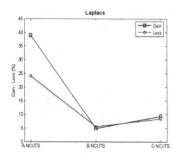

Fig. 4. Percentages of gain and lost of accuracy, for all the data sets. Results are averaged over 100 experiments, varying parameters. We plot results for both smoothing techniques we used: interpolation (Left) and Laplace (Right).

($knn+NBI\text{-}Lap$) and interpolation ($knn+NBI\text{-}Inter$) smoothing, with the parameters described in Table 3. Accuracy of both smoothing techniques is very close (they differ by 0.002, which can not be appreciated in the plot), though interpolation smoothing performed much more better in average. The advantage of $knn+NBI$ over knn is of about 6.5% for both smoothing techniques. Which is a significant improvement over knn alone; furthermore, the gain over the other annotation methods is clearly increased. The advantage of $knn+NBI$ over the closer semi-supervised method (gML10) is of around 11% in average, which is an evident advantage.

You should note that NBI can improve an annotation method, provided the correct label is within the top$-k$ candidate labels returned by such method, we call this improvements the *gain*. We only consider that we have a *gain* when $1\text{-}NN$ misclassified the region. On the other hand, NBI can decrease accuracy of annotation methods as well. This happens when $1\text{-}NN$ selects the correct annotation, but NBI returns an incorrect label, we call this *lost*. In Figure 4 we plot *gain* and *lost*, as defined above, in terms of percentages for the three data sets we considered.

From Figure 4 we can clearly appreciate that the gain is almost always superior to lost, note that each point in the plot is the result of averaging gain and lost over 100 trials, varying parameters for $knn+NBI$. From this plot, it is evident that the gain we obtain with NBI is significant over all data sets, and it is more evident on the $A\text{-}NCUTS$ data set, independently of the smoothing technique used. The gain decreases for the B and C sets due to the fact that we can only apply NBI to a portion of the instances; because not all words are represented in the co-occurrence matrix. In some cases there is a loose in accuracy, however we consider that this could be significantly improved by having a more extensive corpus to estimate the co-occurrence matrix, and considering more robust models such as Markov random fields. Furthermore, a key contribution of this work is that it can be applied to other annotation methods that rank labels for their relevance.

7 Conclusions

In this paper we have presented a method for the improvement of automatic image annotation methods at region level. Our method, *NBI*, is based on the fact that accuracy of annotation methods at the first label is lower than that obtained if we consider the set of the top−k candidate labels as annotations. *NBI* takes advantage of word co-occurrences among the candidate labels for a region and those of the other regions within the same image. Co-occurrence information is obtained off-line from an external collection of captions, which is a novel approach. Experimental results of our method on three subsets of the benchmark Corel collection, give evidence that the use of *NBI*, with *knn* as our annotation method, results in significant error reductions. We also show that the use of different smoothing techniques can affect the performance of *NBI*. Therefore, by building a more robust co-occurrence matrix and by considering more elaborated smoothing techniques we could obtain further improvements with *NBI*. Our method is efficient since we used a naïve Bayesian approach and the co-occurrence matrix is obtained off-line. Furthermore, *NBI* can be used with any other annotation method, provided it ranks labels for their relevance; even when the method does not ranks labels probabilistically, as we have shown here.

Future work includes the use of more robust probabilistic models, just like Markov random fields, for example. The improvement of the co-occurrence matrix is an immediate step towards the enhancement of *NBI*. Finally, we would like to test the *NBI* method with another annotation methods, and in other image collections, such as the *IAPR-TC12* benchmark [14].

Acknowledgements. We would like to thank Kobus Barnard and P. Carbonetto for making available their data and code on image annotation, and M. Grubinger for made available the *IAPR − TC*12 collection. Thanks too, to the members of the *INAOE-TIA-research group* by their comments and suggestions. This work was partially supported by CONACyT under grant 205834.

References

1. Barnard, K., Forsyth, D.: Learning the semantics of words and pictures. In: Proc. ICCV, vol. 2, pp. 408–415. IEEE, Los Alamitos (2001)
2. Blei, D.M., Jordan, M.I.: Modeling annotated data. In: Proc. of the 26th international ACM-SIGIR conf. on Research and development in informaion retrieval, pp. 127–134. ACM Press, New York, NY, USA (2003)
3. Carbonetto, P.: Unsupervised statistical models for general object recognition. Master's thesis, C.S. Department, University of British Columbia (August 2003)
4. Carbonetto, P., de Freitas, N., Barnard, K.: A statistical model for general context object recognition. In: Proc. of 8th ECCV, pp. 350–362 (2005)
5. Carbonetto, P., de Freitas, N., Gustafson, P., Thompson, N.: Bayesian feature eeighting for unsupervised learning. In: Proc. of the HLT-NAACL workshop on Learning word meaning from non-linguistic data, Morristown, NJ, USA, pp. 54–61 (2003)

6. Carneiro, G., Chan, A.B., Moreno, P.J., Vasconcelos, N.: Supervised learning of semantic classes for image annotation and retrieval. IEEE Trans. on PAMI 29(3), 394–410 (2007)
7. Carneiro, G., Vasconcelos, N.: Formulating semantic image annotation as a supervised learning problem. In: Proc. of CVPR, Washington, DC, USA, vol. 2, pp. 163–168. IEEE Computer Society, Los Alamitos (2005)
8. Chen, S.F., Goodman, J.: An empirical study of smoothing techniques for language modeling. In: Proc. of the 34th meeting on Association for Computational Linguistics, Morristown, NJ, USA, pp. 310–318 (1996)
9. Datta, R., Li, J., Wang, J.Z.: Content-based image retrieval - approaches and trends of the new age. In: Proceedings ACM International Workshop on Multimedia Information Retrieval, Singapore. ACM Multimedia, New York (2005)
10. Duda, R.O., Hart, P.E., Stork, D.G.: Pattern Classification, 2nd edn. Wiley-Interscience, Chichester (2000)
11. Duygulu, P., Barnard, K., de Freitas, N., Forsyth, D.: Object recognition as machine translation: Learning a lexicon for a fixed image vocabulary. In: Heyden, A., Sparr, G., Nielsen, M., Johansen, P. (eds.) ECCV 2002. LNCS, vol. 2353, pp. 97–112. Springer, Heidelberg (2002)
12. Iyengar, G., et al.: Joint visual-text modeling for automatic retrieval of multimedia documents. In: Proc. the 13th MULTIMEDIA, pp. 21–30. ACM Press, New York, NY, USA (2005)
13. Ghoshal, A., Ircing, P., Khudanpur, S.: Hmm's for automatic annotation and content-based retrieval of images and video. In: Proc. of the 28th int. conf. on Research and development in information retrieval, New York, NY, USA, pp. 544–551 (2005)
14. Grubinger, M., Clough, P., Leung, C.: The iapr tc-12 benchmark -a new evaluation resource for visual information systems. In: Proc. of the International Workshop OntoImage 2006 Language Resources for CBIR (2006)
15. Hare, J.S., Lewis, P.H., Enser, P.G.B., Sandom, C.J.: Mind the Gap: Another look at the problem of the semantic gap in image retrieval. In: Hanjalic, A., Chang, E.Y., Sebe, N. (eds.) Proceedings of Multimedia Content Analysis, Management and Retrieval, San Jose, California, USA, SPIE, vol. 6073 (2006)
16. Lavrenko, V., Manmatha, R., Jeon, J.: A model for learning the semantics of pictures. In: NIPS, vol. 16. MIT Press, Cambridge, MA (2004)
17. Li, W., Sun, M.: Automatic image annotation based on wordnet and hierarchical ensembles. In: Gelbukh, A. (ed.) CICLING 2006. LNCS, vol. 3878, pp. 417–428. Springer, Heidelberg (2006)
18. Liu, Y., Zhang, D., Lu, G., Ma, W.Y.: A survey of content-based image retrieval with high-level semantics. Pattern Recogn. 40(1), 262–282 (2007)
19. Mitchell, T.: Machine Learning. McGraw-Hill Education, New York (1997)
20. Mori, Y., Takahashi, H., Oka, R.: Image-to-word transformation based on dividing and vector quantizing images with words. In: 1st Int. Worksh. on Multimedia Intelligent Storage and Retrieval Management (1999)
21. Nigam, K., McCallum, A., Thrun, S., Mitchell, T.: Text classification from labeled and unlabeled documents using em. Machine Learning 39, 103–134 (2000)
22. Pan, J., Yang, H., Duygulu, P., Faloutsos, C.: Automatic image captioning. In: Proc. of the ICME (2004)
23. Shi, J., Malik, J.: Normalized cuts and image segmentation. PAMI-IEEE 22(8), 888–905 (2000)
24. Smeulders, A.W.M., Worring, M., Santini, S., Gupta, A., Jain, R.: Content-based image retrieval at the end of the early years. IEEE Trans. on PAMI 22(12), 1349–1380 (2000)

Automatic Image Annotation with Relevance Feedback and Latent Semantic Analysis

Donn Morrison, Stéphane Marchand-Maillet, and Eric Bruno

Centre Universitaire Informatique
Université de Genève, Genève, Switzerland
{donn.morrison, marchand, eric.bruno}@cui.unige.ch
http://viper.unige.ch/

Abstract. The goal of this paper is to study the image-concept relationship as it pertains to image annotation. We demonstrate how automatic annotation of images can be implemented on partially annotated databases by learning image-concept relationships from positive examples via inter-query learning. Latent semantic analysis (LSA), a method originally designed for text retrieval, is applied to an image/session matrix where relevance feedback examples are collected from a large number of artificial queries (sessions). Singular value decomposition (SVD) is exploited during LSA to propagate image annotations using only relevance feedback information. We will show how SVD can be used to filter a noisy image/session matrix and reconstruct missing values.

1 Introduction

Content-based image retrieval is burdened by a dichotomy between user-desired high-level concepts and the low-level descriptions that retrieval systems are capable of indexing. During an interactive query, *relevance feedback (RF)* attempts to narrow this gap by allowing a user to refine the query by selecting positive and negative examples. After each iteration, a model is updated to reflect the modified query and a new result set is returned to the user. Despite the advantages, however, a query session using relevance feedback is cumbersome and the user must possess a priori knowledge about the low-level structure of the desired image: the colours, shapes, and textures it contains.

1.1 Redefining the Query

Keyword-based queries, popularised by internet search engines and text-based document retrieval, are more desirable from a user's perspective. For image retrieval, this changes the field substantially. Where users were previously confined to retrieval by low-level feature similarity (*query by example (QBE)*), they would now be able to specify their queries more naturally using high-level semantics. Where relevance feedback once dominated the narrowing of a query, the augmentation of query terms now stands to take its place.

However, this presents an obvious problem: keyword-based image retrieval can only be realised on accurately and completely annotated databases. Furthermore, indexed keywords must describe the images and/or image regions in many ways. Polysemy

N. Boujemaa, M. Detyniecki, and A. Nürnberger (Eds.): AMR 2007, LNCS 4918, pp. 71–84, 2008.

and synonymy present problems as similar concepts can be described using different terms and different concepts can be described with similar terms. But ultimately, the prohibitive barrier is on the creation of annotated databases themselves. It is infeasible to manually annotate images given the scope and size of image collections nowadays.

This realisation changes the focus of content-based image retrieval from a query problem to that of a semantic extraction problem. This is precisely the goal of this paper: to experiment with a method of propagating image labels onto unannotated images via instances of relevance feedback made during user queries. In this way, an image collection can be incrementally annotated beginning with a small (but sufficiently uniform) subset of labelled images.

1.2   Traditional Image Annotation

Despite suffering problems relating to subjectivity, the manual annotation of image collections, that is having users hand-label the images, is the most accurate method for creating a database on which reliable keyword-based queries can be made. However, most image databases are too large and too complex to facilitate such a task. Some studies successfully harness social aspects of image labelling, such as the ESP Game [1], where users compete to label as many images as possible in a set amount of time, but for specialised databases with sensitive applications in medicine or security, this approach is impractical and manual annotation is beyond reach.

Another popular approach in the literature is the use of semi-automatic annotation methods [2]. Here users play a limited role, effectively managing, correcting, or judging annotations resulting from automatic algorithms. Automatic algorithms must make use of the features contained in the images, as mentioned above: colour, texture, shape, etc. Similarities between images mean that keywords can be shared, but as these approaches largely lack any semantic understanding of the actual content beyond the low-level features, users must provide this high-level information.

A need arises to extract the semantic knowledge users possess about images they view or interact with and apply it at the collection level so that relationships between images are formed. This has been acknowledged in the literature for some time [3,4,5,6,7,8,9], but we see it as an underdeveloped area that needs further activity in order to mature.

The rest of this paper is organised as follows. In Section 2 we review existing automatic annotation techniques in the literature. These include generative models, classification-, and cluster-based approaches. Next, in Section 3 we describe our experiments and the structure of the database used. Section 4 examines our initial results and finally Section 5 concludes with some avenues for improvement and future research.

2   Automatic Image Annotation

2.1   Latent-Space and Generative Models

Automatic image annotation can be approached with a variety of machine learning methods, from supervised classification to probabilistic to clustering. It is common to borrow latent and generative models from text retrieval such as latent semantic analysis

(LSA) [10] and it's probabilistic cousin, PLSA [11]. These two latent-space models are compared in [12]. The authors pose the question of whether annotation by propagation is better than annotation by inference. LSA is shown to outperform PLSA. However, they explain that some of the reasons for this may be that LSA is better at annotating images from uniformly annotated databases.

In a later paper, the authors introduce an improved probabilistic latent model, called *PLSA-words*, which models a set of documents using dual cooperative PLSA models. The intention is to increase the relevance of the captions in the latent space. The process is divided into two stages: parameter learning, where the latent models are trained, and annotation inference, where annotations are projected onto unseen images using the generated models. In the first stage, the first PLSA model is trained on a set of captions and a new latent model is trained on the visual features of the corresponding images. In the second stage, the standard PLSA technique projects a latent variable onto the new image, and annotations of an aspect are assigned if the probability exceeds a threshold [13].

Extensions of PLSA have been described, for example *latent Dirichlet allocation (LDA)*, introduced in [14], which models documents as probabilistic mixtures of topics which are comprised of sets of words [15]. This model was applied to image annotation in a slightly modified version called *correspondence latent Dirichlet allocation (Corr-LDA)* [16]. In this study, the authors compare the algorithm with two standard hierarchical probabilistic mixture models. Three tasks are identified: modelling the joint distribution of the image and it's caption, determining the conditional distribution of words in an image, and determining the conditional distribution of words in an image region. The Corr-LDA model first generates region descriptions from the image using an LDA model. Then corresponding caption words and image regions are selected, based on how the image region was selected.

2.2 Supervised Learning Approaches

In [17] a statistical model using multi-resolution hidden Markov models (MHMMs) is presented for automatic annotation of images. The authors use global features consisting of colour and texture features. Wavelets are used for representing the texture features and the LUV colour space is used for the colour features. Three benefits are given to the usage of the statistical model: simple retraining when new images are added; individual models can be retrained easily as they represent a single concept; likelihood for similarity based on global features. The images are first subsampled into multiple resolutions, each of which are used for different levels of feature extraction. For each concept, a statistical model is built based on the training images. Next, test images are introduced and the system searches a dictionary for the most keywords which have the greatest likelihood of describing the image. These terms are then associated with the image.

In [18], a method (confidence-based dynamic ensemble, or CDE) is proposed which utilises one-class SVMs at the base level to extract a confidence factor on the prediction of a two-class SVM on the classification of an image. This confidence factor is also used to dynamically alter the characteristics of the member classifiers. At the base level, binary SVMs are used to make a distinction on one semantic label. The confidence factor is found by using the one-class SVM, and the prediction is mapped to a posterior probability. At the multi-class level, the confidence factors from the base classifiers are combined to predict a single class. At the bag-level, results from many classifiers are combined using different partitions of the training data in a standard bagging technique. The dynamic ensemble (DE) part of the system takes predictions with low confidence and tries to retrain specialist classifiers using reduced-class training data depending on which classes are most certain. The authors recognise the added complexity, but note that most automatic annotation is done off-line, and that the DE is only applied to low confidence instances, and that the DE only considers the relevant classes.

In [19], salient regions were used as the features for an automatic annotation framework. A statistical model was also used, dubbed the cross-media relevance model, to uncover correlation between visual features and keywords. The model finds the joint probability distribution between image regions and the keywords of the annotated training data. Salient regions are used in place of global image descriptors, and the Scale Invariant Feature Transform (SIFT) feature is also used. A hybrid approach joins the two methods and annotation accuracy is found to be better than LSI (k=4) and vector-space methods.

2.3   Unsupervised Learning Approaches

The combination of short-term and long-term learning is explored in [20] where K-means clustering is used to update a series of one-class support vector machines, each of which corresponds to an instance of relevance feedback during a query. Following the initial query, the nearest neighbour images (in features space and cluster proximity) are returned. After relevance feedback, a one-class SVM is trained on the relevant images. This new SVM becomes the new query. The process is repeated until the session terminates.

User intervention is relied upon in a clustering approach in [2] where the authors employ similarity methods with semi-supervised fuzzy clustering for semi-automatic image annotation. The premise is that user intervention may be required to help accurately define clusters by specifying pairwise relationships (must-link, cannot-link) between instances which are at the borders of automatically defined clusters. This method relies on the assumption that users can easily specify the pairwise constraints on images and that after specifying such constraints the clusters in question are better separated. The centroids of strong clusters are found by isolating and purging spurious small clusters. The method is compared with two other clustering methods: CA and K-means. The authors conclude that as long as the user intervention is minimal and simple, important information can be gleaned from this step.

The work in [21] and [22] builds and improves on a semantic ensemble which uses an ontology such as WordNet for determining a hierarchical representation of the semantic information for automatic annotation. One process specialises in propagating generic semantic information while the other process works to introduce specific knowledge about the document.

[23] describe a system for pruning irrelevant terms from automatically annotated images using word similarity in WordNet. Images are segmented into blobs using the normalised cuts algorithm [24] which are associated with keywords based on the distance between the image and the centroids of the blobs. The similarity of the keywords is

measured using a hybrid approach comprising three WordNet noun distance measures. Scores are combined using Dempster-Shafer Evidence Combination. Words which are viewed as outliers to others in the annotation are pruned.

2.4 Exploiting User Interaction

A different modality can be introduced to harnesses the knowledge generated by users or groups of users interacting with an image database, whether it be browsing or performing longer queries (including but not limited to relevance feedback). By observing these interactions and the associations made between relevant and non-relevant images during a query, semantic themes can start to become apparent. These themes need not be named entities such as words describing objects or concepts, but can simply be relationships between images indicating some level of semantic similarity.

This type of learning is dubbed *inter-query learning* due to the feature space spanning multiple (or all) query sessions. The converse is the traditional *intra-query learning*: the utilisation of relevance feedback examples during the current query only (after the session has ended the weights are discarded). Inter-query learning takes an approach similar to collaborative filtering; interaction (in the form of queries with relevance feedback) is required to increase density in the feature space. It is in this way that a collection can be incrementally annotated. The more interaction and querying, the more accurate the annotations become.

The Viper group produced one of the first studies which looked at inter-query learning [3]. The authors analysed the logs of queries using the *GIFT (GNU Image Finding Tool)* demonstration system over a long period of time and used this information to update the *tf-idf* feature weightings. Images were paired based on two rules: images sharing similar features and also marked relevant have a high weight while images sharing similar features but marked both relevant and irrelevant should have a low weight (indicating a semantic disagreement). Two factors were introduced to manage the relevance feedback information. The first being a measure of the difference between the positively and negatively rated marks for each feature and the second re-weighting the positively and negatively marked features differently such that the ratio is scaled non-linearly.

Later, in [4], the authors focus more formally on annotation. A general framework is described which annotates the images in a collection using relevance feedback instances. As a user browses an image database using a CBIR system, providing relevance feedback as the query progresses, the system automatically annotates images using the relationships described by the user.

Taking a direction toward the fusion of the two modalities, [5] combine inter-query learning with traditional low-level image features to build semantic similarities between images for use in later retrieval sessions. The similarity model between the request and target images are refined during a standard relevance feedback process for the current session. This refinement and fusion is facilitated by a *barycenter*. The paper also discusses the problems with asymmetrical learning, where the irrelevant images are marked irrelevant by the user for a variety of reasons, whereas relevant images are marked relevant only because they relate semantically to the query. Therefore, the authors reduce the relevance of irrelevant images during the fusion of feedback stages. Similarly, in [6], a statistical correlation model is built to create semantic relationships between images based on the co-occurrence frequency that images are rated relevant to a query. These relationships are fused with low-level features (256 colour histogram, colour moments, 64 colour coherence, Tamura coarseness and directionality) to propagate the annotations onto unseen images.

In [7], inter-query learning is used to improve the accuracy of a retrieval system and latent semantic indexing (LSI) is used in a way such that the interactions are the documents and the images correspond to the term vocabulary of the system. The authors perform a validation experiment on image databases consisting of both texture and segmentation data from the MIT and UCI repositories. Random queries were created and two sessions of relevance feedback were conducted to generate the historical information to be processed by LSI. From experiments on different levels of data, they conclude that LSI is robust to a lack of data quality but is highly dependent on the sparsity of interaction data.

This method of exchanging RF instances and images for the documents and term vocabulary was also used in a later study where the authors use long-term learning in the PicSOM retrieval system [8]. PicSOM is based on multiple parallel tree-structured *self-organising maps (SOMs)* and uses MPEG7 content descriptors for features. The authors claim that by the use of SOMs the system automatically picks the most relevant features. They note that the relevance feedback information provided by the users is similar to hidden annotations. Using Corel images with a ground truth set of 6 classes, MPEG7 features scalable colour, dominant colour, colour structure, colour layout, edge histogram, homogeneous texture, and region shape, the authors reported a significant increase in performance.

In [9] long term user interaction with a relevance feedback system is used to make better semantic judgements on unlabelled images for the purpose of image annotation. Relationships between images which are created during relevance feedback can denote similar or dissimilar concepts. The authors also try to improve the learning of semantic features by "a moving of the feature vectors" around a group of concept points, without specifically computing the concept points. The idea is to cluster the vectors around the concept centres.

In this section we have reviewed the many approaches to automatic image annotation. The traditional approaches, such as those which attempt to label images using generative probabilistic models or that rely on document similarity to label images clearly have not succeeded in narrowing the semantic gap. Until the time when these automatic methods are able to recognise and infer semantic concepts, the knowledge required to fill this gap must come from the user.

3   Experimental Framework

For our experiments, a subset of the Corel database was chosen due to its ubiquitous use in the image retrieval community. Ten categories were arbitrarily chosen to reduce the complexity of the data set for the initial experiment: *architecture, beach, bird, cloud, flower, insect, leopard, lizard, mushroom, sunrise/sunset.* For each category there are 20 images, bringing the total number of images in the collection to 200.

Table 1. Concept-category relationships

Concept	Category
landscape	beach
	sunrise/sunset
sky	beach
	cloud
	sunrise/sunset
animals	birds
	insect
	leopard
	lizard
plants	flower
	mushroom
man-made	architecture

We group categories into concepts to build an artificial data set for inter-query learning. Concepts are used to describe semantically similar categories. For example, the concept "landscape" can describe images depicting beaches and sunrise/sunset and "animals" can describe images depicting birds and lizards. We use concepts to model more general themes from relevance feedback examples. Table 1 shows the concept-category relationships used in the experiments.

A pool of 100 artificial relevance feedback sessions was created by setting all images under a concept as relevant to that query. In essence, the matrix created is a groundtruth matrix where all concepts are related to the categories through artificial sessions. This data simulates query sessions where users would have a concept image in mind (for example, images depicting animals), and would construct the query by selecting a number of positive and negative examples.

Thus, a matrix A is created where the columns represent the RF sessions and the rows represent the images [7,8]. Figure 1 shows this matrix. It is highly redundant because of the large number of RF sessions generated and the low number of concepts.

In this experiment, only the positive examples ($A(i,j) == +1$) are used in order to simplify the propagation stage (we will ignore irrelevant concepts for the moment). Next, to simulate missing relevance feedback data, the values of A are randomly dropped (set to 0) to form a new noisy matrix, A_n. Singular value decomposition (SVD) is applied to this matrix to yield:

$$A_n = U \Sigma V^T.$$ (1)

The diagonal matrix Σ contains the singular values. We retain only $k = 5$ concepts from Σ to filter out unimportant concepts and reconstruct A as A_r.

$$A_r = U \Sigma' V^T$$ (2)

With A_n reconstructed as A_r, we now apply a thresholding measure to allow diffusion of relevance feedback examples into cells with missing data. As a result of SVD,

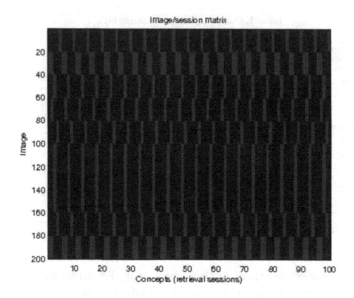

Fig. 1. Complete artificially generated relevance feedback matrix A

cells previously zero will now be non-zero. These values are normalised into the same space as A_n and then thresholded at 0.7, giving:

$$A_r(i, j) = \begin{cases} 1 & \text{where} \quad A_r(i, j) > 0.7 \\ 0 & \text{otherwise} \end{cases} \qquad (3)$$

The result is the reconstructed matrix with values that should minimise the difference from A_n:

$$D_{nr} = \sum_{i,j} |A_n(i, j) - A_r(i, j)| \qquad (4)$$

Based on this reconstructed data, we can propagate image labels from similar concepts. Note that this process does not differentiate between terms at the keyword level. Different keywords in the annotations can describe different parts of the image, some of which may not be present in images under a similar concept. In order to alleviate this, an extension using regions must be employed.

We want to annotate the unlabelled images in the database to allow for keyword-based queries. Image similarities are specified by the user by way of relevance feedback. This alone could be sufficient for labelling, but normally the feature space is very sparse, and some diffusion is needed to propagate image labels throughout the collection.

We start by simulating a uniform partially annotated database. We discard all annotations except for 25% in each concept. Thus, for the concept "sky," we have 15 annotated images out of 60. For each concept in the reconstructed matrix A_r, we determine the most common keywords by image.

Consider the reconstructed matrix A_r. Recall that the rows correspond to images, I_i and the columns correspond to concepts, C_j. Using A_r, the concepts C_j for image I_i

are summed and a vote is cast determining to which concept I_i belongs. There is a case when A_n will be too sparse that reconstruction will yield no concepts for an image I_i. In this case the image can only be labelled when further query sessions have been added to A, or in the case of our artificial situation, when the number of cells deleted from A is reduced.

4   Results and Discussion

4.1   SVD and Missing Value Recovery

Figure 2 shows the effect that incremental random deletions have on the distance from A_n and A_r. Starting with a fully annotated set and incrementally removing data has a non-linear effect on the distance measure. Note that as the deletions approach the maximum, the distance begins to decrease slightly due to the instability of the SVD on a very sparse matrix.

Figure 3 shows A_n, which results from the random cell deletion on A at 80%. In our experiments, the percentage of cell deletion was varied to see how SVD handles incremental missing values. Finally, Figures 4 and 5 show the reconstructed image/session matrix A_r, before and after thresholding, respectively. It can be seen that one category of images (Figure 5, images 61-80) suffers more corruption after reconstruction than the rest, with almost no associated concepts. This is because the category in question, "cloud", belongs to only one concept ("sky"), while the other members of that concept belong to two concepts ("landscape" and "sky"). This causes the "cloud" category to have less influence, and thus, SVD tries to map the "cloud" concept onto these images.

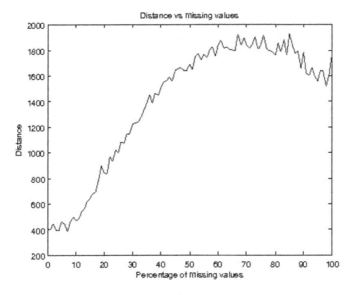

Fig. 2. Distance between A_n and A_r versus percentage of deleted cells

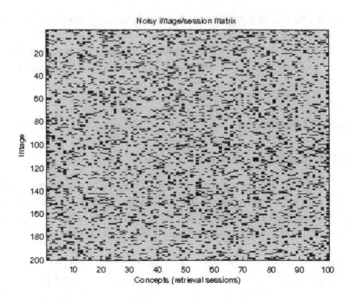

Fig. 3. Noisy image/session matrix A_n with 80% percent cell deletion

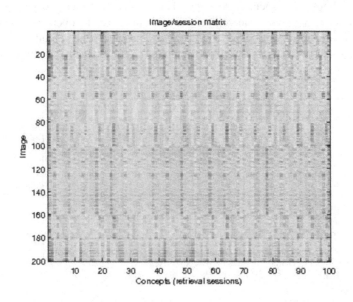

Fig. 4. Reconstructed image/session matrix A_r

4.2   Annotation Propagation

Figure 6 shows some example images which have been labelled using our propagation method. It is apparent that the method blankets images under each concept with

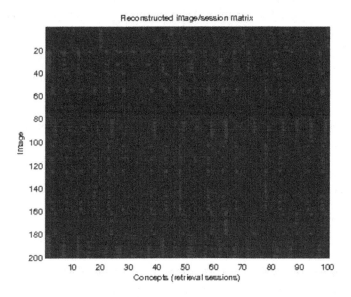

Fig. 5. Thresholded image/session matrix A_r showing reconstruction by SVD

Fig. 6. Automatically labelled images with cell deletions at 80% and SVD threshold of 0.7

words that have the highest distribution. Although this allows some relevant keywords to be propagated onto unlabelled images, the final annotations leave much room for improvement.

An ontology such as WordNet could be used to find parent concepts shared between labels to apply a more general annotation, as was done in [22]. For example, instead of the top-middle image in Figure 6 being labelled "bird tree insect lizard," when it is clearly a leopard, the common parent between "lizard," "bird," and "insect", which is "animal," could be used. This would more naturally model the concepts we have chosen.

This method has a quantization effect on the propagation of image labels due to the use of broad concepts. In the example of architecture in Figure 6, the labels more closely model the image than some of the other examples because the "man-made" concept contains only the "architecture" category. For the "animals" concept, the images are labelled with a high proportion of "lizards," most likely due to the distribution of keywords in the annotations.

In the case of the bottom left-most image in Figure 6, no labels were propagated because the reconstructed matrix was too sparse to determine a concept. As mentioned above, this can be alleviated by adding more relevance feedback examples to the original matrix A which sufficiently cover the concept and involve the image.

5   Conclusion

In this paper we reviewed several state of the art image annotation methods in the literature. The main goal was to determine whether the image-concept relationship, derived from inter-query learning, could be used to annotate images in a partially labelled corpus. We demonstrated how the SVD algorithm responds to incremental cell deletions in the image/session matrix and showed how it can be used with thresholding to reconstruct a matrix with missing values. This reconstructed matrix can be used to annotate unlabelled images in the collection. A set of artificial relevance feedback examples were used as a source of semantic knowledge, alleviating the reliance on low-level features. We have shown that labels can be propagated based on these semantic relationships.

We would like to address some of the drawbacks introduced with this method of label propagation. The first is that the categories are blurred due to the broad (and narrow) scope of the chosen concepts. This can be improved by diversifying the initial image-session matrix A so that there are more concepts or so that there are more than one concept per session. Second, because artificial image-concept data was used, the initial results may be inflated. We hope to acquire a large amount of natural data through long-term use of a retrieval system. This would enable the extraction of more diverse concepts.

We plan to extend the model to utilise low-level image features such as colour, texture, and shape to further improve incremental annotation accuracy. Because keywords are propagated blindly with respect to actual image content, a more accurate approach would specify annotations that correspond to image regions so that irrelevant labels are not assigned. The use of WordNet will also be investigated to find common concepts within the vocabulary.

Acknowledgements

This study was funded by the Swiss NCCR Interactive Multi-modal Information Management (IM2).

References

1. von Ahn, L., Dabbish, L.: Labeling images with a computer game. In: CHI 2004: Proceedings of the SIGCHI conference on Human factors in computing systems, pp. 319–326. ACM Press, New York, NY, USA (2004)
2. Grira, N., Crucianu, M., Boujemaa, N.: Active semi-supervised fuzzy clustering for image database categorization. In: MIR 2005: Proceedings of the 7th ACM SIGMM international workshop on Multimedia information retrieval, pp. 9–16. ACM Press, New York, NY, USA (2005)
3. Mueller, H., Mueller, W., Squire, D.M., Marchand-Maillet, S., Pun, T.: Long-term learning from user behavior in content-based image retrieval. Technical report, Université de Genève (2000)
4. Wenyin, L., Dumais, S., Sun, Y., Zhang, H., Czerwinski, M., Field, B.: Semi-automatic image annotation (2001)
5. Fournier, J., Cord, M.: Long-term similarity learning in content-based image retrieval (2002)
6. Li, M., Chen, Z., Zhang, H.: Statistical correlation analysis in image retrieval (2002)
7. Heisterkamp, D.: Building a latent-semantic index of an image database from patterns of relevance feedback (2002)
8. Koskela, M., Laaksonen, J.: Using long-term learning to improve efficiency of content-based image retrieval (2003)
9. Cord, M., Gosselin, P.H.: Image retrieval using long-term semantic learning. In: IEEE International Conference on Image Processing (2006)
10. Deerwester, S.C., Dumais, S.T., Landauer, T.K., Furnas, G.W., Harshman, R.A.: Indexing by latent semantic analysis. Journal of the American Society of Information Science 41(6), 391–407 (1990)
11. Hofmann, T.: Unsupervised learning by probabilistic latent semantic analysis. IEEE Trans. on PAMI 25 (2000)
12. Monay, F., Gatica-Perez, D.: On image auto-annotation with latent space models. In: Proc. ACM Int. Conf. on Multimedia (ACM MM), Berkeley (2003)
13. Monay, F., Gatica-Perez, D.: Plsa-based image auto-annotation: Constraining the latent space. In: MULTIMEDIA 2004: Proceedings of the 12th annual ACM international conference on Multimedia, pp. 348–351. ACM Press, New York, NY, USA (2004)
14. Blei, D.M., Ng, A.Y., Jordan, M.I.: Latent dirichlet allocation. Journal of Machine Learning Research 3, 993–1022 (2003)
15. Barnard, K., Duygulu, P., Forsyth, D., de Freitas, N., Blei, D., Jordan, M.: Matching words and pictures. Machine Learning Research 3, 1107–1135 (2003)
16. Blei, D.M., Jordan, M.I.: Modeling annotated data. In: SIGIR 2003: Proceedings of the 26th annual international ACM SIGIR conference on Research and development in informaion retrieval, pp. 127–134. ACM Press, New York, NY, USA (2003)
17. Wang, J.Z., Li, J.: Learning-based linguistic indexing of pictures with 2-d mhmms. In: MULTIMEDIA 2002: Proceedings of the tenth ACM international conference on Multimedia, pp. 436–445. ACM Press, New York, NY, USA (2002)
18. Goh, K.S., Chang, E.Y., Li, B.: Using one-class and two-class svms for multiclass image annotation. IEEE Transactions on Knowledge and Data Engineering 17(10), 1333–1346 (2005)

19. Tang, J., Hare, J.S., Lewis, P.H.: Image auto-annotation using a statistical model with salient regions. In: Proceedings of IEEE International Conference on Multimedia & Expo (ICME), Hilton Toronto, Toronto, Ontario, Canada (2006)
20. Gondra, I., Heisterkamp, D.R.: Incremental semantic clustering summarizing inter-query learning in content-based image retrieval via. In: Proceedings of the International Conference on Information Technology: Coding and Computing (ITCC 2004) (2004)
21. Kosinov, S., Marchand-Maillet, S.: Multimedia autoannotation via hierarchical semantic ensembles. In: Proceedings of the Int. Workshop on Learning for Adaptable Visual Systems (LAVS 2004), Cambridge, UK (2004)
22. Kosinov, S., Marchand-Maillet, S.: Hierarchical ensemble learning for multimedia categorization and autoannotation. In: Proceedings of the 2004 IEEE Signal Processing Society Workshop (MLSP 2004), São Luís, Brazil, pp. 645–654 (2004)
23. Jin, Y., Khan, L., Wang, L., Awad, M.: Image annotations by combining multiple evidence & wordnet. In: MULTIMEDIA 2005: Proceedings of the 13th annual ACM international conference on Multimedia, pp. 706–715. ACM Press, New York, NY, USA (2005)
24. Shi, J., Malik, J.: Normalized cuts and image segmentation. IEEE Transactions on Pattern Analysis and Machine Intelligence 22(8), 888–905 (2000)

A Novel Retrieval Refinement and Interaction Pattern by Exploring Result Correlations for Image Retrieval

Rongrong Ji, Hongxun Yao, Shaohui Liu, Jicheng Wang, and Pengfei Xu

VILAB, School of Computer Science, Harbin Institute of Technology, No.92,
West Dazhi Street, Harbin, 150001, China
{rrji,yhx,shaohl}@vilab.hit.edu.cn

Abstract. Efficient retrieval of image database that contains multiple predefined categories (e.g. medical imaging databases, museum painting collections) poses significant challenges and commercial prospects. By exploring category correlations of retrieval results in such scenario, this paper presents a novel retrieval refinement and feedback framework. It provides users a novel perceptual-similar interaction pattern for topic-based image retrieval. Firstly, we adopts Pairwise-Coupling SVM (PWC-SVM) to classify retrieval results into predefined image categories, and reorganizes them into category-based browsing topics. Secondly, in feedback interaction, category operation is supported to capture users' retrieval purpose fast and efficiently, which differs from traditional relevance feedback patterns that need elaborate image labeling. Especially, an Asymmetry Bagging SVM (ABSVM) network is adopted to precisely capture users' retrieval purpose. And user interactions are accumulated to reinforce our inspections of image database. As demonstrated in experiments, remarkable feedback simplifications are achieved comparing to traditional interaction patterns based on image labeling. And excellent feedback efficiency enhancements are gained comparing to traditional SVM-based feedback learning methods.

Keywords: image retrieval, image classification, relevance feedback, support vector machine, pairwise coupling, bagging.

1 Introduction

Content-based image retrieval (CBIR) is a technique that effectively retrieves images based on their visual contents [1]. Over the past decade, many efforts have been carried out to enhance the retrieval precision and recall of CBIR systems [2]. However, few attentions are concerned on investigating result correlations and representing retrieval result in a more perceptual similar manner. Better representation leads to more efficient and effective user browsing, which can inspire user passions in interaction engagement. Traditional CBIR methods simply return to user the most similar retrieval results without any post-processing. The correlations between query results is out of consideration.

In many cases, the image databases are consisted of image categories that can be predefined to certain degree, in which image category is known beforehand but only a

N. Boujemaa, M. Detyniecki, and A. Nürnberger (Eds.): AMR 2007, LNCS 4918, pp. 85–94, 2008.

very limited number of category images can obtained for training. In such case, fixed image pre-classification is not a feasible solution for user browsing since the classification precision and recall are very limited. However, online classification of retrieval results, which can assist user navigation by topic-based image representation, is feasible. For instance, images in many medical databases are of finite kinds of imaging modalities and anatomic regions. Similar examples can be found in, e.g. , remote-sense satellite image database (landforms can be predefined), art museum painting collections (consists of portraitures, landscape, tachisme paintings et. al.), sports news image database (sports image such as soccer, baseball, tennis can be predefined beforehand). In such scenario, the design of CBIR browsing and interaction pattern can be improved by integrating domain-specific knowledge. Especially, in such cases, users maybe request category search and wish the search result to be represented in a topic-specific manner. Similar but not identical researches can be found in textual retrieval [16] [17]. In unsupervised scenario, clustering-driven retrieval refinement is an ad hoc research area [18]. For instance, Vivisimo (*http://vivisimo.com*) is a search engine that automatically clusters search results into representative categories.

Fig. 1. Clustering-Based retrieval result representation in Vivisimo

To the best of our knowledge, clustering & categorizing-based refinement in image retrieval is also becoming a new research hot-spot. For instance, some interactive search engines participating in the TRECVID benchmark offer such functionality. And some of them (e.g., Columbia, IBM) also feature cluster-based re-ranking of results. Chen [12] developed a cluster-based image retrieval system: CLUE to automatically cluster content-based search results by unsupervised learning. And Lee [13] indexed objects based on shape and grouped retrieval results into a set of clusters, in which cluster is represented by a prototype based on the learning of the users' specific preference.

Furthermore, the relevance feedback mechanism can be further simplified and improved using predefined category knowledge in above-mentioned scenario. To integrate human supervision into retrieval, traditional relevance feedback schemes [3-5, 14] need users to manually label certain amount of positive/negative example images. However, in many cases, users are reluctant to provide sufficient feedback images, since this labeling procedure is tedious and burdensome. Thus it affects the efficiency of RF learning algorithms. As a result, the poor RF learning results would cause users to end their retrieval tasks with a failure.

To address these issues in above-mentioned scenario, this paper proposes a novel retrieval refinement and feedback learning framework, which leads to a new user browsing and interaction pattern. Our target is to facilitate user browsing and enhance interaction efficiency. Firstly, pre-categorized images are utilized for Pairwise-Coupling SVM training, which produces a set of one-to-one category classifiers. In retrieval, the initial similarity ranking results (Top k most similar images) are classified into their corresponding image categories. Both top k ranking results and top m ranking categories are returned to the users. In RF procedure, category selection and labeling is available (No selection indicates the appearing image categories are all negative examples). The image similarities are re-ranked using the user-provided positive and negative image categories. Especially, an asymmetry bagging SVM (ABSVM) network is adopted in category-based RF learning. Finally, in a successful retrieval, the query image is added into its positive labeled category in training collection. Fig.2 shows our refinement system framework.

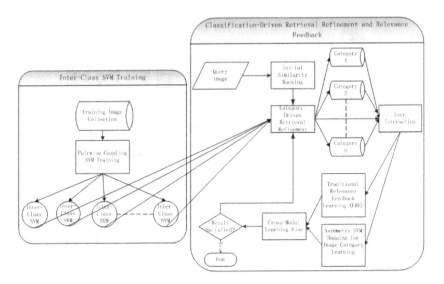

Fig. 2. Category-Based Retrieval Refinement and Relevance Feedback Framework

Three innovations distinguish our category-based retrieval framework from the other CBIR schemes:

1. Classification-based retrieval refinement (PWC-SVM) to group and represent results in a perceptual similar topic-based interface.
2. Support category-level feedback interaction to efficiently and effectively capture users' retrieval purpose.

3.   Adopt asymmetry bagging SVM network to address the issues of sample insufficiency and sample asymmetry in feedback learning.

The rest of this paper is organized as follows: Section.2 proposes our retrieval result refinement algorithm based on Pairwise-Coupling SVM. Section.3 presents our classification-based RF learning strategy using asymmetric SVM bagging network. The experimental results are shown in Section.4. And finally this paper concludes in Section 5.

2   Category-Based Retrieval Result Refinement Using Pairwise-Coupling SVM

Our refinement algorithm concerns on category search in the database which consists of image categories that can be predefined to some degree. Such scenario is prevalent in many specific image databases (Medical image database, gene image database, museum painting collections). Since the image category can be defined beforehand, category information can be adopted to design a refinement scheme to group and represent results in a perceptual similar topic-based interface, which will largely simplify and accelerate user retrieval.

Fig. 3. Category Refinement System Interface

Assume that m image categories can be defined beforehand in a category-based image database. We can utilize this category information to train decision rules that classify retrieval result images into their corresponding categories. Consequently, the retrieval results is consisted of not only top k relevant images but also their top n frequently appeared categories. In RF operation, users can either mark positive/negative images or just simply select their interesting image category. As shown in Fig.3, the initial retrieval result is shown in the top right image window.

Once clicking a category in the left textual list (which presents the name of the top n category), an image browsing window would be presented to the users in the bottom right image window, which contains the retrieval results with the selected category. Users can further select misclassified image inside each category. In this scenario, an active user can participate as much as possible to achieve his goal (Select both feedback categories and the misclassified images); while a "lazy" user without specified knowledge only needs to select positive category (one operation) to conduct the relevance feedback learning.

Our scheme adopts a Pairwise-Coupling SVM (PWC-SVM) framework to classify images to their corresponding categories. After initial retrieval, the top k most similar images are further classified into their corresponding categories using a PWC-SVM framework (Tab.1). And the top n most frequently appeared categories are returned to the users.

In such framework, SVM is selected as the inter-class classifier. SVM is an effective binary classifier and widely used in the RF learning of content-based image retrieval [5] [7]. It aims at separating two classes in feature space by an optimal hyperplane, where the maximum geometric margin gains [6]. But as a binary classifier, it is unsuitable to be applied directly to image categorization scenario, which is a multiple class classification problem. Generally, there are two strategies adopted to extend binary classifiers to multiple-class situation:

1. One-To-All: For each class, train an intra-class classifier whose classification result indicates the confidence (scope [0,1]) that whether the test sample belongs to this class or not. For each test sample, these classifiers of all categories are used to gain the classification results, in which the class with the highest output is selected as the classification result.

2. One-To-One: For each category, train (m-1) pairwise classifiers (inter-class) between current class and the rest classes (Totally m classes). For each test sample, the confidence level of each class is the majority voting result of its corresponding (m-1) classifiers (each between (0, 1)). The class with highest accumulated outputs is selected as the classification result. This is called PWC (Pairwise-Coupling), which combines the outputs of all classifiers to form prediction. And it has gained more concerns due to its good generalization ability [9, 10].

In our category-based retrieval framework, the Pairwise-Coupling (one-to-one) strategy is adopted to extend binary SVM into multiple-class scenario (Tab.1). There are totally C_m^2 SVM classifiers to be trained.

Table 1. PWC SVM Retrieval Result Classification

Input: retrieval result images $I_1...I_k$, pairwise SVM classifiers $C_{01}, C_{02},...,C_{m(m-1)}$
  For each retrieval result image I_i
  Begin
    Utilize its (m-1) corresponding SVM classifiers $C_{i1}, C_{i2},...,C_{i(m-1)}$ to classify I_i
    to its corresponding category
  End
Output: The top n categories with the n highest accumulated classification values
  among the result images.

3   Category-Level Feedback Learning Using Asymmetric Bagging SVM Network

The distinction between our RF learning algorithm and traditional schemes lies in: users' category selection may be the only interaction information available for retrieval system. Furthermore, in such scenario, the training examples (images from one positive category and other $(n-1)$ negative categories) are strongly asymmetric.

As pointed out by Tao [5], the SVM classifier is unstable on a small training set. And its optimal classification hyperplane may be biased when the numbers of the

Table 2. Asymmetry SVM Bagging for Image Category Confidence Calculation

Input: Positive Image Category Cp and its corresponding training images $Ip_1...Ip_e$, Negative Image Category Cn_i ($i=1$ to n, and $Cn_i\neq$positive category), and their corresponding training images $In1_1...In1_f...Inm_1...Inm_f$. classifier C (SVM)

    For bootstrapping interval k from 1 to n
Begin
  Begin

        Train SVM C_k between positive image category Cp and negative image category Cn_k

  End
  Construct the final classifier C_{final} by aggregation of all C_k. Its output (rank 0 to $(m-1)$) indicates the confidence level that an image belongs to the positive category
End
Output: C_{final} to determine the category belonging of each image

Consequently, the category-level correlations are integrated into traditional image-level RF learning schemes to re-rank resulting images as follows:

Table 3. Classification-Based Similarity Re-ranking

Input: images in the database: $I_1...I_h$, category classifier: C_{final}
  For each image I_i ($i = 1$ to h)
  Begin
    Using a traditional RF learning method to re-rank its similarity S_i of the query image (In our experiments both FRE [11] and SVM are investigated)
    Calculate its confidence level Ca_i which indicates to what degree this image belongs to the positive image category.
    Re-calculate the similarity of S_i: $S_i = S_i/(Ca_i + 1)$
  End
  Re-Rank all the images in the database and return to the user the most similar k images
Output: the most similar k images and their most frequently appeared image category calculated using Tab.2

positive and negative samples are asymmetric. To solve this problem, an asymmetry SVM bagging network is adopted for category-level relevance feedback learning. The asymmetry bagging idea [5] is adopted to overcome the problem of sample asymmetry in SVM training. Different from Tao, our algorithm utilizes this bagging procedure to image category classification. And such classification is further integrated into traditional RF learning algorithms to enhance system performance.

4 Experimental Results and Discussion

Our experiments are conducted on a subset of COREL image database, with over 2000 general purpose images belonging to 20 classes (100 each). 16 images of each topic (Totally 320 images) are randomly selected, half for training and half for query test.

Our experimental evaluation aims at verifying the efficiency of our categorization-based retrieval refinement and interaction scheme. Consequently , for simplicity, a 264-dimensional feature vector is extracted from each image, in which the former 256 dimension features are the auto-correlogram [15] in RGB color space (We quantize RGB color space into 64 bins and based on which the pixel correlation within distance 1,3,5,7 are extracted and calculated to form a 256-dimentional feature.) and the later 8 dimension features are the features of texture co-occurrence matrix [8] (weighted mixed by 8:256).

Table 4. Average RF Operations in Top 100 Results

Category	Traditional RF			Category	Our Method		
	1st	2nd	3rd		1st	2nd	3rd
eagle	49	67	83	train	12	15	14
car	25	43	66	pyramid	8	7	10
tiger	28	41	57	sunrise	11	13	13
fish	35	52	56	sailboat	16	23	23
rose	48	64	75	bear	21	17	19

Our first experiment is the demonstration of our PWC-SVM based category-level retrieval refinement scheme. Tab.4 presents the average RF operation in top *100* retrieval results between traditional image-level RF pattern and our category-based method. As shown in Tab.4, users' average RF operations can be greatly reduced comparing to traditional RF strategies. Our method only needs users to label image categories and the misclassified images in each category.

Our second experiment is the demonstration of ABSVM network in category-based feedback learning. To measure its performance, two classical and efficient baseline feedback learning algorithms are implemented: 1. Rui's feature reweighting (FRE) RF learning method [11] and 2. SVM Based RF learning. Both of these two methods are conducted over the same data scope as our ABSVM category RF. They need users to manually label all positive/negative images in top 100 returning images (The tedious RF operations can be demonstrated by their average operation times in left of Tab.4).

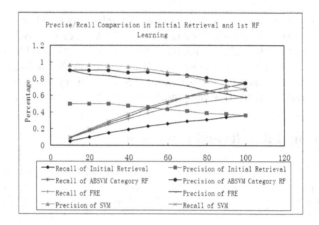

Fig. 4. P-R Comparison in Initial Retrieval and 1st RF Learning

As shown in Fig.4-6, in despite of much fewer RF operations and mis-labeling images, our ABSVM category-RF learning scheme is still excellent comparing to SVM-based image-level RF methods, which is commonly used in state-of-art systems (In image-level SVM, elaborated manually labeling is demanded in top 100 images, which is extremely tedious and burdensome). Promising retrieval Precision & Recall enhancements are gained comparing to traditional RF schemes (both FRE and SVM). In addition, from users' point of view, this pattern is more semantically meaningful and straightforward.

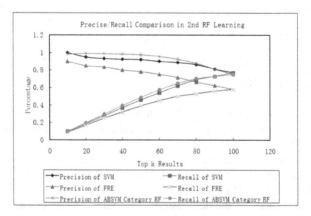

Fig. 5. P-R Comparison in 2nd RF Learning

It should be noted that other well-explored learning and ranking schemes can be easily integrated into our refinement and category-RF frameworks to further enhance system performance., due to its good extensibility and generalization ability.

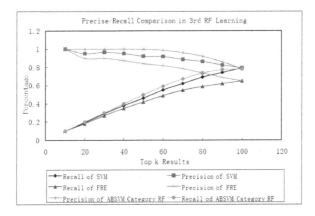

Fig. 6. P-R Comparison in 3rd RF Learning

5 Conclusion

This paper proposes a novel classification-driven retrieval refinement and interaction pattern by exploring result correlations for category image retrieval. Our framework supports topic-based perceptual similar result representation and category-level feedback operation. Especially, a PWC-SVM strategy is proposed for category-based result post-processing and an asymmetry SVM bagging network is integrated into traditional RF learning methods to enhance learning efficiency in category search. Our scheme provides a general idea for category search in domain-specific image database, which can be easily integrated by other sophisticated or state-of-art feature extraction or feedback learning schemes to further enhance system performance.

Acknowledgments. This research is supported by State 863 High Technology R&D Project of China, No. 2006AA01Z197; the Program for New Century Excellent Talents in University (NCET-05-03 34); Natural Science Foundation of China (No. 60472043) and Natural Science Foundation of Heilongjiang Province (No.E2005-29).

References

1. Smeulders, A., Worring, M., Santini, S., Gupta, A., Jain, R.: Content-Based Image Retrieval at the End of the Early Years. IEEE Trans. on Pattern Analysis and Machine Intelligence 22(12), 1349–1380 (2000)
2. Veltkamp, R.C., Tanase, M.: Content-Based Image Retrieval Systems: A Survey, Technical report UU-CS-2000-34, Department of Computing Science, Utrecht University 34 (October 2000)
3. Gong, Y., Zhang, H.J., Chua, T.C.: An image database system with content capturing and fast image indexing abilities. In: Proc. IEEE Int. Conference on Multimedia Computing and Systems, Boston, 14-19 May, pp. 121–130 (1994)

4. Su, Z., Zhang, H., Li, S.: Relevance Feedback in Content-Based Image Retrieval: Bayesian Framework, Feature Subspaces and Progressive Learning. IEEE Tran. on Image Processing 12(3), 8 (2003)
5. Tao, D., Tang, X., Li, X., Wu, X.: Asymmetric Bagging and Random Subspace for Support Vector Machines-Based Relevance Feedback in Image Retrieval. IEEE Trans. on Pattern Analysis and Machine Intelligence 28(7) (July 2006)
6. Burges, J.C.: A Tutorial on Support Vector Machines for Pattern Recognition. Data Mining and Knowledge Discovery 2(2), 121–167 (1998)
7. Tong, S., Chang, E.: Support Vector Machine Active Learning for Image Retrieval. In: Proceeding of ACM International Con. on Multimedia, pp. 107–118 (2001)
8. Haralick, R.M., Shanmugam, K., Dinstein, I.: Texture features for image classification. IEEE Tran. on System Man Cybern 3, 610–621 (1973)
9. Rahman, M.M., Bhattacharya, P., Desai, B.C.: A Framework for Medical Image Retrieval using Machine Learning & Statistical Similarity Matching Techniques with Relevance Feedback, IEEE Trans. on Information Tech. in Biomedicine (accepted for future publication)
10. Wu, T., Lin, C.J., Weng, R.C.: Probability Estimates for Multi-Class Classification by Pairwise Coupling. Int. Journal on Machine Learning Research 10(5), 975–1005 (2004)
11. Rui, Y., Huang, T.S., Mehrotra, S., Ortega, M.: Relevance Feedback: A Power Tool for Interactive Content-based Image Retrieval. IEEE Trans. Circuits and Systems for Video Technology 8(5), 644–655 (1998)
12. Chen, Y., Wang, J.Z., Krovertz, R.: CLUE: Cluster-Based Retrieval of Image by Unsupervised Learning. IEEE Trans. on Image Processing 14(8), 1187–1201 (2005)
13. Lee, K.-M., Nike Street, W.: Cluster-Driven Refinement for Content-Based Digital Image Retrieval. IEEE Trans. on Multimedia 6(6), 817–927 (2004)
14. Tao, D., Tang, X., Li, X., Rui, Y.: Direct Kernel Biased Discriminant Analysis: A New Content-based Image Retrieval Relevance Feedback Algorithm. IEEE Trans. on Multimedia 8(4), 716–727 (2006)
15. Huang, J., Kumar, S.R., Mitra, M., Zhu, W.J., Zabin, R.: Image Indexing using Color Correlogram. In: Proceedings of IEEE Conference on Computer Vision and Pattern Recognition, San Juan, PR, January, pp. 762–768 (1997)
16. Cui, H., Heidorn, P.B., Zhang, H.: An Approach to Automatic Classification of Text for Information Retrieval. In: The 2nd ACM/IEEE-CS Joint Conference on Digital Libraries, Portland, Oregon
17. Karanikolas, N., Skourlas, C., Christopoulou, A., Alevizos, T.: Medical Text Classification based on Text Retrieval techniques. In: MEDINF 2003, Craiova, Romania, October 9 - 11 (2003)
18. Liu, X., Gong, Y., Xu, W., Zhu, S.: Document clustering with cluster refinement and model selection capabilities. In: Proceedings of ACM SIGIR, SESSION: Clustering, Tampere, Finland, pp. 191–198 (2002)

User Modelling for Interactive User-Adaptive Collection Structuring

Andreas Nürnberger and Sebastian Stober

Institute for Knowledge and Language Engineering,
Faculty of Computer Science
Otto-von-Guericke-University Magdeburg, D-39106 Magdeburg, Germany
{nuernb,stober}@iws.cs.uni-magdeburg.de

Abstract. Automatic structuring is one means to ease access to document collections, be it for organization or for exploration. Of even greater help would be a presentation that adapts to the user's way of structuring and thus is intuitively understandable. We extend an existing user-adaptive prototype system that is based on a growing self-organizing map and that learns a feature weighting scheme from a user's interaction with the system resulting in a personalized similarity measure. The proposed approach for adapting the feature weights targets certain problems of previously used heuristics. The revised adaptation method is based on quadratic optimization and thus we are able to pose certain contraints on the derived weighting scheme. Moreover, thus it is guaranteed that an optimal weighting scheme is found if one exists. The proposed approach is evaluated by simulating user interaction with the system on two text datasets: one artificial data set that is used to analyze the performance for different user types and a real world data set – a subset of the banksearch dataset – containing additional class information.

1 Introduction

In many domains users are interested in information that they cannot clearly specify, e.g. by some keywords. For example, a journalist might be researching the background of his current article or someone might look for new music that fits his taste. In such everyday exploratory search scenarios, usually large data collections are accessed. Structuring is one means to ease these tasks, especially if it reflects the user's personal interests and thus is intuitively understandable. Unfortunately, except for the user's own collections, personalized structuring is not generally available.

In previous work, we presented an user-adaptive retrieval system considering the task of organizing an unstructured collection. An initially unpersonalized structure is learned with a growing self-organizing map which provides an overview of the collection. The user can then work with this representation, search and access objects and move items on the map that he feels should be located elsewhere. From this user interaction, an individual feature weighting scheme for similarity computation that represents the user's organization preferences is continuously derived and used to adapt the collection organization.

N. Boujemaa, M. Detyniecki, and A. Nürnberger (Eds.): AMR 2007, LNCS 4918, pp. 95–108, 2008.

Previously, we used greedy heuristics to learn this feature weighting scheme [7,5,6]. Using these heuristics, however, caused several problems: Since the values of the feature weights could not be limited, extreme weighting schemes often occured. Furthermore, the heuristics could not formally guarantee that all manually moved objects are assigned to their target, and no additional constraints could be formulated that could e.g. increase the interpretability of the result.

To address these problems, we have revised our adaptation method by using quadratic optimization to derive the feature weights. This allows the introduction of additional constraints on the feature weights and moreover guarantees to find an optimal weighting scheme if it exists.

The remainder of this paper is organized as follows: Section 2 reviews crucial aspects of the user-adaptive retrieval prototype. In Section 3, the new method for weight adaptation is introduced. Subsequently, the experimental setup for evaluation is explained in Section 4. Section 5 presents and discusses the results of the experiments. Finally, we draw conclusions and point out directions for future research in Section 6.

2   An Interactive Retrieval System Based on a Self-organizing Map

In the following we review our adaptive retrieval system that we previously introduced in [7]. We first decribe, how documents are preprocessed and represented. Section 2.3 outlines, how the initial clustering is computed. Finally, the generic principle of the adaptation algorithm is explained in Section 2.4.

2.1   Document Preprocessing and Representation

To be able to cluster text document collections, we have to map the text files to numerical feature vectors. Therefore, we first applied standard preprocessing methods, i.e., stopword filtering and stemming (using the Porter Stemmer [8]), encoded each document using the vector space model [11] and finally selected a subset of terms as features for the clustering process with a greedy heuristics. These processing are briefly described in the following.

In the vector space model text documents are represented as vectors in an m-dimensional space, i.e., each document j is described by a numerical feature vector $\boldsymbol{x}_j = (x_{j1}, \ldots, x_{jm})$. Each element of the vector represents a word of the document collection, i.e., the size of the vector is defined by the number of words of the complete document collection.

For a given document j x_{jk} defines the importance of the word k in this document with respect to the given document collection C. Large feature values are assigned to terms that are frequent in relevant documents but rare in the whole document collection [10]. Thus a feature x_{jk} for a term k in document j is computed as the term frequency tf_{jk} times the inverse document frequency idf_k, which describes the term specificity within the document collection.

In [9] a scheme for computation of the features was proposed that has meanwhile proven its usability in practice. Besides term frequency and inverse document frequency (defined as $\text{idf}_k = \log(n/n_k)$), a length normalization factor is used to ensure that all documents have equal chances of being retrieved independent of their lengths:

$$x_{jk} = \frac{\text{tf}_{jk} \log \frac{n}{n_k}}{\sqrt{\sum_{l=1}^{m} \left(\text{tf}_{jl} \log \frac{n}{n_l} \right)^2}}, \tag{1}$$

where n is the size of the document collection C, n_k the number of documents in C that contain term k, and m the number of terms that are considered.

Based on this scheme a document j is described by an m-dimensional vector $\boldsymbol{x}_j = (x_{j1}, \ldots, x_{jm})$ of term features and the similarity S of two documents (or the similarity of a document and a query vector) can be computed based on the inner product of the vectors (by which—if we assume normalized vectors—the cosine between the two document vectors is computed), i.e.

$$S(\boldsymbol{x}_j, \boldsymbol{x}_k) = \sum_{l=1}^{m} x_{jl} \cdot x_{kl}. \tag{2}$$

For a more detailed discussion of the vector space model and weighting schemes see, for instance, [1,10,11].

2.2 Index Term Selection

To reduce the number of words in the vector description we applied a simple method for keyword selection by extracting keywords based on their entropy. For each word k in the vocabulary the entropy as defined by [4] was computed:

$$W_k = 1 + \frac{1}{\log_2 n} \sum_{j=1}^{n} p_{jk} \log_2 p_{jk} \quad \text{with} \quad p_{jk} = \frac{\text{tf}_{jk}}{\sum_{l=1}^{n} \text{tf}_{lk}}, \tag{3}$$

where tf_{jk} is the frequency of word k in document j, and n is the number of documents in the collection. Here the entropy gives a measure how well a word is suited to separate documents by keyword search. For instance, words that occur in many documents will have low entropy. The entropy can be seen as a measure of the importance of a word in the given domain context. As index words a number of words that have a high entropy relative to their overall frequency have been chosen, i.e. of words occurring equally often those with the higher entropy can be preferred. Empirically this procedure has been found to yield a set of relevant words that are suited to serve as index terms [3].

However, in order to obtain a fixed number of index terms that appropriately cover the documents, we applied a greedy strategy: From the first document in the collection the term with the highest relative entropy is select as an index term. Then, this document and all other documents containing this term are marked. From the first of the remaining unmarked documents again the term with the highest relative entropy is selected as an index term. Then again, this document and all other documents containing this term are marked. This is repeated until all documents have been marked. Subsequently, the documents are unmarked and the process is started all over again. It can be terminated when the desired number of index terms have been selected.

2.3 Initial Clustering

Representing documents as described in the preceding section and using the cosine similarity measure, documents can be clustered by the growing self-organizing map approach presented in [7]. The algorithm starts with a small initial grid composed of hexagon cells, where each hexagon refers to a cluster and is represented by a randomly initialized prototype feature vector. Each document is then assigned to the most similar cluster in the grid resulting in an update of the respective prototype and to some extend of the surrounding prototypes (depending on a neighborhood function). Having all documents assigned to the grid, the inner cluster distance can be computed. The clusters where it exceeds some predefined threshold are split resulting in a grown map. This process is repeated until no more cells need to or can be split or an empty cell occurs (i.e. a cluster with no assigned documents). It results in a two-dimensional topology preserving the neighborhood relations of the high dimensional feature space. I.e. not only documents within the same cluster are similar to each other but also documents of clusters in the neighborhood are expected to be more similar than those in more distant clusters. Using such a growing approach ensures that only as many clusters are created as are actually needed.

2.4 User-Adaptivity

The algorithm outlined in Section 2.3 works in an unsupervised manner. It depends only on the choice of the features for representation and the initial similarity measure how documents are grouped. However, the user has often a better intuition of a "correct" clustering. In cases where he does not agree on the cluster assignment for a specific document, the user can change it by dragging the document from a cell and drop it onto a different cell of the grid. In online mode, the system will immediately react and modify the map, whereas in batch mode it will wait until the user manually triggers the modification after he has made several reassignments.

The remapping is performed by introducing feature weights that are used during the similarity computation. The basic idea is to change the feature weights for the similarity computation in such a way that the documents moved by the user are now assigned to the desired clusters, i.e. the prototypes defining the new cluster centers are more similar to the moved objects than the prototpyes defining the original cluster centers.

While in prior work we used greedy heuristics to learn local or global weights for each feature, i.e. weights that influence the importance of a term with respect to the whole map or just with respect to a cell (see, e.g., [7,5,6]), we propose in this work an optimization approach based on quadratic optimization as described in the following. This approach works much more stable than the heuristics and it is also possible to define constraints on the weight vector.

3   Quadratic Optimization

The problem of dragging documents as described above can be mapped to a problem of cluster reassignement: Assume a document d that is assigned to a cluster c_1, i.e. for the similarity holds

$$sim(c_1, d) < sim(c_i, d) \qquad \forall i \neq 1. \tag{4}$$

If c_1 is dragged by a user to a cluster c_2 we have to adapt the underlying similarity measure such that now

$$sim(c_2, d) < sim(c_i, d) \qquad \forall i \neq 2 \tag{5}$$

holds. If we assume that a user reassigns more than one document, a similar constraint has to be defined for each reassigned document. In the following, this process is described more formally.

3.1   Formalization

In order to solve the reassignement problem as described above using a quadratic problem solver, we have to formulate our problem at hand appropriately. Therefore, we make the following assumptions:

Let $w := (w_0, w_1, ..., w_m)$ be the weight vector used during similarity computation, x_j be a document vector describing a document d_j as defined above and s_j be a vector defining a cluster prototype. Then we can define a weighted similarity computation between document and protoype as follows:

$$S(x_j, s_k) = \sum_{l=1}^{m} x_{jl} \cdot w_l \cdot s_{kl}. \tag{6}$$

Thus, we can modify the influence of specific features (here words) during similarity computation. If we initialize all weights w_l with 1 we obtain the standard inner product as defined above.

The task of our optimization problem is to increase the similarity of a document to a target prototype t_i (this is the cluster cell to which a user has moved a document) such that this similarity is bigger than the similarity to all other prototypes s_k, in particular to the prototype of the cell to which the document was initially assigned. Using the weighted similarity measure, this means that we have to change the weights such that

$$\sum_{l=1}^{m} x_{jl} \cdot w_l \cdot t_{il} > \sum_{l=1}^{m} x_{jl} \cdot w_l \cdot s_{kl} \qquad \forall k \neq i. \tag{7}$$

Note that the change of the weight vector w should be as small as possible in order to avoid too much corruption of the initial cluster assignments. Therefore, we demand that the sum over all (quadratic) deviations of the weights from their initial value 1 should be minimal (Eq. 8) and further that the weights should be non-negative (Eq. 9) and the sum of all weights should always be m (Eq. 10).

If we furthermore assume, that we like to ensure that several documents can be reassigned at the same time, we can now formulate this problem as a quadratic optimization problem, i.e. we are looking for weights, such that we minimize

$$\min_{w \in \Re^m} \sum_{l=1}^{m} (w_l - 1)^2 \tag{8}$$

subject to the constraints

$$w_l \geq 0 \qquad \forall 1 \leq l \leq m \tag{9}$$

$$\sum_{l=1}^{m} w_l = m \tag{10}$$

$$\sum_{l=1}^{m} x_{jl} \cdot w_l \cdot t_{1l} > \sum_{l=1}^{m} x_{jl} \cdot w_l \cdot s_{kl} \qquad \forall k \neq i$$

$$\sum_{l=1}^{m} x_{jl} \cdot w_l \cdot t_{2l} > \sum_{l=1}^{m} x_{jl} \cdot w_l \cdot s_{kl} \qquad \forall k \neq i \tag{11}$$

$$\vdots$$

$$\sum_{l=1}^{m} x_{jl} \cdot w_l \cdot t_{rl} > \sum_{l=1}^{m} x_{jl} \cdot w_l \cdot s_{kl} \qquad \forall k \neq i.$$

Here, Eq. 10 prevents very large weight values and Eq. 11 ensures that all r documents that were moved by a user are assigned to the cluster cell specified by the user.

3.2 Remarks

The changes of the underlying similarity measure based on the user's mappings might lead to a reassignment of further documents. This is intended, since we assume that the resulting weight changes define the structuring criteria of the user. This way, moving just a small number of object manually, many others could be relocated automatically as a result of the adaption which saves additional effort for the user.

The contraints defined by Eq. 11 can also be used to fix documents to specific clusters, i.e. prevent them from being moved to other cluster cells during user interaction with the system and the resulting weight adaptations. This can be especially useful, if a user likes to ensure that typical objects are used as stable reference landmarks in the mapping.

4   Experimental Setup

We conducted two experiments in which we simulate the user interaction with the system. The general approach chosen is as follows:

```
modify objects by adding random features
learn map on modified objects
repeat
  select an object o to be moved
  select most similar cell c for o according to user
  move o to c
until o could not be moved
```

Given a set of objects described by some specific features, we assume that a user would consider all of these features to be equally important and ignore any other features when comparing the objects. A similarity measure according to the user's preferences would then just compare the relevant features. Consequently, the initial similarity measure on the object set (weighting all features equally) is regarded as ground truth.

In the first step, we add some "noise" to the object descriptions by adding random features.[1] Because the GSOM learning algorithm would ignore noisy features that do not contain any information, the random feature values are obtained as follows: Assuming that n features are to be added, random prototype vectors for n groups are generated. These vectors are randomly initialized with zeros and ones, where the proability for a one is $\log n/n$. Afterwards, a gaussian random number with a mean of 0.2 and standard deviation of 1.0 is added, thus "blurring" the prototype vectors. For each object to be modified, a prototype vector is randomly selected. The feature values to be added to the object's description are then generated by (again) adding a gaussian random number with a mean of 0.2 and standard deviation of 1.0 to the respective feature value of the prototype vector. This empirically derived procedure results in enough information to significantly influence the map learning algorithm.

As a result of the added noise, the assignment of the objects to the map differs from the simulated user's point of view. Iteratively, he selects an objects on the map, moves it to the best position according to his ground truth similarity measure and lets the map update its feature weights. This process is repeated until the selected object could not be moved because it is already at the desired position or due to limitations of the adaptation algorithm that we will discuss later in Section 5.1.[2] In the following, we give details on the specific experiments, particularly on the datasets, the methods for object selection and the evaluation measures used.

4.1 Experiment 1

The first experiment was conducted on the dataset that has been already used in [3] It comprises 1914 text documents taken from a news archive that covers several

---

[1] Just masking out features instead of adding random ones does not work. Due to the sparse nature of the document vectors, masking only few index terms already results in documents that cannot be compared according to the user's preferences because they have no index terms anymore. However, to provide the adaption algorithm with enough "room" for improvement, it would be necessary to mask many index terms.

[2] It can happen very early in the process that the selected object is already at its best position. Therefore, we checked not only one but up to 1% of all objects on the map.

Table 1. Relations of the four scenarios for user simulation

		cell selection	
		greedy	random
object selection	greedy	scenario 1	scenario 3
	random	scenario 2	scenario 4

scientific topics. The documents in the dataset had been already preprocessed and 800 index terms had been selected using the method described in Section 2.2.

For selection of the object to move, we distinguish between the following four scenarios of user action simulation whose relations are depicted in Table 1:

1. *Greedy selection of cell and object:* First, the cell with the lowest average pairwise (ground truth) similarity of the contained objects is chosen for further investigation. Within this cell, the object with the lowest average pairwise (ground truth) similarity with all other objects in the same cell is selected to be moved.
2. *Greedy selection of cell and random selection of object:* The cell is chosen as in the previous scenario. However, an arbitrary object is selected from this cell.
3. *Random selection of cell and greedy selection of object:* Here, the cell is chosen randomly whereas the object to be moved is selected from this cell by the greedy approach used in scenario 1.
4. *Random selection of cell and random selection of object:* In this scenario, both, the cell and the object to be moved from the cell, are selected randomly.

Note that scenario 3 appears to be the one that comes closest to the real use case where a user does not look into all cells before picking an object to be moved but within a specific cell tends to select the object that fits least into the cell according to his preferences.

For the evaluation of the adaptation algorithm, we utilze the average *top-10 precision* of the similarity measure on the object set: A ranked top-10 list of similar objects is computed for each object according to the system's current similarity measure and compared with a ground truth top-10 list. The percentage of matches is computed – ignoring the order of the ranking – and averaged over all objects. This measure resembles a user's natural way of assessing a retrieval result where the correct order of relevance is less important than the actual number of highly relevant objects within the first few items of a result list.

4.2   Experiment 2

In this experiment we use a subset[3] of the Banksearch dataset [12], a pre-classified dataset containing 11,000 web pages from 11 different categories grouped into 4

---

[3] A subset was taken to reduce the computational effort of the evalution.

high-level topics (finance, programming, science, sports). The dataset used in this experiment has been constructed as follows: 100 documents (i.e. 10%) were selected for each of the 11 categories. The doucments were preprocessed with the same methods as the dataset in experiment 1. After index term selection, documents with less than 5 index terms were removed resulting in a set of 947 documents described by 800 index terms.

In contrast to the first dataset, each document additionally contains information about its topic class. This information is not used during training of the map, however it is utilized to select the object to be moved. Analogously to the first experiment, we regard four scenarios but replace the greedy heuristic by one that is based on the class information: For each cell the majority and minority class(es) are determined and the cell with the highest difference in the frequencies of these classes is selected. Further, during the object selection step only those objects belonging to a minority class of the cell are considered. Finally, only those cells can be selected as target cell that have a majority class that matches the class of the object to move.

This experiment resembles a use case where the user tries to sort objects according to (subjective) classes unknown to the system. Apart from the top-n precision that has also been applied here, we use the well-known evaluation measures *purity, inverse purity* and *f-measure* as e.g. described in [2]. These measures return values in the interval $[0, 1]$, with 1 being the optimal value. The purity measures the homogeneity of the resulting clusters and is 1, iff for each cluster all contained objects belong to the same class. Whereas, the inverse purity – also known as *microaveraged precision* – measures how stable the pre-defined classes are when split up into clusters. It is 1, iff for each class all belonging objects are grouped into a single cluster. The F-measure is similar to the inverse purity. However, it punishes overly large clusters, as it includes the individual precision of these clusters into the evaluation.

5   Results

5.1   Experiment 1

The results for experiment 1 are shown in Figure 1. For all scenarios and noise levels the top-10 precision increased significantly to a value between 0.82 and 0.97 with a mean of 0.93. As expected, with an increasing level of noise in the data, more objects need to be moved manually in order to reach an acceptable degree of adaptation, yet – except for the highest noise level (100 random features) – moving at most 1% of all objects was sufficient. This may, however, be very much dependent on the object representation used. For text retrieval, feature vectors are very sparse. This is probably disadvantageous for the adaptation algorithm, as to adapt a feature's weight, the feature needs to be present (i.e. non-zero) in a moved object. Using feature vectors that are less sparse could result in faster adaptation.

Surprisingly, the scenarios that used partly or fully random selection of the object to move did not yield significantly worse results than the fully greedy

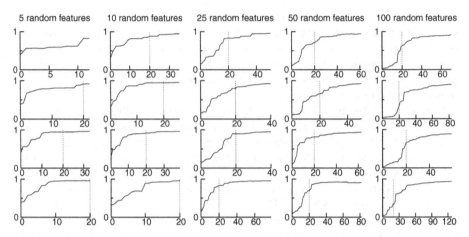

Fig. 1. Top-10 precision for experiment 1 with varying noise levels (number of random features) against the number of iterations (number of manually moved objects) for the four user simulation scenenarios (from top to bottom): (1) Greedy selection of cell and object, (2) Greedy selection of cell and random selection of object, (3) Random selection of cell and greedy selection of object, and (4) Random selection of cell and object. The dotted vertical line at 20 iterations marks the point where 1% of the collection has been moved manually by the simulated user.

one. In some cases their maximum top-10 precision was even slightly better and sometimes they converged faster to a good adaptation. Mostly, however, they did not terminate as quickly, but this is not a problem because it only refers to the simulation method and not to the adaptation algorithm itself.

On the other hand, the simulation sometimes terminated a little too early, leaving still room for improvement as e.g. can be seen for scenario 1 with 5 or 10 random features. In about half of the cases the simulated user just did not find any object to move (within the 1% analyzed). However, for the other half, the adaptation algorithm was not able to compute new weights because adding the constraints for the object to move caused an inconsistency in the system. I.e. there is no feature weighting scheme such that the manually moved objects are assigned to the map as desired by the user. This is a limitation of the proposed adaptation algorithm that needs to be overcome in some way to not put the user acceptance of the system at risk.

Further, a side-effect could be observed, that we want to illustrate by an example, where the user simulation terminated early because of an inconsistency in the system: Figure 2 shows the changes of the feature weights for scenario 1 with 10 random features. The mean weight of the random features decreases to values close to zero but still leaving some non-zero weights because of the early termination. At the same time, the mean weight of the other features slightly increases due to the additional weight mass from the random features. However, as the minima and maxima indicate, there are always some extreme weights. Figure 3 shows a histogram of the weights for the original (i.e. non-random)

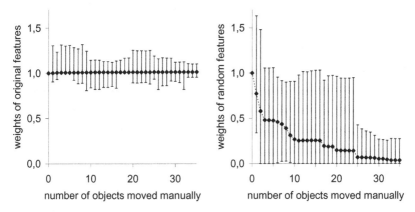

Fig. 2. Weights (mean, maximum and minimum) for original (left) and added random (right) features after each iteration for scenario 1 (greedy selection of cell and object) with 10 random features

features after the last iteration. The weights that differ significantly from the mean refer to index terms of the manually moved objects. They were especially "emphasized" by the adaptation algorithm as only they can be used to decide on the assignment of the manually moved objects to the map. Consequently, the resulting histogram in Figure 3 differs from the ideal one where alle weights are equal. However, as the adaptation algorithm favors weights close to 1.0 that difference is rather small. It is further possible, that the values of the random features to some extend correlate with the non-random ones and accidentally capture some aspects of subgroups. Though this is rather unlikely in general, it may cause side-effects in specific cases. However, this is caused by the evaluation method and thus will not occur in real world applications.

5.2 Experiment 2

In this experiment, we again obtained similar results for all scenarios. Thus, we confine ourselves in the following on the discussion of the results for scenario 1 (i.e. greedy object selection). Figure 4 shows the results on the second dataset using the 4 top-level topics and the 11 low-level categories of the banksearch dataset as classes. In all test cases the final value for purity, inverse purity and

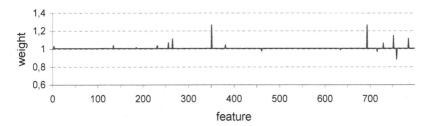

Fig. 3. Histogram of the weights for the original features after the last iteration for scenario 1 (greedy selection of cell and object) with 10 random features

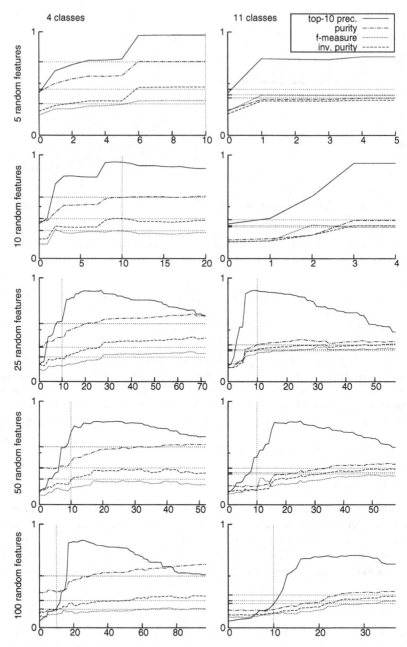

Fig. 4. Performance of the adaption method in experiment 2, using the 4 top-level topics and the 11 low-level categories of the banksearch dataset as classes, with varying noise levels (number of random features) plotted against the number of iterations (number of manually moved objects). Cell and object where selected greedily (scenario 1). The three dotted horizontal marker lines depict (from top to bottom) the baseline values for purity, f-measure and inverse purity. The dotted vertical line at 10 iterations marks the point where 1% of the collection has been moved manually by the simulated user.

f-measure came close to or exceeded the baseline value, that was obtained by setting the weights of the random features to 0 and equally distributing the weight mass on the remaining feature weights. The baseline values could be exceeded by some extend through adaptation because here the additional class information was used which was unknown to the map learning algorithm that solely worked on the index terms as features. Especially, the greedy heuristic applied for object selection favours cells with low purity. On the other hand, the top-10 precision only increases up to some point. From there it slowly decreases again. This is because the weight adaptation is not approximating a map that was learned only on the original objects (i.e. without the noise) what would optimize top-10 precision, but instead, tries to separate the classes.

6   Conclusions

In this contribution we presented a method for feature weight adaptation in order to learn user specific structuring criteria. The approach is based on quadratic optimization and ensures that an optimal weighting scheme can be found if it exists. Furthermore, we evaluated the proposed method on two datasets by simulating the interaction of a user with the system. Therefore, we modelled different user types that simulated typical and worst case behaviors. We have shown that the system was able to derive appropriate solutions for all scenarios.

In future work we will modify the optimization strategy such that at least a sub-optimal solution is returned if no optimal one can be found. This is especially important for scenarios where the users structering criteria can not be represented by the available document features.

References

1. Greiff, W.R.: A theory of term weighting based on exploratory data analysis. In: 21st Annual International ACM SIGIR Conference on Research and Development in Information Retrieval. ACM Press, New York, NY (1998)
2. Hotho, A., Nürnberger, A., Paaß, G.: A brief survey of text mining. GLDV-Journal for Computational Linguistics and Language Technology 20(1), 19–62 (2005)
3. Klose, A., Nürnberger, A., Kruse, R., Hartmann, G.K., Richards, M.: Interactive text retrieval based on document similarities. Physics and Chemistry of the Earth, Part A: Solid Earth and Geodesy 25(8), 649–654 (2000)
4. Lochbaum, K.E., Streeter, L.A.: Combining and comparing the effectiveness of latent semantic indexing and the ordinary vector space model for information retrieval. Information Processing and Management 25(6), 665–676 (1989)
5. Nürnberger, A., Detyniecki, M.: Weighted self-organizing maps - incorporating user feedback. In: Artificial Neural Networks and Neural Information Processing - ICANN/ICONIP 2003, Proc. of the joined 13th Int. Conf. (2003)
6. Nürnberger, A., Detyniecki, M.: Externally growing self-organizing maps and its application to e-mail database visualization and exploration. Applied Soft Computing 6(4), 357–371 (2006)

7. Nürnberger, A., Klose, A.: Improving clustering and visualization of multimedia data using interactive user feedback. In: Proc. of the 9th Int. Conf. on Information Processing and Management of Uncertainty in Knowledge-Based Systems (IPMU 2002) (2002)
8. Porter, M.: An algorithm for suffix stripping. Program, 130–137 (1980)
9. Salton, G., Allan, J., Buckley, C.: Automatic structuring and retrieval of large text files. Communications of the ACM 37(2), 97–108 (1994)
10. Salton, G., Buckley, C.: Term weighting approaches in automatic text retrieval. Information Processing & Management 24(5), 513–523 (1988)
11. Salton, G., Wong, A., Yang, C.S.: A vector space model for automatic indexing. Communications of the ACM 18(11), 613–620 (1975) (see also TR74-218, Cornell University, NY, USA)
12. Sinka, M., Corne, D.: A large benchmark dataset for web document clustering. In: Soft Computing Systems: Design, Management and Applications. Frontiers in Artificial Intelligence and Applications, vol. 87, pp. 881–890 (2002)

Searching for Music Using Natural Language Queries and Relevance Feedback

Peter Knees[1] and Gerhard Widmer[1,2]

[1] Dept. of Computational Perception, Johannes Kepler University Linz, Austria
[2] Austrian Research Institute for Artificial Intelligence (OFAI)
peter.knees@jku.at

Abstract. We extend an approach to search inside large-scale music collections by enabling the user to give feedback on the retrieved music pieces. In the original approach, a search engine that can be queried through free-form natural language text is automatically built upon audio-based and Web-based similarity measures. Features for music pieces in the collection are derived automatically by retrieving relevant Web pages via Google queries and using the contents of these pages to construct *term vectors*. The additional use of information about acoustic similarity allows for reduction of the dimensionality of the vector space and characterization of audio pieces with no associated Web information. With the incorporation of *relevance feedback*, the retrieval of pieces can be adapted according to the preferences of the user and thus compensate for inadequately represented initial queries. The approach is evaluated on a collection comprising about 12,000 pieces by using semantic tags provided by *Audioscrobbler* and a user study which also gives further insights into users search behaviors.

1 Introduction

When searching for (popular) music, users' options are currently very limited. Existing music search systems, i.e. the search systems offered by commercial music portals, make use of meta-data like artist, album name, track name, or year as well as arbitrarily determined, subjective meta-information like genre or style to index their music repository. As a consequence, when searching for music, the customer must already have a very precise conception of the expected result set. In fact, none of these systems allows its users to formulate natural language queries that *describe* the music they intend to find. For example, instead of just finding tracks that are assigned to the genre Rock, a user could want to formulate a query like *"rock with great riffs"* to emphasize the importance of energetic guitar phrases in the desired music pieces. Another example would be the query *chicago 1920*, which could express the intention to find Jazz pieces originating from this particular area and time.

To address the shortcomings of current search systems, in [1] we proposed a method to build a music search engine that is capable of processing arbitrary queries. For each piece in a music collection, features are derived automatically

N. Boujemaa, M. Detyniecki, and A. Nürnberger (Eds.): AMR 2007, LNCS 4918, pp. 109–121, 2008.

from relevant Web pages by constructing *term vector* representations using standard Information Retrieval methods. Furthermore, a state-of-the-art audio similarity measure is incorporated to characterize audio pieces with no (or little) Web information associated. Thus, we combine information about the *context* of music with information about the *content*.

However, although the musical, or more general, the cultural context of music pieces can be captured to a certain extent with this method, there are still limitations. One obvious problem is the appropriate translation of queries into the term vector space of music pieces to calculate similarities to all retrievable pieces. Furthermore, we have to deal with the fact that users are actually not accustomed to use free-form text input to search for music. Even if these issues can be sorted out in the near future, the problem of individual concepts and intentions behind the issued queries remains. For example, different users will have different expectations of the resulting pieces for the query *folk*. Some users may aim to retrieve music pieces from american singers and songwriters, while others may intend to find all sorts of folkloristic music. While these user specific interests may not be adequately expressible via a query, getting explicit feedback on the relevance of the retrieved pieces from the users can give extremely valuable information to disambiguate query meaning and clarify the original intention.

In this paper, we incorporate Rocchio's relevance feedback method to adapt the retrieval of music pieces to the user's preferences. Not only that the retrieval process can increasingly accommodate to users expectations, the approach can also help to compensate for inadequately translated initial queries that would otherwise result in low performance.

2   Related Work

In the following, we review music information retrieval systems that enable cross-media retrieval, i.e. in our case, systems that allow queries consisting of arbitrary natural language text, e.g. descriptions of sound, mood, or cultural events, and return music pieces that are semantically related to this query. Compared to the number of presented *query-by-example* systems (e.g. [2,3]), the number of systems allowing for this form of query is very little. Beside our own approach [1], the most elaborate work has been presented in [4]. The system is supported by a semantic ontology which integrates meta-data as well as automatically extracted acoustic properties of the music pieces and defines relations between these informations. In the end, the system allows for semantic queries like *"something fast from..."* or *"something new from..."*. In [5], the music search engine *Search Sounds*[1] is presented. A special crawler that focuses on a set of "audio blogs" is used to find blog entries consisting of music files with associated explanations. The related textual information can then be used to match text queries to actual music pieces. Furthermore, acoustically similar pieces can be discovered by means of content-based audio analysis. Another system that opts to enhance music search with additional semantic information is Squiggle [6]. Queries

---

[1] http://www.searchsounds.net

are matched against meta-data provided from the freely available community databases MusicMoz[2] and MusicBrainz[3]. Based on this data, related queries are proposed, for example, searching for *rhcp* results in zero hits, but suggests to search for the band "Red Hot Chili Peppers".

A system that is not limited to a fixed set of predefined meta-data is the recommendation service last.fm[4]. Last.fm monitors each user's listening preferences by integrating into music player applications. Based on the collected data, similar artists or tracks are identified and can be recommended to other users. Additionally, users can assign tags to the tracks in their collection. These tags provide a valuable source of information on how people perceive and describe music. A drawback of the system is that the assigned tags are highly inconsistent and noisy, cf. [1].

Beside music information systems that deal solely with popular music, there exist a number of search engines that use specialized (focused) crawlers to find all types of sounds on the Web. The traced audio files are indexed using contextual information extracted from the text surrounding the links to the files. Examples of such search engines are Aroooga [7] and FindSounds[5].

3   Technical Realization

In Sections 3.1 to 3.5, we review our technique to build a natural language search engine for music as published in [1]. Instead of describing every step in detail, we will solely present the settings that yielded best results during evaluation. In Section 3.6, we describe the straight-forward incorporation of Rocchio's relevance feedback technique into our system.

3.1   Web-Based Features

We rely on the Web as our primary source of information. While previous work exploiting Web data for Music Information Retrieval operates solely on the artist level (e.g. [8,9]), we try to derive descriptors for individual tracks. To this end, we opt to gather as much track specific information as possible while preserving a high number of available Web pages (via artist related pages) by joining results of three queries issued to Google for each track in the collection:

1. "*artist*" music
2. "*artist*" "*album*" music review
3. "*artist*" "*title*" music review -lyrics

While the first query is intended to provide a stable basis of artist related documents, the second and third query target more specific pages (reviews of the album and the track, respectively). For each query, at most 100 of the top-ranked

---

[2] http://www.musicmoz.org
[3] http://www.musicbrainz.org
[4] http://www.last.fm
[5] http://www.findsounds.com

Web pages are retrieved and added to the set of pages relevant to the track. All retrieved pages are cleaned from HTML tags and stop words in six languages[6].

For each music piece m and each term t appearing in the retrieved pages, we count tf_{tm}, the number of occurrences (term frequency) of term t in documents related to m, as well as df_{tm}, the number of pages related to m in which the term t occurred (document frequency). All terms with $df_{tm} \leq 2$ are removed from m's term set. Finally, we count mpf_t the number of music pieces that contain term t in their set (music piece frequency). For pragmatic reasons, we further remove all terms that co-occur with less than 0.1% of all music pieces. For our evaluation collection, this results in a vector space with about 78,000 dimensions. To calculate the weight $w(t, m)$ of a term t for music piece m, we use a straight forward modification of the well-established term frequency × inverse document frequency (*tf* × *idf*) function [10]:

$$w(t, m) = \begin{cases} (1 + \log_2 tf_{tm}) \log_2 \frac{N}{mpf_t} & \text{if } tf_{tm} > 0 \\ 0 & \text{otherwise} \end{cases} \quad (1)$$

where N is the overall number of music pieces in the collection. From the given definition, it can be seen that all Web pages related to a music piece are treated as one large document. Furthermore, the resulting term weight vectors are Cosine normalized to remove the influence of the length of the retrieved Web pages as well as the different numbers of retrieved pages per track.

3.2   Audio-Based Similarity

In addition to the context-based Web features, information on the content of the music is derived by following a well-established procedure, e.g. [11,12]: For each audio track, 19 Mel Frequency Cepstral Coefficients (*MFCCs*) are computed on short-time audio segments (called *frames*) to describe the spectral envelope of each frame. Thus, perceived acoustical similarity is assessed by modeling *timbral* properties. For MFCC calculation, we use the definition given in [13]:

$$c_n = \frac{1}{2\pi} \times \int_{\omega=-\pi}^{\omega=+\pi} \log\left(S\left(e^{j\omega}\right)\right) \cdot e^{j\omega \cdot n} d\omega \quad (2)$$

According to [14], a Single Gaussian Model with full covariance matrix is sufficient to model the distribution of MFCCs. This facilitates computation and comparison of the distribution models, since a symmetrized *Kullback-Leibler divergence* can be calculated on the means and covariance matrices in order to derive a similarity measure.

However, applying the Kullback-Leibler divergence entails some undesirable consequences [15,16], e.g., it can be observed that some pieces ("hubs") are frequently "similar" (i.e. have a small distance) to many other pieces in the

---

[6] English, German, Spanish, French, Italian, and Portuguese.

collection without actually sounding similar, while on the other side, some pieces are never similar to others. Furthermore, the Kullback-Leibler divergence is no metric since it does not fulfill the triangle inequality. To deal with these issues, we apply a simple rank-based correction called *Proximity Verification* [16]. As a consequence, all further steps presented here will be based on the ranking information of the audio similarity measure only.

3.3 Dimensionality Reduction

For dimensionality reduction of the feature space, we use the χ^2 test (e.g. [17]). Since we have no class information (e.g. genre) available, we make use of the derived audio similarity. For each track, we define a 2-class term selection problem and use the χ^2 test to find those terms that discriminate s, the group of the 100 most similar tracks, from d, the group of the 100 most dissimilar tracks. For each track, we calculate

$$\chi^2(t,s) = \frac{N(AD - BC)^2}{(A + B)(A + C)(B + D)(C + D)} \tag{3}$$

where A is the number of documents in s which contain term t, B the number of documents in d which contain t, C the number of documents in s without t, D the number of documents in d without t, and N the total number of examined documents. The number of documents refers to the document frequency from Section 3.1. We found to yield best results when joining into a global list the 50 terms of each track's calculation that have highest $\chi^2(t,s)$ values and occur more frequently in s than in d. After feature selection, for our collection, 4,679 dimensions remain.

3.4 Vector Adaptation

Another application of the information provided by the audio similarity measure is the modification of the term vector representations toward acoustically similar pieces. This step is mandatory for tracks for which no related information could be retrieved from the Web. For all other tracks, the intention is to enforce those dimensions that are typical among acoustically similar tracks. To this end, a simple Gauss weighting over the $n = 10$ most similar tracks is performed for each piece. Modified weights of term t for music piece m are defined as

$$gauss_n(t,m) = \sum_{i=0}^{n} \frac{1}{\sqrt{2\pi}} e^{-\frac{(i/2)^2}{2}} \cdot w(t, sim_i(m)), \tag{4}$$

where $sim_i(m)$ denotes the ith most similar track to m according to audio similarity and $sim_0(m)$ is m itself. Vectors are again Cosine normalized after term weight adaptation.

3.5   Querying the Music Search Engine

Finding those tracks that are most similar to a natural language query is a non trivial task. In [1], queries are translated to vector space representations by adding the extra constraint *music*, sending them to Google and constructing a term vector from the 10 top-most Web pages returned. The resulting query vector can then be compared to the music pieces in the collection by calculating *Euclidean distances* on the Cosine normalized vectors. Based on the distances, a *relevance ranking* can be obtained which forms the response to the query.

This method has two major drawbacks. First, it depends on the availability of Google, i.e. to query the local database, the Internet must be accessible, and second, the response time of the system increases by the time necessary to perform the on-line retrieval. To by-pass these shortcomings, we utilize the Web pages retrieved for term vector creation to create an off-line index that can be used instead of Google. For our purpose, we configured the Java-based open source search engine *Nutch*[7] to index the off-line collection of documents. Since information on in- and out-links is not available for the stored documents, *Nutch* calculates the document relevances for a query solely on the basis of a *tf* × *idf* variant.[8]

3.6   Relevance Feedback

Relevance feedback is an iterative process in which the user is presented with a ranked list of the music pieces that are most similar to the query. After examination of the list, the user marks those pieces which are relevant in his/her opinion (*explicit relevance feedback*).[9] The intention is to modify the query vector such that it moves toward the relevant and away from the non-relevant pieces. Since both music pieces and queries are representable as weighted term vectors, we can easily incorporate Rocchio's relevance feedback method to adapt search results according to users' preferences [18]. Thus, based on the relevance judgments, we calculate the modified query vector q_m by

$$q_m = \alpha\, q + \frac{\beta}{|D_r|} \sum_{\forall d_j \in D_r} d_j - \frac{\gamma}{|D_n|} \sum_{\forall d_j \in D_n} d_j, \tag{5}$$

where q is the original query vector constructed from the stored Web pages, D_r the set of relevant music pieces (according to the user) among the retrieved pieces, and D_n the set of non-relevant pieces among the retrieved pieces (cf. [19]). The parameters α, β, and γ can be used to tune the impacts of original vector, relevant pieces, and non-relevant pieces, respectively. For our experiments, we

---

[7] http://lucene.apache.org/nutch/

[8] Note that due to time constraints, only a subset (approx. 100,000 documents) of the stored files (consisting solely of the pages returned for the *"artist" music* queries) has been indexed.

[9] For future work also implicit relevance feedback could be deployed by measuring e.g. the time a user is listening to the returned tracks.

decided to assign equal values to all parameters, i.e. $\alpha = \beta = \gamma = 1$. The modified vector is again Cosine normalized. Based on the new query vector, new results are presented to the user in the next step. The effect of relevance feedback (modification after 20 pieces) can be seen in Table 3 for the example query *speed metal*.

Note that, in contrast to information retrieval systems for text documents that often benefit from additional techniques like *query expansion* [20], our system is currently restricted to the query vector modification step due to the two-layered query processing.

4   Evaluation

In this section, the performance of our extended music search engine is evaluated. For reasons of comparability, we evaluate the impact of relevance feedback on the evaluation collection from [1]. The collection comprises 12,601 different tracks by 1,200 artists. Evaluation is carried out on the same set of related Web pages using the same semantic tags. Additionally, we report on a user study that has been conducted to uncover the impact of relevance feedback.

4.1   Evaluation against Audioscrobbler Ground Truth

As in [1], we utilize the track specific tag information provided by last.fm/Audioscrobbler for evaluation. Although this method has severe shortcomings (for a discussion see [1]), for lack of a real golden standard, using last.fm/Audioscrobbler tags is still a viable option. The same set of 227 test queries is used to evaluate the performance of our system. As reference values, we include the best performing method from [1] which was obtained by pruning the vector space to 4,679 dimensions, Gaussian smoothing over ten nearest neighbors and query construction by invoking Google.

To measure the impact of relevance feedback, for each test query we construct two rankings. The first is the standard ranking for the whole collection based on a query vector constructed from the offline-index of Web pages. For the second ranking, we simulate relevance feedback by starting with the first 20 results obtained through an off-line based query vector. The next 20 results are then calculated from the query vector modified according to the relevances of the already seen music pieces, and so on.

We measure the quality of the rankings obtained with the different retrieval approaches by calculating the *precision at 11 standard recall levels* for the three compared retrieval methods, cf. [19]. This measure is useful to observe precision over the course of a ranking. Since we evaluate the system using a set of 227 queries, we calculate the average of the precision values at each recall level after interpolating to the 11 standard values. The resulting plots are depicted in Figure 1. Not surprisingly, the usage of relevance feedback has a very positive effect on the precision of the returned music pieces. Starting from the same level (about 0.49 precision at recall level 0.0) the traditional approach without relevance feedback drops to 0.34 precision at recall level 0.1, while relevance feedback boosts precision to 0.52. Also for all other recall levels this trend is

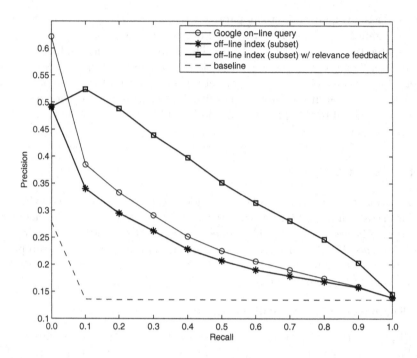

Fig. 1. Precision at 11 standard recall levels (average over all 227 test queries) for the different retrieval approaches

clearly visible. Beside this, it can also be seen that the values of the off-line index approach without relevance feedback are thoroughly below the values of the on-line approach that uses Google for query vector construction.

For further comparisons, we average single value summaries over all queries. The *average precision at seen relevant documents* indicates the ability of the different settings to retrieve relevant documents quickly. A similar measure is *R-Precision*. It corresponds to the precision at the Rth position in the ranking, where R is the number of relevant documents for the query. For both measures, the approach utilizing relevance feedback yields the highest values. Finally, we calculate the *precision after 10 documents*. Since returning 10 results is the default for nearly all search engines, we think it is valuable to examine how many relevant music pieces can be expected "at first sight". This setting is only meaningful to compare the on-line Google query approach and the off-line index approaches. As expected, Google performs better here (about every second piece among the first ten is relevant in average). Using the off-line index, in average 4 returned music pieces among the first ten are relevant. This complies with the results obtained by means of a user study presented in the next section.

Table 1. IR measures for different retrieval approaches (average over all 227 test queries). The first column shows values obtained by constructing query vectors via Google. The second column displays the values obtained by using the constructed off-line index instead. The third column shows the obtained values for relevance feedback enabled (off-line query).

	Google query	off-line query	off-line/RF
Avg. prec. at seen relevant docs	25.29	22.99	**35.80**
R-Precision	26.41	23.48	**37.66**
Precision after 10 documents	**49.56**	39.74	39.74

4.2 Evaluation Via User Experiments

We conducted a small user study with 11 participants to assess the impact of the relevance feedback under less artificial conditions. To this end, each participant was asked to submit 5 queries of choice to the system. For each query, in total 100 results, whose relevance to the query had to be judged, were presented in groups of 20 (thus, a run consisted of 5 feedback iterations). Additionally, each query had to be evaluated twice. In one run, the ranking was not influenced by the ratings at all, i.e. the first 100 retrieval results without relevance feedback have been presented in groups of 20. In the other run, relevance feedback was enabled. Thus, the ratings of the documents had a direct influence on the following 20 results. Whether the first or the second run was presented first was chosen randomly for each query to avoid learning effects. Furthermore, the users were told to evaluate two different feedback strategies. The fact that one run included no

Table 2. Results of the user study over 5 iterations. In each iteration, 55 queries have been evaluated (the maximum achievable number of relevant retrieved pieces for each query is 20; the maximum achievable number per iteration is thus 1,100). For comparison between results obtained with relevance feedback and results obtained without, the more advantageous values are set in bold typeface.

	iter.1	iter.2	iter.3	iter.4	iter.5	total
No relevance feedback						
relevant retrieved/iter. (mean)	7.13	**5.02**	4.05	3.76	3.71	4.73
relevant retrieved/iter. (sum)	392	**276**	223	207	204	1,302
cumulative relevant retr. (sum)	392	**668**	891	1,098	1,302	1,302
queries with all relevant	9	**3**	3	2	1	0
queries with no relevant	22	**26**	25	28	30	17
With relevance feedback						
relevant retrieved/iter. (mean)	7.22	4.15	**6.47**	**5.73**	**6.18**	**5.95**
relevant retrieved/iter. (sum)	397	228	**356**	**315**	**340**	**1,636**
cumulative relevant retr. (sum)	397	625	**981**	**1,296**	**1,636**	**1,636**
queries with all relevant	8	1	**6**	**4**	**5**	0
queries with no relevant	23	27	**20**	**23**	**22**	**11**

Table 3. Results for the example query *speed metal*. Bold entries indicate relevant pieces according to the tags provided by last.fm. Query update after 20 results.

	no relevance feedback	with relevance feedback
1.	Deicide - Dead But Dreaming	Deicide - Dead But Dreaming
2.	Deicide - Trifixion	Deicide - Trifixion
3.	Deicide - Repent To Die	Deicide - Repent To Die
4.	Skitzo - Kill With a Vengeance (live)	Skitzo - Kill With a Vengeance (live)
5.	Deicide - In Hell I Burn	Deicide - In Hell I Burn
6.	**Iron Savior - Protector**	**Iron Savior - Protector**
7.	Entombed - Chief Rebel Angel	Entombed - Chief Rebel Angel
8.	Deicide - Satan Spawn, The Caco-Daemon	Deicide - Satan Spawn, The Caco-Daemon
9.	**Iron Savior - Warrior**	**Iron Savior - Warrior**
10.	**Nightwish - Nightshade Forests**	**Nightwish - Nightshade Forests**
11.	**Powergod - Back To Attack**	**Powergod - Back To Attack**
12.	Deicide - Oblivious To Evil	Deicide - Oblivious To Evil
13.	**Steel Prophet - Unseen**	**Steel Prophet - Unseen**
14.	**Steel Prophet - The Ides Of March**	**Steel Prophet - The Ides Of March**
15.	**Steel Prophet - Messiah**	**Steel Prophet - Messiah**
16.	**Steel Prophet - Goddess Arise**	**Steel Prophet - Goddess Arise**
17.	**Steel Prophet - Ghosts Once Past**	**Steel Prophet - Ghosts Once Past**
18.	Deicide - Behead The Prophet	Deicide - Behead The Prophet
19.	Deicide - Revocate The Agitator	Deicide - Revocate The Agitator
20.	**Steel Prophet - Dawn Of Man**	**Steel Prophet - Dawn Of Man**
21.	**Steel Prophet - 07-03-47**	**Steel Prophet - 07-03-47**
22.	Deicide - Holy Deception	**Steel Prophet - Mysteries Of Inquity**
23.	**Steel Prophet - Mysteries Of Inquity**	**Powergod - Metal Church**
24.	Deicide - Sacrificial Suicide	**Powergod - Burning the Witches**
25.	**Powergod - Madhouse**	**Iron Savior - Paradise**
26.	Crematory - Lost In Myself - Trance Raymix	**Powergod - Madhouse**
27.	Tiamat - Cain	**Powergod - Bleed for the gods**
28.	**Powergod - Bleed for the gods**	**Iron Savior - For The World (Live)**
29.	**Powergod - Ruler Of The Wasteland**	**Iron Savior - Brave New World**
30.	**Powergod - Burning the Witches**	**Iron Savior - Mindfeeder**
31.	**Powergod - Metal Church**	**Powergod - Stars**
32.	Crematory - Through My Soul	**Powergod - Ruler Of The Wasteland**
33.	Crematory - Reign Of Fear	**Powergod - Esper**
34.	**Powergod - Soldiers Under Command**	**Stratovarius - Rebel**
35.	Tiamat - Carry Your Cross An Ill Carry...	**Powergod - Soldiers Under Command**
36.	**Powergod - Stars**	**Iron Savior - Crazy (Ltd Ed Bonus**
37.	Crematory - Revolution	**Iron Savior - Iron Savior (Live)**
38.	Crematory - Red Sky	Electric Six - She's White
39.	Entombed - Left Hand Path (Outro)	**Powergod - Salvation**
40.	Monoide - One year after first love	**Powergod - Prisoner**
41.	**Finntroll - Ursvamp**	**Powergod - The Eagle & The Rainbow**
42.	**Finntroll - Grottans Barn**	**Powergod - Anybody Home**
43.	**Powergod - Esper**	**Powergod - Lost Illusions**
44.	**Iron Savior - For The World (Live)**	**Powergod - Tor With The Hammer**
45.	**Finntroll - Fiskarens Fiende**	**Iron Savior - Riding On Fire (Live)**
46.	**Finntroll - Nattfodd**	**Powergod - Red Rum**
47.	**Finntroll - Trollhammaren**	**Powergod - Steel The Light**
48.	Chicks on Speed - Procrastinator	**Iron Savior - No Heroes**
49.	Deicide - Crucifixation	**Powergod - I Am A Viking**
50.	Entombed - Say It In Slugs	**Powergod - Into The Battle**
51.	**Iron Savior - Mindfeeder**	**Powergod - Kill With Power**
52.	Crematory - Dreams	**Powergod - Mean Clean Fighting Machine**
53.	Tiamat - Light In Extension	**Powergod - Children Of Lost Horizons**
54.	Deicide - Mephistopheles	**Powergod - I'm On Fire**
55.	**Iron Savior - Brave New World**	**Powergod - Gods Of War**
56.	Tiamat - Nihil	**Powergod - No Brain No Pain**
57.	**Iron Savior - Paradise**	**Powergod - Observator**
58.	Crematory - Human Blood	**Powergod - Evilution Part I**
59.	Entombed - Something Out Of Nothing	**Powergod - Powergod**
60.	**Stratovarius - Rebel**	Corvus Corax - Bitte Bitte

Table 4. 55 queries issued by users in the user study

"plastic band"	jazz
80ies synth pop	latin pop
ac/dc	mass in b minor
acdc	melodic metal with opera singer as
american folk	front woman
angry samoans	metal
barbie girl	metallica
cello	ndw
comedy	neomedieval music
dancehall	new orleans
don't dream it's over	new zork scene
drude	no new york
eurodance	nur die besten sterben jung
female electro	oldies slow jazz
filmmusik	postmodern
gangsta	punk
german hip hop	punk rock
ghost dog	rammstein music with strong keyboard
green day	rem
groove	schoenheitsfehler
guitar rock brit pop	sicherheitsmann
happy sound	soundtrack
hard rock fast guns'n roses	vienna electro dj
heavy metal with orchestra	violin
herr lehmann	weilheim
in extremo live	wie lieblich sind deine wohnungen
indie rock	world
industrial rock trent reznor	zztop

feedback strategy at all was concealed. The 55 different queries issued by the participants can be found in Table 4.

Since obtaining users' relevance judgments for all pieces in the collection for all queries is infeasible, other measures than those used in Section 4.1 have to be applied to illustrate the impact of relevance feedback, e.g. those proposed in [20]. Table 2 displays the results of the user study. Interestingly, for the first iteration, results are not consistent. Obviously, users have considered different tracks to be relevant in the first and in the second run (even if only very sporadically). Nevertheless, the general trend of better results when using relevance feedback can be observed in the user study.

5   Conclusions and Future Work

We successfully incorporated relevance feedback into a search engine for large music collections that can be queried via natural language text input. One of the central challenges of our method is to assign semantically related information to individual music pieces. We opt to accomplish this by finding relevant information on the Web. The extracted text-based information is complemented by audio-based similarity, which leads to improved results of the retrieval due to the reduced dimensionality of the feature space. Information about the acoustic similarity is also mandatory to describe music pieces for which no related pages can be found on the Web. Due to the chosen vector space model, Rocchio's relevance feedback could be integrated smoothly. The conducted evaluations showed that relevance feedback provides a valuable extension to the system in that it adapts to users' preferences.

Since relevance feedback has a positive impact on the system's performance, we can conclude that the vector space representations of the music pieces are well suited to model the similarity between pieces. To further advance the system, the translation of queries into the term vector space has to be improved. Starting with better initial results is also mandatory for the acceptance of the system since people usually judge the quality based on the first results.

Finally, for future work, we plan to break the dependency on external search engines to further improve the applicability of the system. To this end, we aim at developing a Web crawler focused on music-related Web pages to create an page index specific to our task. Furthermore, we will also investigate alternative methods of obtaining relevance rankings.

Acknowledgments

Special thanks are due to all volunteers that helped evaluating the search engine. This research is supported by the Austrian Fonds zur Förderung der Wissenschaftlichen Forschung (FWF project number L112-N04) and the Vienna Science and Technology Fund (WWTF project CIO10 "Interfaces to Music"). The Austrian Research Institute for Artificial Intelligence (OFAI) acknowledges financial support by the Austrian ministries BMBWK and BMVIT.

References

1. Knees, P., Pohle, T., Schedl, M., Widmer, G.: A Music Search Engine Built upon Audio-based and Web-based Similarity Measures. In: Proceedings of the 30th annual international ACM SIGIR conference on research and development in information retrieval (SIGIR 2007), Amsterdam, The Netherlands (2007)
2. Maddage, N.C., Li, H., Kankanhalli, M.S.: Music structure based vector space retrieval. In: SIGIR 2006: Proceedings of the 29th annual international ACM SIGIR conference on Research and development in information retrieval (2006)
3. Ghias, A., Logan, J., Chamberlin, D., Smith, B.C.: Query by humming: musical information retrieval in an audio database. In: Proceedings of the 3rd ACM International Conference on Multimedia (MULTIMEDIA 1995), San Francisco, California, United State (1995)
4. Baumann, S., Klüter, A., Norlien, M.: Using natural language input and audio analysis for a human-oriented MIR system. In: Proceedings of the 2nd International Conference on Web Delivering of Music (WEDELMUSIC 2002), Darmstadt, Germany (2002)
5. Celma, O., Cano, P., Herrera, P.: Search Sounds: An audio crawler focused on weblogs. In: Proceedings of the 7th International Conference on Music Information Retrieval (ISMIR 2006), Victoria, B.C., Canada (2006)

 6. Celino, I., Della Valle, E., Cerizza, D., Turati, A.: Squiggle: A semantic search engine for indexing and retrieval of multimedia content. In: Proceedings of the 1st International Workshop on Semantic-enhanced Multimedia Presentation Systems (SEMPS 2006), Athens, Greece (2006)
 7. Knopke, I.: AROOOGA: An audio search engine for the World Wide Web. In: Proceedings of the 2004 International Computer Music Conference (ICMC 2004), Miami, USA (2004)
 8. Whitman, B., Lawrence, S.: Inferring Descriptions and Similarity for Music from Community Metadata. In: Proceedings of the 2002 International Computer Music Conference (ICMC 2002), Gotheborg, Sweden, pp. 591–598 (2002)
 9. Knees, P., Pampalk, E., Widmer, G.: Artist Classification with Web-based Data. In: Proceedings of 5th International Conference on Music Information Retrieval (ISMIR 2004), Barcelona, Spain, pp. 517–524 (2004)
10. Salton, G., Buckley, C.: Term-weighting approaches in automatic text retrieval. Information Processing and Management 24(5), 513–523 (1988)
11. Aucouturier, J.J., Pachet, F., Sandler, M.: The Way It Sounds: Timbre Models for Analysis and Retrieval of Music Signals. IEEE Transactions on Multimedia 7(6), 1028–1035 (2005)
12. Pampalk, E.: Computational Models of Music Similarity and their Application to Music Information Retrieval. PhD thesis, Vienna University of Technology (2006)
13. Aucouturier, J.J., Pachet, F.: Music Similarity Measures: What's the Use? In: Proceedings of the 3rd International Conference on Music Information Retrieval (ISMIR 2002), Paris, France, IRCAM, pp. 157–163 (2002)
14. Mandel, M., Ellis, D.: Song-Level Features and Support Vector Machines for Music Classification. In: Proceedings of the 6th International Conference on Music Information Retrieval (ISMIR 2005), London, UK (2005)
15. Aucouturier, J.J.: Ten Experiments on the Modelling of Polyphonic Timbre. PhD thesis, University of Paris 6 (2006)
16. Pohle, T., Knees, P., Schedl, M., Widmer, G.: Automatically Adapting the Structure of Audio Similarity Spaces. In: Proceedings of 1st Workshop on Learning the Semantics of Audio Signals (LSAS 2006), Athens, Greece (2006)
17. Yang, Y., Pedersen, J.O.: A comparative study on feature selection in text categorization. In: Fisher, D.H. (ed.) Proceedings of ICML 1997, 14th International Conference on Machine Learning, Nashville, US, pp. 412–420. Morgan Kaufman Publishers, San Francisco, US (1997)
18. Rocchio, J.J.: Relevance feedback in information retrieval. In: Salton, G. (ed.) The SMART Retrieval System – Experiments in Automatic Document Processing, Prentice Hall Inc., Englewood Cliffs, NJ, USA (1971)
19. Baeza-Yates, R., Ribeiro-Neto, B.: Modern Information Retrieval. Addison-Wesley, Reading, Massachusetts (1999)
20. Harman, D.: Relevance Feedback Revisited. In: Proceedings of the 15th annual international ACM SIGIR conference on Research and development in information retrieval (SIGIR 1992), Copenhagen, Denmark (1992)

Automatically Detecting Members and Instrumentation of Music Bands Via Web Content Mining

Markus Schedl[1] and Gerhard Widmer[1,2]

[1] Department of Computational Perception
Johannes Kepler University
Linz, Austria
markus.schedl@jku.at
http://www.cp.jku.at
[2] Austrian Research Institute for Artificial Intelligence
Vienna, Austria
gerhard.widmer@jku.at
http://www.ofai.at

Abstract. In this paper, we present an approach to automatically detecting music band members and instrumentation using web content mining techniques. To this end, we combine a named entity detection method with a rule-based linguistic text analysis approach extended by a rule filtering step. We report on the results of different evaluation experiments carried out on two test collections of bands covering a wide range of popularities. The performance of the proposed approach is evaluated using precision and recall measures. We further investigate the influence of different query schemes for the web page retrieval, of a critical parameter used in the rule filtering step, and of different string matching functions which are applied to deal with inconsistent spelling of band members.

1 Introduction and Context

Automatically retrieving textual information about music artists is a key question in text-based music information retrieval (MIR), which is a subfield of multimedia information retrieval. Such information can be used, for example, to enrich music information systems or music players [14], for automatic biography generation [1], to enhance user interfaces for browsing music collections [9,6,11,16], or to define similarity measures between artists, a key concept in MIR. Similarity measures enable, for example, creating relationship networks [3,13] or recommending unknown artists based on the favorite artists of the user (recommender systems) [17] or based on arbitrary textual descriptions of the artist or music (music search engines) [8].

Here, we present an approach that was developed for – but is not restricted to – the task of finding the members of a given music band and the respective instruments they play. In this work, we restrict instrument detection to the standard line-up of most Rock bands, i.e. we only check for singer(s), guitarist(s), bassist(s), drummer(s), and keyboardist(s). Since our approach relies

N. Boujemaa, M. Detyniecki, and A. Nürnberger (Eds.): AMR 2007, LNCS 4918, pp. 122–133, 2008.
© Springer-Verlag Berlin Heidelberg 2008

on information provided on the web by various companies, communities, and interest groups (e.g. record labels, online stores, music information systems, listeners of certain music genres), it adapts to changes as soon as new or modified web pages incorporating the changes become available. Deriving (member, instrument)-assignments from web pages is an important step towards building a music information system whose database is automatically populated by reliable information found on the web, which is our ultimate aim.

The approach presented in this paper relates to the task of *named entity detection (NED)*. A good outline of the evolution of NED can be found in [2]. Moreover, [2] presents a knowledge-based approach to learning rules for NED in structured documents like web pages. To this end, document-specific extraction rules are generated and validated using a database of known entity names. In [10], information about named entities and non-named entity terms are used to improve the quality of new event detection, i.e. the task of automatically detecting, whether a given story is novel or not. The authors of [15] use information about named entities to automatically extract facts and concepts from the web. They employ methods including domain-specific rule learning, identifying subclasses, and extracting elements from lists of class instances.

The work presented in [4] strongly relates to our work as the authors of [4] propose a pattern-based approach to finding instances of concepts on web pages and classify them according to an ontology of concepts. To this end, the page counts returned by *Google* for search queries containing hypothesis phrases are used to assign instances to concepts. For the general geographic concepts (e.g. city, country, river) and well-known instances used in the experiments in [4], this method yielded quite promising results.

In contrast, the task which we address in this paper, i.e. assigning (member, instrument)-pairs to bands, is a more specific one. Preliminary experiments on using the page counts returned for patterns including instrument, member, and band names yielded very poor results. In fact, querying such patterns as exact phrases, the number of found web pages was very small, even for well-known bands and members. Using conjunctive queries instead did not work either as the results were, in this case, heavily distorted by famous band members frequently occurring on the web pages of other bands. For example, *James Hetfield*, singer and rhythm guitarist of the band *Metallica*, occurs in the context of many other Heavy Metal bands. Thus, he would likely be predicted as the singer (or guitarist) of a large number of bands other than *Metallica*. Furthermore, the page counts returned by *Google* are only very rough estimates of the actual number of web pages. For these reasons, we elaborated an approach that combines the power of *Google*'s page ranking algorithm [12] (to find the top-ranked web pages of the band under consideration) with the precision of a rule-based linguistic analysis method (to find band members and assign instruments to them).

The remainder of this paper is organized as follows. Section 2 presents details of the proposed approach. In Section 3, the test collection used for our experiments is introduced. Subsequently, the conducted experiments are presented and the evaluation results are discussed in Section 4. Finally, Section 5 draws conclusions and points out directions for future research.

2   Methodology

The basic approach comprises four steps: *web retrieval, named entity detection, rule-based linguistic analysis*, and *rule selection*. Each of these are elaborated on in the following.

2.1   Web Retrieval

Given a band name B, we use *Google* to obtain the URLs of the 100 top-ranked web pages, whose content we then retrieve via *wget*[1]. Trying to restrict the query results to those web pages that actually address the music band under consideration, we add domain-specific keywords to the query, which yields the following four query schemes:

- *"B"+music* (abbreviated as M in the following)
- *"B"+music+review* (abbreviated as MR in the following)
- *"B"+music+members* (abbreviated as MM in the following)
- *"B"+lineup+music* (abbreviated as LUM in the following)

By discarding all markup tags, we eventually obtain a plain text representation of each web page.

2.2   Named Entity Detection

We employ a quite simple approach to NED, which basically relies on *detecting capitalization* and on *filtering*. First, we extract all *2-, 3-, and 4-grams* from the plain text representation of the web pages as we assume that the complete name of a band member comprises at least two and at most four single names, which holds for our test collection as well as for the vast majority of band members in arbitrary collections. Subsequently, some basic filtering is performed. We exclude those N-grams whose substrings contain only one character and retain only those N-grams whose tokens all have their first letter in upper case and all remaining letters in lower case. Finally, we use the *iSpell English Word Lists*[2] to filter out those N-grams which contain at least one substring that is a common speech word. The remaining N-grams are regarded as potential band members.

2.3   Rule-Based Linguistic Analysis

Having determined the potential band members, we perform a linguistic analysis to obtain the actual instrument(s) of each member. Similar to the approach proposed in [7] for finding hyponyms in large text corpora, we define the following rules and apply them on the potential band members (and the surrounding text as necessary) found in the named entity detection step.

---

[1] *http://www.gnu.org/software/wget*
[2] *http://wordlist.sourceforge.net*

1. M plays the I
2. M who plays the I
3. R M
4. M is the R
5. M, the R
6. M (I)
7. M (R)

In these rules, M is the potential band member, I is the instrument, and R is the role M plays within the band (singer, guitarist, bassist, drummer, keyboardist). For I and R, we use synonym lists to cope with the use of multiple terms for the same concept (e.g. *percussion* and *drums*). We further count on how many of the web pages each rule applies for each M and I (or R).

2.4   Rule Selection According to Document Frequencies

These counts are document frequencies (DF) since they indicate, for example, that on 24 of the web pages returned for the search query "Primal Fear"+music *Ralf Scheepers* is said to be the singer of the band according to rule 6 (on 6 pages according to rule 3, and so on). The extracted information is stored as a set of quadruples (member, instrument, rule, DF) for every band. Subsequently, the DF given by the individual rules are summed up over all (member, instrument)-pairs of the band, which yields (member, instrument, $\sum$DF)-triples. To reduce uncertain membership predictions, we filter out the triples whose $\sum$DF values are below a threshold t_{DF}, both expressed as a fraction of the highest $\sum$DF value of the band under consideration. To give an example, this filtering would exclude, in a case where the top-ranked singer of a band achieves an accumulated rule DF ($\sum$DF) of 20, but no potential drummer scores more than 1, all potential drummers for any $t_{DF} > 0.05$. Thus, the filtering would discard information about drummers since they are uncertain for the band.

   In preliminary experiments for this work, after having performed the filtering step, we predicted, for each instrument, the (member, instrument)-pair with the highest $\sum$DF value. Unfortunately, this method allows only for a $1 : m$ assignment between members and instruments. In general, however, an instrument can be played by more than one band member within the same band. To address this issue, for the experiments presented here, we follow the approach of predicting all (member, instrument)-pairs that remain after the filtering according to DF step described above. This enables an $m : n$ assignment between instruments and members.

3   Test Collection

To evaluate the proposed approach, we compiled a ground truth based on one author's private music collection. As this is a labor-intensive and time-consuming task, we restricted the dataset to 51 bands, with a strong focus on the genre *Metal*. The chosen bands vary strongly with respect to their popularity (some

Table 1. A list of all band names used in the experiments

Angra	Annihilator	Anthrax
Apocalyptica	Bad Religion	Black Sabbath
Blind Guardian	Borknagar	Cannibal Corpse
Century	Crematory	Deicide
Dimmu Borgir	Edguy	Entombed
Evanescence	Finntroll	Gamma Ray
Green Day	Guano Apes	Hammerfall
Heavenly	HIM	Iron Maiden
Iron Savior	Judas Priest	Krokus
Lacuna Coil	Lordi	Majesty
Manowar	Metal Church	Metallica
Motörhead	Nightwish	Nirvana
Offspring	Pantera	Paradise Lost
Pink Cream 69	Powergod	Primal Fear
Rage	Regicide	Scorpions
Sepultura	Soulfly	Stratovarius
Tiamat	Type O Negative	Within Temptation

are very well known, like *Metallica*, but most are largely unknown, like *Powergod*, *Pink Cream 69*, or *Regicide*). A complete list of all bands in the ground truth can be found in Table 1. We gathered the current line-up of the bands by consulting *Wikipedia*[3], *allmusic*[4], *Discogs*[5], or the band's web site. Finally, our ground truth contained 240 members with their respective instruments. We denote this dataset, that contains the current band members at the time we conducted the experiments (March 2007), as M_c in the following.

Since we further aimed at investigating the performance of our approach on the task of finding members that already left the band, we created a second ground truth dataset, denoted M_f in the following. This second dataset contains, in addition to the current line-up of the bands, also the former band members. Enriching the original dataset M_c with these former members (by consulting the same data sources as mentioned above), the number of members in M_f adds up to 499.

4   Evaluation

We performed different evaluations to assess the quality of the proposed approach. First, we calculated precision and recall of the predicted (member, instrument)-pairs on the ground truth using a fixed t_{DF} threshold. To get an impression of the goodness of the recall values, we also determined the upper bound for the recall achievable with the proposed method. Such an upper bound

---

[3] *http://www.wikipedia.org*

[4] *http://www.allmusic.com*

[5] *http://www.discogs.com*

exists since we can only find those members whose names actually occur in at least one web page retrieved for the artist under consideration. Subsequently, we investigate the influence of the parameter t_{DF} used in the rule filtering according to document frequencies. We performed all evaluations on both ground truth datasets M_c and M_f using each of the four query schemes.

We further employ three different string comparison methods to evaluate our approach. First, we perform *exact string matching*. Addressing the problem of different spelling for the same artist (e.g. the drummer of *Tiamat*, *Lars Sköld*, is often referred to as *Lars Skold*), we also evaluate the approach on the basis of a *canonical representation* of each band member. To this end, we perfom a mapping of similar characters to their stem, e.g. *ä, à, á, å, æ* to *a*. Furthermore, to cope with the fact that many artists use nicknames or abbreviations of their real names, we apply an *approximate string matching* method. According to [5], the so-called *Jaro-Winkler similarity* is well suited for personal first and last names since it favors strings that match from the beginning for a fixed prefix length (e.g. *Edu Falaschi* vs. *Eduardo Falaschi*, singer of the Brazilian band *Angra*). We use a *level two distance function* based on the Jaro-Winkler distance metric, i.e. the two strings to compare are broken into substrings (first and last names, in our case) and the similarity is caluclated as the combined similarities between each pair of tokens. We assume that the two strings are equal if their Jaro-Winkler similarity is above 0.9. For calculating the distance, we use the open-source Java toolkit *SecondString*[6].

4.1 Precision and Recall

We measured precision and recall of the predicted (member, instrument)-pairs on the ground truth. Such a (member, instrument)-pair is only considered correct if both the member and the instrument are predicted correctly. We used a threshold of $t_{DF} = 0.25$ for the filtering according to document frequencies (cf. Subsection 2.4) since according to preliminary experiments, this value seemed to represent a good trade-off between precision and recall.

Given the set of correct (band member, instrument)-assignments T according to the ground truth and the set of assignments predicted by our approach P, precision and recall are defined as $p = \frac{|T \cap P|}{|P|}$ and $r = \frac{|T \cap P|}{|T|}$, respectively. The results given in Table 2 are the average precision and recall values (over all bands in each of the ground truth sets M_c and M_f).

4.2 Upper Limits for Recall

Since the proposed approach relies on information that can be found on web pages, there exists an upper bound for the achievable performance. A band member that never occurs in the set of the 100 top-ranked web pages of a band obviously cannot be detected by our approach. As knowing these upper bounds is crucial to estimate the goodness of the recall values presented in Table 2,

---

[6] *http://secondstring.sourceforge.net*

Table 2. Overall precision and recall of the predicted (member, instrument)-pairs in percent for different query schemes and string distance functions on the ground truth sets M_c (upper table) and M_f (lower table). A filtering threshold of $t_{DF} = 0.25$ was used. The first value indicates the precision, the second the recall.

Precision/Recall on M_c		
exact	*similar char*	*L2-JaroWinkler*
M 46.94 / 32.21	50.27 / 34.46	53.24 / 35.95
MR 42.49 / 31.36	45.42 / 33.86	48.20 / 35.32
MM 43.25 / 36.27	44.85 / 37.23	47.44 / 37.55
LUM 32.48 / 27.87	33.46 / 29.06	34.12 / 29.06

Precision/Recall on M_f		
exact	*similar char*	*L2-JaroWinkler*
M 63.16 / 23.33	68.16 / 25.25	72.12 / 26.38
MR 52.42 / 21.33	55.63 / 23.12	59.34 / 24.82
MM 60.81 / 26.21	63.66 / 27.45	67.32 / 27.64
LUM 43.90 / 19.22	44.88 / 19.75	46.80 / 20.08

we analyzed how many of the actual band members given by the ground truth occur at least once in the retrieved web pages, i.e. for every band B, we calculate the recall, on the ground truth, of the N-grams extracted from B's web pages (without taking information about instruments into account). We verified that no band members were erroneously discarded in the N-gram selection phase. The results of these upper limit calculations using each query scheme and string matching function are depicted in Table 3 for both datasets M_c and M_f.

4.3   Influence of the Filtering Threshold t_{DF}

We also investigated the influence of the filtering threshold t_{DF} on precision and recall. Therefore, we conducted a series of experiments, in which we successively increased the value of t_{DF} between 0.0 and 1.0 with an increment of 0.01. The resulting precision/recall-plots can be found in Figures 1 and 2 for the ground truth datasets M_c and M_f, respectively. In these plots, only the results for exact string matching are presented for reasons of lucidity. Employing the other two, more tolerant, string distance functions just shifts the respective plots upwards. Since using low values for t_{DF} does not filter out many potential band members, the recall values tend to be high, but at the cost of lower precision. In contrast, high values of t_{DF} heavily prune the set of (member, instrument)-predictions and therefore generally yield lower recall and higher precision values.

4.4   Discussion of the Results

Taking a closer look at the overall precision and recall values given in Table 2 reveals that, for both datasets M_c and M_f, the query scheme M yields the highest precision values (up to more than 72% on the dataset M_f using Jaro-Winkler string matching), whereas the more specific scheme MM is able to

Table 3. Upper limits for the recall achievable on the ground truth datasets M_c (upper table) and M_f (lower table) using the 100 top-ranked web pages returned by *Google*. These limits are denoted for each of the search query scheme and string distance function. The values are given in percent.

Upper Limits for Recall on M_c			
	exact	*similar char*	*L2-Jaro Winkler*
M	56.00	57.64	63.44
MR	50.28	53.53	60.92
MM	58.12	59.69	66.33
LUM	55.80	58.62	66.26
Upper Limits for Recall on M_f			
	exact	*similar char*	*L2-Jaro Winkler*
M	52.97	55.15	62.01
MR	47.41	49.59	56.29
MM	56.40	57.62	64.08
LUM	55.21	57.27	64.11

achieve a higher recall on the ground truth (a maximum recall of nearly 38% on the dataset M_f using Jaro-Winkler string matching). The LUM scheme performs worst, independent of the used dataset and string distance function. The MR scheme performs better than LUM, but worse than M and MM with respect to both precision and recall.

Comparing the precision and recall values obtained using the dataset M_c with those obtained using M_f not surprisingly shows that for M_f the recall drops as this dataset contains more than double the number of band members as M_c and also lists members who spent a very short time with a band. For the same reasons, the precision is higher for the dataset M_f since obviously the chance to correctly predict a member is larger for a larger ground truth set of members.

Interestingly, comparing the upper limits for the recall for the two ground truth datasets (cf. Table 3) reveals that extending the set of the current band members with those who already left the band does not strongly influence the achievable recall (despite the fact that the number of band members in the ground truth set increases from 240 to 499 when adding the former members). This is a strong indication that the 100 top-ranked web pages of every band, which we use in the retrieval process, contain information about the current as well as the former band members to almost the same extent. We therefore conclude that using more than 100 web pages is unlikely to increase the quality of the (member, instrument)-predictions.

Regarding Figures 1 and 2, which depict the influence of the filtering parameter t_{DF} on the precision and recall values using the datasets M_c and M_f respectively, reveals that, for the dataset M_c, the query schemes M, MR, and MM do not stongly differ with respect to the achievable performance. Using the dataset M_f, in constrast, the results for the scheme MR are considerably worse than that for M and MM. It seems that album reviews (which are captured by the MR scheme) are more likely to mention the current band members than the

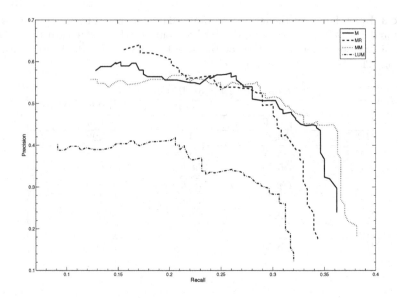

Fig. 1. Precision/recall-plot for the dataset M_c using the different query schemes and exact string matching

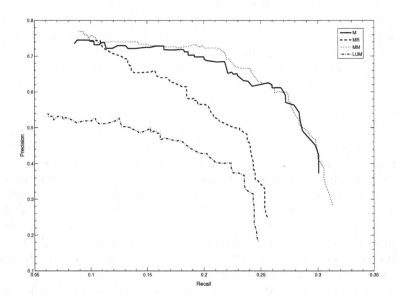

Fig. 2. Precision/recall-plot for the dataset M_f using the different query schemes and exact string matching

former ones. This explanation is also supported by the fact that the highest precision values on the dataset M_c are achieved with the MR scheme. Furthermore, the precision/recall-plots illustrate the worse performance of the LUM scheme, independently of the filtering threshold t_{DF}.

To summarize, taking the upper limits for the recall into account (cf. Table 3), the recall values achieved with the proposed approach as given in Table 2 are quite promising, especially when considering the relative simplicity of the approach. Basically, the query scheme M yields the highest precision while the scheme MM yields the highest recall.

5   Conclusions and Future Work

We presented an approach to detecting band members and instruments they play within the band. To this end, we employ the techniques *N-gram extraction*, *named entity detection*, *rule-based linguistic analysis*, and *filtering according to document frequencies* on the textual content of the top-ranked web pages returned by *Google* for the name of the band under consideration. The proposed approach eventually predicts (member, instrument)-pairs. We evaluated the approach on two sets of band members from 51 bands, one containing the current members at the time this research was carried out, the other additionally including all former members. We presented and discussed precision and recall achieved for different search query schemes and string matching methods.

As for future work, we will investigate more sophisticated approaches to named entity detection. Employing machine learning techniques, e.g. to estimate the reliability of the rules used in the linguistic text analysis step, could also improve the quality of the results. We further aim at deriving complete band histories (by searching for dates when a particular artist joined or left a band), which would allow for creating time-dependent relationship networks. Under the assumption that bands which share or shared some members are similar to some extent, these networks could be used to derive a similarity measure. An application for this research is the creation of a domain-specific search engine for music artists, which is our ultimate aim.

Acknowledgments

This research is supported by the Austrian Fonds zur Förderung der Wissenschaftlichen Forschung (FWF) under project number L112-N04 and by the Vienna Science and Technology Fund (WWTF) under project number CI010 (Interfaces to Music). The Austrian Research Institute for Artificial Intelligence acknowledges financial support by the Austrian ministries BMBWK and BMVIT.

References

1. Alani, H., Kim, S., Millard, D.E., Weal, M.J., Hall, W., Lewis, P.H., Shadbolt, N.R.: Automatic Ontology-Based Knowledge Extraction from Web Documents. IEEE Intelligent Systems 18(1) (2003)

2. Callan, J., Mitamura, T.: Knowledge-Based Extraction of Named Entities. In: Proceedings of the 11th International Conference on Information and Knowledge Management (CIKM 2002), McLean, VA, USA, pp. 532–537. ACM Press, New York (2002)
3. Cano, P., Koppenberger, M.: The Emergence of Complex Network Patterns in Music Artist Networks. In: Proceedings of the 5th International Symposium on Music Information Retrieval (ISMIR 2004), Barcelona, Spain (October 2004)
4. Cimiano, P., Handschuh, S., Staab, S.: Towards the Self-Annotating Web. In: Proceedings of the 13th International Conference on World Wide Web (WWW 2004), pp. 462–471. ACM Press, New York, NY, USA (2004)
5. Cohen, W.W., Ravikumar, P., Fienberg, S.E.: A Comparison of String Distance Metrics for Name-Matching Tasks. In: Proceedings of the IJCAI 2003 Workshop on Information Integration on the Web (IIWeb 2003), Acapulco, Mexico, August 2003, pp. 73–78 (2003)
6. Goto, M., Goto, T.: Musicream: New Music Playback Interface for Streaming, Sticking, Sorting, and Recalling Musical Pieces. In: Proceedings of the 6th International Conference on Music Information Retrieval (ISMIR 2005), London, UK (September 2005)
7. Hearst, M.A.: Automatic Acquisition of Hyponyms from Large Text Corpora. In: Proceedings of the 14th Conference on Computational Linguistics, Nantes, France, August 1992, vol. 2, pp. 539–545 (1992)
8. Knees, P., Pohle, T., Schedl, M., Widmer, G.: A Music Search Engine Built upon Audio-based and Web-based Similarity Measures. In: Proceedings of the 30th Annual International ACM SIGIR Conference on Research and Development in Information Retrieval (SIGIR 2007), Amsterdam, The Netherlands, July 23-27 (2007)
9. Knees, P., Schedl, M., Pohle, T., Widmer, G.: An Innovative Three-Dimensional User Interface for Exploring Music Collections Enriched with Meta-Information from the Web. In: Proceedings of the ACM Multimedia 2006 (MM 2006), Santa Barbara, California, USA, October 23-26 (2006)
10. Kumaran, G., Allan, J.: Text Classification and Named Entities for New Event Detection. In: Proceedings of the 27th Annual International ACM SIGIR Conference on Research and Development in Information Retrieval (SIGIR 2004), pp. 297–304. ACM Press, New York, NY, USA (2004)
11. Mörchen, F., Ultsch, A., Nöcker, M., Stamm, C.: Databionic Visualization of Music Collections According to Perceptual Distance. In: Proceedings of the 6th International Conference on Music Information Retrieval (ISMIR 2005), London, UK (September 2005)
12. Page, L., Brin, S., Motwani, R., Winograd, T.: The PageRank Citation Ranking: Bringing Order to the Web. In: Proceedings of the Annual Meeting of the American Society for Information Science (ASIS 1998), January 1998, pp. 161–172 (1998)
13. Schedl, M., Knees, P., Widmer, G.: Discovering and Visualizing Prototypical Artists by Web-based Co-Occurrence Analysis. In: Proceedings of the Sixth International Conference on Music Information Retrieval (ISMIR 2005), London, UK (September 2005)
14. Schedl, M., Pohle, T., Knees, P., Widmer, G.: Assigning and Visualizing Music Genres by Web-based Co-Occurrence Analysis. In: Proceedings of the 7th International Conference on Music Information Retrieval (ISMIR 2006), Victoria, Canada (October 2006)

15. Shinyama, Y., Sekine, S.: Named Entity Discovery Using Comparable News Articles. In: Proceedings of the 20th International Conference on Computational Linguistics (COLING 2004), Morristown, NJ, USA. Association for Computational Linguistics, p. 848 (2004)
16. Vignoli, F., van Gulik, R., van de Wetering, H.: Mapping Music in the Palm of Your Hand, Explore and Discover Your Collection. In: Proceedings of the 5th International Symposium on Music Information Retrieval (ISMIR 2004), Barcelona, Spain (October 2004)
17. Zadel, M., Fujinaga, I.: Web Services for Music Information Retrieval. In: Proceedings of the 5th International Symposium on Music Information Retrieval (ISMIR 2004), Barcelona, Spain (October 2004)

A System for Automatic Chord Transcription from Audio Using Genre-Specific Hidden Markov Models

Kyogu Lee

Center for Computer Research in Music and Acoustics
Stanford University, Stanford CA 94305, USA
kglee@ccrma.stanford.edu

Abstract. We describe a system for automatic chord transcription from the raw audio using genre-specific hidden Markov models trained on audio-from-symbolic data. In order to avoid enormous amount of human labor required to manually annotate the chord labels for ground-truth, we use symbolic data such as MIDI files to automate the labeling process. In parallel, we synthesize the same symbolic files to provide the models with the sufficient amount of observation feature vectors along with the automatically generated annotations for training. In doing so, we build different models for various musical genres, whose model parameters reveal characteristics specific to their corresponding genre. The experimental results show that the HMMs trained on synthesized data perform very well on real acoustic recordings. It is also shown that when the correct genre is chosen, simpler, genre-specific model yields performance better than or comparable to that of more complex model that is genre-independent. Furthermore, we also demonstrate the potential application of the proposed model to the genre classification task.

1 Introduction

Extracting high-level information of musical attributes such as melody, harmony, key or rhythm from the raw audio is very important in music information retrieval (MIR) systems. Using such high-level musical information, users can efficiently and effectively search, retrieve and navigate through a large collection of musical audio. Among those musical attributes, chords play a key role in Western tonal music. A musical chord is a set of simultaneous tones, and succession of chords over time, or chord progression, forms the core of harmony in a piece of music. Hence analyzing the overall harmonic structure of a musical piece often starts with labeling every chord at every beat or measure.

Recognizing the chords automatically from audio is of great use for those who want to do harmony analysis of music. Once the harmonic content of a piece is known, a sequence of chords can be used for further higher-level structural analysis where themes, phrases or forms can be defined.

Chord sequences with the timing of chord boundaries are also a very compact and robust mid-level representation of musical signals, and have many potential

N. Boujemaa, M. Detyniecki, and A. Nürnberger (Eds.): AMR 2007, LNCS 4918, pp. 134–146, 2008.

applications, which include music identification, music segmentation, music similarity finding, mood classification and audio summarization. Chord sequences have been successfully used as a front end to the audio cover song identification system in [1], where a dynamic time warping algorithm was used to compute the minimum alignment cost between two frame-level chord sequences. For these reasons and others, automatic chord recognition has recently attracted a number of researchers in the music information retrieval community.

Hidden Markov models (HMMs) are very successful for speech recognition, and they owe such high performance largely due to gigantic databases accumulated over decades. Such a huge database not only helps estimate the model parameters appropriately, but also enables researchers to build richer models, resulting in better performance. However, there is very few such database available for music applications. Furthermore, the acoustical variance in a piece of music is far greater than that in speech in terms of its frequency range, timbre due to instrumentation, dynamics, and/or tempo, and thus a even more data is needed to build the generalized models.

It is very difficult to obtain a large set of training data for music, however. First of all, it is nearly impossible for researchers to acquire a large collection of musical recordings. Secondly, hand-labeling the chord boundaries in a number of recordings is not only an extremely time consuming and laborious task but also involves performing harmony analysis by someone with a certain level of expertise in music theory or musicology.

In this paper, we propose a method of automating the daunting task of providing the machine learning models with a huge amount of labeled training data for supervised learning. To this end, we use symbolic music documents such as MIDI files to generate chord names and precise chord boundaries, as well as to create audio files. Audio and chord-boundary information generated this way are in perfect alignment, and we can use them to estimate the model parameters. In addition, we build a separate model for each musical genre, which, when a correct genre model is selected, turns out to outperform a generic, genre-independent model. The overall system is illustrated in Figure 1.

There are several advantages to this approach. First, a great number of symbolic music files are freely available, often the times categorized by genres. Second, we do not need to manually annotate chord boundaries with chord names to obtain training data. Third, we can generate as much data as needed with the same symbolic files but with different musical attributes by changing instrumentation, tempo, or dynamics when synthesizing audio. This helps avoid overfitting the models to a specific type of music. Fourth, sufficient training data enables us to build richer models for better performance.

This paper continues with a review of related work in Section 2; in Section 3, we describe the feature vector we used to represent the state in the models; in Section 4, we explain the method of obtaining the labeled training data, and describe the procedure of building our models; in Section 5, we present experimental results with discussions, and draw conclusions followed by directions for future work in Section 6.

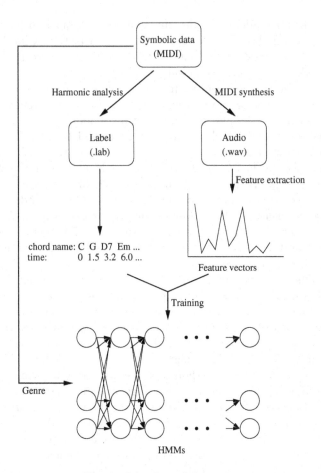

Fig. 1. Overview of the system

2   Related Work

Several systems have been proposed for chord recognition from the raw wave-form. Some systems use a simple pattern matching algorithm [2,3,4] while others use more sophisticated machine learning techniques such as hidden Markov models or Support Vector Machines [5,6,7,8,9]. Our approach is closest to two previous works.

Sheh and Ellis proposed a statistical learning method for chord segmentation and recognition [5]. They used the hidden Markov models (HMMs) trained by the Expectation-Maximization (EM) algorithm, and treated the chord labels as hidden values within the EM framework. In training the models, they used only the chord sequence as an input to the models, and applied the forward-backward algorithm to estimate the model parameters. The frame accuracy they obtained was about 76% for segmentation and about 22% for recognition, respectively. The poor performance for recognition may be due to insufficient training data compared with a large set of classes (just 20 songs to train the model with 147 chord types). It is also possible that the flat-start initialization in the EM algorithm yields incorrect chord boundaries resulting in poor parameter estimates.

Bello and Pickens also used HMMs with the EM algorithm to find the crude transition probability matrix for each input [6]. What was novel in their approach was that they incorporated musical knowledge into the models by defining a state transition matrix based on the key distance in a circle of fifths, and avoided random initialization of a mean vector and a covariance matrix of observation distribution. In addition, in training the model's parameter, they selectively updated the parameters of interest on the assumption that a chord template or distribution is almost universal regardless of the type of music, thus disallowing adjustment of distribution parameters. The accuracy thus obtained was about 75% using beat-synchronous segmentation with a smaller set of chord types (24 major/minor triads only). In particular, they argued that the accuracy increased by as much as 32% when the adjustment of the observation distribution parameters is prohibited. Even with the high recognition rate, it still remains a question if it will work well for all kinds of music.

The present paper expands our previous work on chord recognition [8,9,10]. It is founded on the work of Sheh and Ellis or Bello and Pickens in that the states in the HMM represent chord types, and we try to find the optimal path, *i.e.*, the most probable chord sequence in a maximum-likelihood sense using a *Viterbi* decoder. The most prominent difference in our approach is, however, that we use a *supervised learning* method; *i.e.*, we provide the models with feature vectors as well as corresponding chord names with precise boundaries, and therefore model parameters can be directly estimated without using an EM algorithm when a single Gaussian is used to model the observation distribution for each chord. In addition, we propose a method to automatically obtain a large set of labeled training data, removing the problematic and time consuming task of manual annotation of precise chord boundaries with chord names. Furthermore, this large data set allows us to build genre-specific HMMs, which not only increase the chord recognition accuracy but also provide genre information.

3   System

Our chord transcription system starts off by performing harmony analysis on symbolic data to obtain label files with chord names and precise time boundaries. In parallel, we synthesize the audio files with the same symbolic files using a sample-based synthesizer. We then extract appropriate feature vectors from audio which are in perfect sync with the labels and use them to train our models.

3.1   Obtaining Labeled Training Data

In order to train a supervised model, we need a large number of audio files with corresponding label files which must contain chord names and boundaries. To automate this laborious process, we use symbolic data to generate label files as well as to create time-aligned audio files. To this end, we first convert a symbolic file to a format which can be used as an input to a chord-analysis tool. Chord analyzer then performs harmony analysis and outputs a file with root information and note names from which complete chord information (*i.e.*, root and its sonority – major, minor, or diminished) is extracted. Sequence of chords are used as pseudo ground-truth or labels when training the HMMs along with proper feature vectors.

We used symbolic files in MIDI (Musical Instrument Digital Interface) format. For harmony analysis, we used the Melisma Music Analyzer developed by Sleator and Temperley [11]. Melisma Music Analyzer takes a piece of music represented by an event list, and extracts musical information from it such as meter, phrase structure, harmony, pitch-spelling, and key. By combining harmony and key information extracted by the analysis program, we can generate label files with sequence of chord names and accurate boundaries.

The symbolic harmony-analysis program was tested on a corpus of excerpts and the 48 fugue subjects from the *Well-Tempered Clavier*, and the harmony analysis and the key extraction yielded an accuracy of 83.7% and 87.4%, respectively [12].

We then synthesize the audio files using Timidity++. Timidity++ is a free software synthesizer, and converts MIDI files into audio files in a WAVE format.[1] It uses a sample-based synthesis technique to create harmonically rich audio as in real recordings. The raw audio is downsampled to 11025 Hz, and 6-dimensional tonal centroid features are extracted from it with the frame size of 8192 samples and the hop size of 2048 samples, corresponding to 743 ms and 186 ms, respectively.

3.2   Feature Vector

Harte and Sandler proposed a 6-dimensional feature vector called *Tonal Centroid*, and used it to detect harmonic changes in musical audio [13]. It is based on the Harmonic Network or *Tonnetz*, which is a planar representation of pitch relations where pitch classes having close harmonic relations such as fifths, major/minor thirds have smaller Euclidean distances on the plane.

The Harmonic Network is a theoretically infinite plane, but is wrapped to create a 3-D Hypertorus assuming enharmonic and octave equivalence, and therefore there are just 12 chromatic pitch classes. If we reference C as a pitch class 0, then we have 12 distinct points on the circle of fifths from 0-7-2-9-···-10-5, and it wraps back to 0 or C. If we travel on the circle of minor thirds, however, we come back to a referential point only after three steps as in 0-3-6-9-0. The circle of major thirds is defined in a similar way. This is visualized in Figure 2. As shown in Figure 2, the six dimensions are viewed as three coordinate pairs $(x1, y1), (x2, y2)$, and $(x3, y3)$.

Using the aforementioned representation, a collection of pitches like chords is described as a single point in the 6-D space. Harte and Sandler obtained a 6-D tonal centroid vector by projecting a 12-bin tuned chroma vector onto the three circles in the equal tempered Tonnetz described above. By calculating the

---

[1] http://timidity.sourceforge.net/

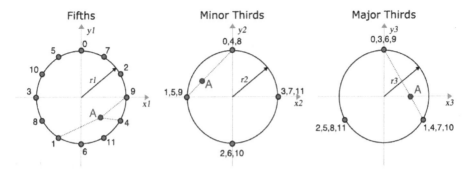

Fig. 2. Visualizing the 6-D Tonal Space as three circles: fifths, minor thirds, and major thirds from left to right. Numbers on the circles correspond to pitch classes and represent nearest neighbors in each circle. Tonal Centroid for A major triad (pitch class 9,1, and 4) is shown at point A (adapted from Harte and Sandler [13]).

Euclidean distance between successive analysis frames of tonal centroid vectors, they successfully detect harmonic changes such as chord boundaries from musical audio.

While a 12-dimensional chroma vector has been widely used in most chord recognition systems, it was shown that the tonal centroid feature yielded far less errors in [10]. The hypothesis was that the tonal centroid vector is more efficient and more robust because it has only 6 dimensions, and it puts emphasis on the interval relations such as fifths, major/minor thirds, which are key intervals that comprise most of musical chords in Western tonal music.

3.3   Hidden Markov Model

A hidden Markov model [14] is an extension of a discrete Markov model, in which the states are *hidden* in the sense that an underlying stochastic process is not directly observable, but can only be observed through another set of stochastic processes.

We recognize chords using 36-state HMMs. Each state represents a single chord, and the observation distribution is modeled by Gaussian mixtures with diagonal covariance matrices. State transitions obey the first-order Markov property; *i.e.*, the future is independent of the past given the present state. In addition, we use an ergodic model since we allow every possible transition from chord to chord, and yet the transition probabilities are learned.

In our model, we have defined three chord types for each of 12 chromatic pitch classes according to their sonorities – major, minor, and diminished chords – and thus we have 36 classes in total. We grouped triads and seventh chords with the same root into the same category. For instance, we treated E minor triad and E minor seventh chord as just E minor chord without differentiating the triad and the seventh. We found this class size appropriate in a sense that it lies between overfitting and oversimplification.

With the labeled training data obtained from the symbolic files, we first train our models to estimate the model parameters. Once the model parameters are learned, we then extract the feature vectors from the real recordings, and apply the Viterbi algorithm to the models to find the optimal path, *i.e.*, chord sequence, in a maximum likelihood sense.

3.4   Genre-Specific HMMs

In [10], when tested with various kinds of input, Lee and Slaney showed that the performance was greatest when the input audio was of the same kind as the training data set, suggesting the need to build genre-specific models. This is because not only different instrumentation causes the feature vector to vary, but also the chord progression, and thus the transition probabilities are very different from genre to genre.

We therefore built an HMM for each genre. While the genre information is not contained in the symbolic data, most MIDI files are categorized by their genres, and we could use them to obtain different training data sets by genres. We defined six musical genres including keyboard, chamber, orchestral, rock, jazz, and blues. We acquired the MIDI files for classical music – keyboard, chamber, and orchestral – from `http://www.classicalarchives.com`, and others from a few websites including `http://www.mididb.com`, `http://www.thejazzpage.de`, and `http://www.davebluesybrown.com`. The total number of MIDI files and synthesized audio files used for training is 4,212, which correspond to 348.73 hours of audio and 6,758,416 feature vector frames. Table 1 shows the training data sets used to train each genre model in more detail.

Figure 3 shows the 36×36 transition probability matrices for rock, jazz, and blues model after training. Although they are all strongly diagonal because the rate at which chord changes is usually longer than the frame rate, we still can observe the differences among them. For example, the blues model shows higher transition probabilities between the tonic (I) and the dominant (V) or subdominant (IV) chord than the other two models, which are the three chords almost exclusively used in blues music. This is indicated by darker off-diagonal lines 5 or 7 semitones apart from the main diagonal line. In addition, compared with the rock or blues model, we find that the jazz model reveals more

Table 1. Training data sets for each genre model

Genre	# of MIDI/Audio files	# of frames	Audio length (hours)
Keyboard	393	1,517,064	78.28
Chamber	702	1,224,209	63.17
Orchestral	319	1,528,796	78.89
Rock	1,046	1,070,752	55.25
Jazz	1,037	846,006	43.65
Blues	715	571,589	29.49
All	4,212	6,758,416	348.73

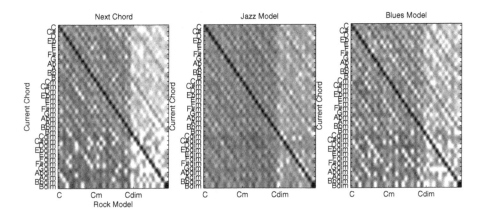

Fig. 3. 36×36 transition probability matrices of rock (left), jazz (center), and blues (right) model. For viewing purpose, logarithm was taken of the original matrices. Axes are labeled in the order of major, minor, and diminished chords.

frequent transitions to the diminished chords, as indicated by darker last third region, which are rarely found in rock or blues music in general.

We can also witness the difference in the observation distribution of the chord for each genre, as shown in Figure 4. Figure 4 displays the mean tonal centroid vectors and covariances of C major chord in the keyboard, chamber, and in the orchestral model, respectively, where the observation distribution of the chord was modeled by a single Gaussian.

We believe these unique properties in model parameters specific to each genre will help increase the chord recognition accuracy when the correct genre model is selected.

4   Experimental Results and Analysis

4.1   Evaluation

We tested our models' performance on the two whole albums of Beatles (CD1: *Please Please Me*, CD2: *Beatles For Sale*) as done by Bello and Pickens [6], each of which contains 14 tracks. Ground-truth annotations were provided by Harte and Sandler at the Digital Music Center at University of London in Queen Mary.[2]

In computing scores, we only counted exact matches as correct recognition. We tolerated the errors at the chord boundaries by having a time margin of one frame, which corresponds approximately to 0.19 second. This assumption is fair since the segment boundaries were generated by human by listening to audio, which cannot be razor sharp.

---

[2] http://www.elec.qmul.ac.uk/digitalmusic/

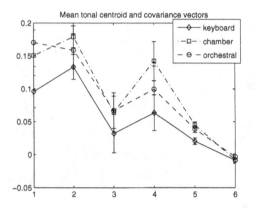

Fig. 4. Mean tonal centroid vectors and covariances of C major chord in keyboard, chamber, and orchestral model

To examine the dependency of the test input on genres, we first compared the each genre model's performance on the same input material. In addition to 6 genre models described in Section 3.4, we built a universal model without genre dependency where all the data were used for training. This universal, genre-independent model was to investigate the model's performance when no prior genre information of the test input is given.

4.2   Results and Discussion

Table 2 shows the frame-rate accuracy in percentage for each genre model. The number of Gaussian mixtures was one for all models. The best results are shown in boldface.

From the results shown in Table 2, we can notice a few things worthy of further discussions. First of all, the performance of the classical models – keyboard, chamber, and orchestral model – is much worse than that of other models. Second, the performance of the rock model came 2nd out of all 7 models, which proves our hypothesis that the model of the same kind as the test input outperforms the others. Third, even though the test material is generally classified

Table 2. Test results for each model with major/minor/diminished chords (36 states, % accuracy)

Model	Beatles CD1	Beatles CD2	Total
Keyboard	38.674	73.106	55.890
Chamber	30.557	73.382	51.970
Orchestral	18.193	57.109	37.651
Rock	45.937	77.294	61.616
Jazz	43.523	76.220	59.872
Blues	**48.483**	**79.598**	**64.041**
All	24.837	68.804	46.821

Table 3. Test results for each model with major/minor chords only (24 states, % accuracy)

Model	Beatles CD1	Beatles CD2	Total
Keyboard	43.945	73.414	58.680
Chamber	43.094	79.593	61.344
Orchestral	37.238	77.133	57.186
Rock	**60.041**	**84.289**	**72.165**
Jazz	44.324	76.107	60.216
Blues	52.244	80.042	66.143
All	51.443	80.013	65.728

as rock music, it is not striking that the blues model gave the best performance considering that rock music has its root in blues music. Particularly, early rock music like Beatles' was greatly affected by blues music. This again supports our hypothesis.

Knowing that the test material does not contain any diminished chord, we did another experiment with the class size reduced down to just 24 major/minor chords instead of full 36 chord types. The results are shown in Table 3.

With fewer chord types, we can observe that the recognition accuracy increased by as much as 20% for some model. Furthermore, the rock model outperformed all other models, again verifying our hypothesis on genre-dependency. This in turn suggests that if the type of the input audio is given, we can adjust the class size of the corresponding model to increase the accuracy. For example, we may use 36-state HMMs for classical or jazz music where diminished chords are frequently used, but use only 24 major/minor chord classes in case of rock or blues music, which rarely uses diminished chords.

Finally, we investigated the universal, genre-independent model in further detail to see the effect of the model complexity. This is because in practical situations, the genre information of the input is unknown, and thus there is no choice but to use a universal model. Although the results shown in Table 2 and Table 3 indicate a general, genre-independent model performs worse than a genre-specific model of the same kind as the input, we can build a richer model for potential increase in performance since we have much more data. Figure 5 illustrates the performance of a universal model as the number of Gaussian mixture increases.

As shown in Figure 5, the performance increases as the model gets more complex and richer. To compare the performance of a complex, genre-independent 36-state HMM with that of a simple, genre-specific 24-state HMM, overlaid is the performance of a 24-state rock model with only one mixture. Although increasing the number of mixtures also increases the recognition rate, it fails to reach the rate of a rock model with just one mixture. This comparison is not fair in that a rock model has only 24 states compared with 36 states in a universal model, resulting in less errors particularly because not a single diminished

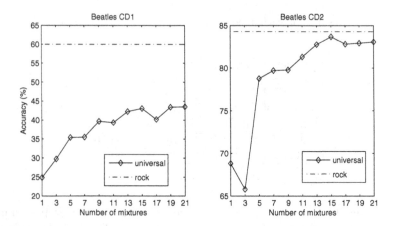

Fig. 5. Chord recognition performance of a 36-state universal model with the number of mixtures as a variable (solid) overlaid with a 24-state rock model with one mixture (dash-dot)

chord is included in the test material. As stated above, however, given no prior information regarding the kind of input audio, we can't take the risk of using a 24-state HMM with only major/minor chords because the input may be classical or jazz music in which diminished chords appear quite often.

The above statements therefore suggest that genre identification on the input audio must be preceded in order to be able to use genre-specific HMMs for better performance. It turns out, however, that we don't need any other sophisticated genre classification algorithms or different feature vectors like MFCC, which is almost exclusively used for genre classification. Given the observation sequence from the input, when there are several competing models, we can select the correct model by choosing one with the maximum likelihood using a forward-backward algorithm also known as a Baum-Welch algorithm. It is exactly the same algorithm as one used in isolated word recognition systems described in [14]. Once the model is selected, we can apply the Viterbi decoder to find the most probable state path, which is identical to the most probable chord sequence. Using this method, our system successfully identified 24 tracks as rock music out of total 28 tracks, which is 85.71% accuracy. What is noticeable and interesting is that the other four songs are all misclassified as blues music in which rock music is known to have its root. In fact, they all are very blues-like music, and some are even categorized as "bluesy".

Our results compare favorably with other state-of-the-art system by Bello and Pickens [6]. Their performance with Beatles' test data was 68.55% and 81.54% for CD1 and CD2, respectively. However, they went through a pre-processing stage of beat detection to perform a tactus-based analysis/recognition. Without a beat-synchronous analysis, their accuracy drops down to 58.96% and 74.78% for each CD, which is lower than our results with a rock model which are 60.04% and 84.29%.

5   Conclusion

In this paper, we describe a system for automatic chord transcription from the raw audio. The main contribution of this work is the demonstration that automatic generation of a very large amount of labeled training data for machine learning models leads to superior results in our musical task by enabling richer models like genre-specific HMMs. By using the chord labels with explicit segmentation information, we directly estimated the model parameters in HMMs.

In order to accomplish this goal, we have used symbolic data to generate label files as well as to synthesize audio files. The rationale behind this idea was that it is far easier and more robust to perform harmony analysis on the symbolic data than on the raw audio data since symbolic files such as MIDI files contain noise-free pitch and time information for every note. In addition, by using a sample-based synthesizer, we could create audio files which have harmonically rich spectra as in real acoustic recordings. This labor-free procedure to obtain a large amount of labeled training data enabled us to build richer models like genre-specific HMMs, resulting in improved performance with much simpler models than a more complex, genre-independent model.

As feature vectors, we used 6-dimensional tonal centroid vectors which proved to outperform conventional chroma vectors for the chord recognition task in previous work by the same author.

Each state in HMMs was modeled by a multivariate, single Gaussian or Gaussian mixtures completely represented by mean vectors and covariance matrices. We have defined 36 classes or chord types in our models, which include for each pitch class three distinct sonorities – major, minor, and diminished. We treated seventh chords as their corresponding root triads, and disregarded augmented chords since they very rarely appear in Western tonal music. We reduced the class size down to 24 without diminished chords for some models – for instance, for rock or blues model – where diminished chords are very rarely used, and we could observe great improvement in performance.

Experimental results show that the performance is best when the model and the input are of the same kind, which supports our hypothesis on the need for building genre-specific models. This in turn indicates that although the models are trained on synthesized data, they succeed to capture genre-specific musical characteristics seen in real acoustic recordings. Another great advantage of present approach is that we can also predict the genre of the input audio by computing the likelihoods of different genre models as done in isolated word recognizers. This way, we not only extract chord sequence but also identify musical genre at the same time, without using any other algorithms or feature vectors.

Even though the experiments on genre identification yielded high accuracy, the test data contained only one type of musical genre. In the near future, we plan to expand the test data to include several different genres to fully examine the viability of genre-specific HMMs. In addition, we consider higher-order HMMs for future work because chord progressions based on Western tonal music theory show such higher-order characteristics. Therefore, knowing two or more preceding chords will help to make a correct decision.

Acknowledgment

The author would like to thank Moonseok Kim and Jungsuk Lee at McGill University for fruitful discussions and suggestions regarding this research.

References

1. Lee, K.: Identifying cover songs from audio using harmonic representation. In: Extended abstract submitted to Music Information Retrieval eXchange task, BC, Canada (2006)
2. Fujishima, T.: Realtime chord recognition of musical sound: A system using Common Lisp Music. In: Proceedings of the International Computer Music Conference, Beijing. International Computer Music Association (1999)
3. Harte, C.A., Sandler, M.B.: Automatic chord identification using a quantised chromagram. In: Proceedings of the Audio Engineering Society, Spain. Audio Engineering Society (2005)
4. Lee, K.: Automatic chord recognition using enhanced pitch class profile. In: Proceedings of the International Computer Music Conference, New Orleans, USA (2006)
5. Sheh, A., Ellis, D.P.: Chord segmentation and recognition using EM-trained hidden Markov models. In: Proceedings of the International Symposium on Music Information Retrieval, Baltimore, MD (2003)
6. Bello, J.P., Pickens, J.: A robust mid-level representation for harmonic content in music signals. In: Proceedings of the International Symposium on Music Information Retrieval, London, UK (2005)
7. Morman, J., Rabiner, L.: A system for the automatic segmentation and classification of chord sequences. In: Proceedings of Audio and Music Computing for Multimedia Workshop, Santa Barbar, CA (2006)
8. Lee, K., Slaney, M.: Automatic chord recognition using an HMM with supervised learning. In: Proceedings of the International Symposium on Music Information Retrieval, Victoria, Canada (2006)
9. Lee, K., Slaney, M.: Automatic chord recognition from audio using a supervised HMM trained with audio-from-symbolic data. In: Proceedings of Audio and Music Computing for Multimedia Workshop, Santa Barbara, CA (2006)
10. Lee, K., Slaney, M.: Acoustic Chord Transcription and Key Extraction From Audio Using Key-Dependent HMMs Trained on Synthesized Audio. IEEE Transactions on Audio, Speech and Language Processing 16(2), 291–301 (2008)
11. Sleator, D., Temperley, D.: The Melisma Music Analyzer (2001), http://www.link.cs.cmu.edu/music-analysis/
12. Temperley, D.: The cognition of basic musical structures. The MIT Press, Cambridge (2001)
13. Harte, C.A., Sandler, M.B.: Detecting harmonic change in musical audio. In: Proceedings of Audio and Music Computing for Multimedia Workshop, Santa Barbara, CA (2006)
14. Rabiner, L.R.: A tutorial on hidden Markov models and selected applications in speech recognition. Proceedings of the IEEE 77(2), 257–286 (1989)

Information Fusion in Multimedia Information Retrieval

Jana Kludas, Eric Bruno, and Stephane Marchand-Maillet

University of Geneva, Switzerland
jana.kludas@cui.unige.ch
http://viper.unige.ch/

Abstract. In retrieval, indexing and classification of multimedia data an efficient information fusion of the different modalities is essential for the system's overall performance. Since information fusion, its influence factors and performance improvement boundaries have been lively discussed in the last years in different research communities, we will review their latest findings. They most importantly point out that exploiting the feature's and modality's dependencies will yield to maximal performance. In data analysis and fusion tests with annotated image collections this is undermined.

1 Introduction

The multi modal nature of multimedia data creates an essential need for information fusion for its classification, indexing and retrieval. Fusion has also great impact on other tasks such as object recognition, since all objects exist in multi modal spaces. Information fusion has established itself as an independent research area over the last decades, but a general formal theoretical framework to describe information fusion systems is still missing [14].

One reason for this is the vast number of disparate research areas that utilize and describe some form of information fusion in their context of theory. For example, the concept of data or feature fusion, which forms together with classifier and decision fusion the three main divisions of fusion levels, initially occurred in multi-sensor processing. By now several other research fields found its application useful. Besides the more classical data fusion approaches in robotics, image processing and pattern recognition, the information retrieval community discovered some years ago its power in combining multiple information sources [23].

The roots of classifier and decision fusion can be found in the neural network literature, where the idea of combining neural network outputs was published as early as 1965 [10]. Later its application expanded into other fields like econometrics as forecast combining, machine learning as evidence combination and also information retrieval in page rank aggregation [23].

In opposite to the early application areas of data, classifier and decision fusion, researchers were for a long time unclear about which level of information fusion is to be preferred and more generally, how to design an optimal information fusion strategy for multimedia processing systems.

N. Boujemaa, M. Detyniecki, and A. Nürnberger (Eds.): AMR 2007, LNCS 4918, pp. 147–159, 2008.

This can be seen in recently published approaches that solve similar tasks and nevertheless use different information fusion levels. Examples using classifier fusion are multimedia retrieval [28], multi-modal object recognition [12], multibiometrics [15] and video retrieval [29]. Concerning data fusion, the applications that can be named are multimedia summarization [1], text and image categorization [7], multi-modal image retrieval [27] and web document retrieval [19]. Other problems of interest are the determination of fusion performance improvement compared to single source systems and the investigation of its suspected influence factors like dependency and accuracy of classifiers and data.

Compared to other application fields of information fusion, there is in multimedia a limited understanding of the relations between basic features and abstract content description [26]. Many scientists have approached this problem in the past empirically and also attempted to justify their findings in theoretical frameworks. Lately the information fusion community did important progress in fusion theory that have not yet been considered for multimedia retrieval tasks.

In this paper we give first (Section 2) a review on information fusion in a generic context and what is important in practice for fusion system design. The section includes a discussion on influence factors of fusion effectiveness and the design of an optimal fusion system. In section 3, the task of semantic classification of keyword annotated images is analyzed in order to suggest ways of future research for an appropriate fusion strategy in accordance with the latest findings in information fusion. The paper also confirms this with experimental results.

2   General Overview on Information Fusion

The JDL working group defined information fusion as "an information process that associates, correlates and combines data and information from single or multiple sensors or sources to achieve refined estimates of parameters, characteristics, events and behaviors" [13]. Several classification schemes for information fusion systems have been proposed in literature, whereby the one from the JDL group is probably the most established. This functional model represents components of a fusion system in 4 core levels of fusion (L0-L3) and 2 extension levels (L4,L5). Here L0-L3 are the data or feature association and there above the object, situation, and impact refinement. The extension levels (L4, L5) consist of the process and the user refinement.

In [2], an overview of information fusion scenari in the context of multi modal biometrics is given, which can be easily adapted to general tasks. Hence in information fusion the settings that are possible are: (1) single modality and multiple sensors, (2) single modality and multiple features, (3) single modality and multiple classifiers and (4) multi modalities. Where in the latter case for each modality one of the combinations (1)-(3) can be applied. The multi modal fusion can be done serial, parallel or hierarchical. For completeness reasons, we add a scenario found in [15]: single modality and multiple sample, which is of importance in information retrieval approaches like bagging.

The gain of information fusion is differentiated in [14]: "By combining low level features it is possible to achieve a more abstract or a more precise representation of the world". This difference in the fusion goal is also covered in the Durrant-Whyte classification of information fusion strategies [13], which refers to complementary, cooperative and competitive fusion. In the first case, the information gain results from combining multiple complementary information sources to generate a more complete representation of the world. Here, the overall goal is to exploit the sources diversity or complementarity in the fusion process. The cooperative and competitive fusion provide a reduced overall uncertainty and hence also increased robustness in fusion systems by combining multiple information sources or multiple features of a single source respectively. These latter strategies utilize the redundancy in information sources. Since the sum of complementarity and redundancy of a source equals a constant, it is only possible to optimize a fusion system in favor of the one or the other [3].

In general the benefit of fusion, presuming a proper fusion method, is that the influence of unreliable sources can be lowered compared to reliable ones [18]. This is of a high practical relevance, because during system design it is often not clear how the different features and modalities will perform in real world environments.

Further aspects of information fusion like the system architecture (distributed, centralized) and utilization of certain mathematical tools (probability and evidence theory, fuzzy set and possibility theory, neural networks, linear combination) can be found in an older review on information fusion [11], but their detailed presentation is out of the scope of this paper.

2.1 Information Fusion System Design

Based on the theory presented before in the practice of system design the following points have to be considered: sensors or sources of information, choice of features, level, strategy and architecture of fusion processing and if further background or domain knowledge can be comprised [14]. The choice of sensors and information sources is normally limited by the application. The available sources should be considered in regard to their inhered noise level, cost of computation, diversity in between the set and its general ability to describe and distinguish the aimed at patterns.

During feature selection, one must realize that feature values of different modalities can encounter a spectrum of different feature types: continuous, discrete and even symbolic. That is why modality fusion is more difficult and complex [30], i.e. especially for joint fusion at data level, where a meaningful projection of the data to the result space has to be defined. But also in the case of only continuous features observed from different modalities the information fusion is not trivial, because nonetheless an appropriate normalization has to be applied [2].

The most common location of fusion are at data/feature, classifier/score level and decision level. Hence, a decision between low level or high level fusion must be taken, but also hybrid algorithms that fuse on several levels are possible. An exception is presented in [25], where the authors fuse kernel matrices. In [14] the authors proved, with the help of their category theory framework, that classifier and decision fusion are just special cases of data fusion. Furthermore they stated that a correct fusion system is always at least as effective as any of its parts, because, due to fusion several sources, more information about the problem is involved. The emphasize is here on 'correct', so inappropriate fusion can lead to a performance decrease. Attention should be payed to the difference between data fusion and data concatenation. The latter is circumventing the data alignment problem and thus is not having the power of data fusion. But it can be an easy and sufficient solution for compatible feature sets.

Many publications so far treated the topic data versus decision fusion by investigating the pros and conc of each fusion type. Data fusion can, due to the data processing inequality, achieve the best performance improvements [17], because at this early stage of processing the most information is available. Complex relations in data can be exploited during fusion, provided that their way of dependence is known. Drawbacks in data and feature fusion are problems due to the 'curse of dimensionality', its computationally expensiveness and that it needs a lot of training data.

The opposite is true for decision fusion. It can be said to be throughout faster because each modality is processed independently which is leading to a dimensionality reduction. Decision fusion is however seen as a very rigid solution, because at this level of processing only limited information is left.

The fusion strategy is mostly determined by the considered application. For example, all sensor integration, image processing, multi modal tracking tasks and the like execute cooperative fusion since they exploit temporal or spatial co-occurrence of feature values.

However, for information retrieval systems the situation is not as trivial. For example, three different effects in rank aggregation tasks can be exploited with fusion [4]:

(1) Skimming effect: the lists include diverse and relevant items
(2) Chorus effect: the lists contain similar and relevant items
(3) Dark Horse effect: unusually accurate result of one source

According to the theory presented in the last section, it is impossible to exploit all effects within one approach because the required complementary (1) and cooperative (2) strategy are contradictory.

The task of multi modal information retrieval and classification, e.g. joint processing of images aligned with texts or annotated with keywords, was approached in the past with success using cooperative strategies like LSI, which uses feature co-occurence matrices, or mixture models, which exploit the feature's joint probabilities [19]. The same is true for complementary ensemble methods, that train classifiers for each modality separately and fuse them afterwards [5].

2.2   Performance Improvement Boundaries

The lack of a formal theory framework for information fusion caused a vibrant discussion in the last years about the influences on fusion results and especially on theoretical achievable performance improvement boundaries compared to single source systems. Early fusion experiments have shown thorough performance improvement. Later publications accumulated that reported about ambivalent fusion results, mostly, where ensemble classifier were outperformed by the best single classifier. So the information fusion community began to empirically investigate suspected influence factors such as diversity, dependency and accuracy of information sources and classifiers. Based on the experiments explanations for the fusion result ambiguity and mostly application specific upper and lower bounds of performance improvements were found. This section will summarize their findings.

First investigations of these problems were undertaken in competitive fusion on behalf of decorrelated neural network ensembles [20], that outperformed independently trained ones. The overall reduced error is achieved due to negative correlated errors[1] in the neural networks, that average out in combination. [6] confirmed that more diverse classifiers improve the ensemble performance.

The bias-variance decomposition of the mean square error of the fusion result serves as theoretical explanation: more training lowers the bias, but gives rise to variance of the fusion result. The bias-variance-covariance relation is an extension of the former decomposition [16], that shows theoretically that dependencies between classifiers increase the generalization error compared to independent ones. So this strategy achieves a more precise expectation value in the result due to averaging over the inputs.

A theoretical study on complementary fusion [15] applied to multibiometrics found its lower bound of performance improvement for highly correlated modalities and the upper bound for independent ones. This strategy works only for truly complementary tasks, which means that it is aimed at independent patterns in the data, as in a rank aggregation problem where the combined lists contain a significant number of unique relevant documents [22]. Here, the opposite of the bias-variance decomposition for averaging applies: more training rises the bias (ambiguity) and lowers the variance of the result. But the influence of the classifier's bias, variance and their number, affects the fusion result not as much as dependency [10]. For this fusion strategy high level or late fusion is most efficient, since there are no dependencies that can be exploited at data level.

In practice often independence between the fusion inputs is assumed for simplicity reasons or in reference to the diversity of involved modalities. But this is not true i.e. for modalities in multibiometrics [15] and most certainly also not for modalities of other applications, even though it may contain only small dependencies. Applying in this situations high level fusion will hence never yield the maximum theoretical possible fusion performance improvement, because the information reduction caused by processing makes it impossible to exploit data dependencies completely in late fusion.

---

[1] Negative correlated errors are here referred to as being signals with an opposite developing of their values, not that only negative correlation coefficients are found between the signals.

On the other hand, data level fusion can have blatant disadvantages in practice due to the 'curse-of-dimensionality' [12] and perform badly towards generalization, modeling complexity, computational intensity and need of training data. A solution for the trade off data versus classifier fusion, can be a hybrid system fusing on several levels.

Empirical tests that investigate optimal features in an approach to fuse visual clues from different sources, hence cooperative fusion, showed that they should be redundant in their values, but complementary in their errors [8]. In [17] fusion performance is investigated on behalf of a multi modal binary hypothesis testing problem as e.g. used in multibiometrics. Considering the error exponents for the dependence and independence assumption for the modalities, it is found that the dependent case gives the upper performance improvement bound, and the case of independence the lower.

A comparison of a complementary and cooperative classifier fusion applied to multibiometrics [21] showed a slight performance advantage for the cooperative fusion approach that exploits the modalities dependencies. Admittedly, this gain over the complementary fusion is small, which is due to the little dependencies between the modalities. Furthermore, it needs a lot of training data to estimate the correlation matrix. So in practice there is a trade off between performance improvement and computational cost, whereas the independence assumption often will achieve sufficient results. The authors [21] show as well that class-dependent training of classifiers can help to improve the system's ability to discriminate the classes and hence improve the over all performance.

After having reviewed the fundamentals of information fusion, the next section will analyze first the data of a multi modal classification task, specifically of keyword annotated images. Some simple fusion test undermine the presented information fusion theory and should lead the way to develop an efficient solution to the problem.

3   Data Analysis Towards Effective Multi-media Information Retrieval

Due to the high interest in multimedia processing in the past many multi modal collections have been made available to the research communities. Here 2 examples of them are investigated. The Washington database contains 21 image classes of locations like Australia and Italy, but also semantic concepts like football and cherry trees. Most of the images are manually annotated with a few keywords (1-10). Classes with no annotation were left out of the tests. So we experimented with 16 classes that contained in all 675 images, which are nearly equally distributed over the classes.

The second collection is a subset of the Corel database, for which [9] created keyword annotations. The final set contains 1159 images in 49 classes, where the images are unequally distributed over the classes. They form similar concepts as in the Washington collection. An important characteristic of this data collection is that the annotations also include complete nonsense keyword sets, which makes it similar to what one would expect in real world data.

For preprocessing, GIFT features [24] (color and texture histograms) of all images and term-frequency vectors of their annotations were computed. Hence each data sample in the Washington collection is described by 624 features (166 color, 120 texture and 338 text) and in the Corel collection by 2035 features (166 color, 120 texture and 1749 text), where, of course, the textual features are very sparse.

Figure 1 shows the absolute correlation matrices over the feature vectors of the Washington and Corel collection respectively. Bright areas represent feature pairs with high correlation (positive and negative) and darker areas low correlation and hence independence. The significantly correlated feature pairs can be numbered with 17% in the simpler Washington and only 3% in the Corel collection. This tendency of decrease in correlation we expect to be enforced in even noisier real world data.

Since in fusion inter modal dependencies are of a special interest, the average correlation coefficients for both collections are given in table 1. Additionally, the

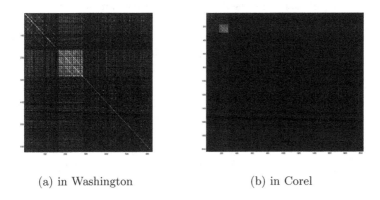

(a) in Washington   (b) in Corel

Fig. 1. Absolute correlation matrices of features in Washington and Corel collection

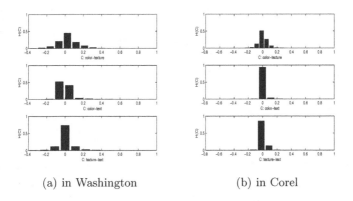

(a) in Washington   (b) in Corel

Fig. 2. Histograms of correlation matrices of Washington and Corel collection

respective histograms are pictured in figure 2. The average decencies turn out to be close to zero, since a nearly equal amount of positive and negative correlation is contained. The maximum correlation coefficients can be found between the histograms and textual features (Wash/Corel color-text: 0.85/0.99, texture-text: 0.74/0.76), whereas between color and texture histogram itself smaller dependencies appear (color-texture: 0.54/0.41). These dependencies between the modalities should be exploited in order to develop an efficient multi modal information fusion system.

Another interesting and not yet explained process is the propagation of the feature dependencies to the classifier outcome. Their dependencies are given in the bottom line of table 1. One can say that there is found again the stronger dependence between the histograms and the text modality. Even though here the dependency between color and texture is not as much smaller as in the feature set.

3.1   Information Fusion Experiments

For the fusion experiments we used a support vector machine (SVM) classifier with rbf kernel as described in [5]. First we compared several simple fusion approaches: (1) hierarchical SVM, which consists of one SVM classifier for each modality and then as well a SVM classifier to fuse their results, (2) concatenated data and SVM, which uses all modalities concatenated as classifier input, (3) averaging the classifier outputs of the modalities, (4) weighted sum, which is the same as (3), but weights the best modality (text) more than the others and (5) majority vote of the classifier outcomes.

The tests were run as one-against-all classifications, where 7 positive and 7 negative samples for the Washington collection and 5 positive and 7 negative samples for the Corel collection were used to train the classifiers. Thereafter their performance is evaluated by applying the classifiers to the remaining data samples. The classification error, false alarm rate (false negative) and miss rate (false positive) are given in percent and are averaged over all classes of each collection.

The experimental results for the Washington and Corel collection are given in table 2 and 3 respectively. For both collections the hierarchical fusion, a learning based approach, performs superior to all other approaches considering the overall classification error, but the classification results in the positive class (false alarm) are throughout better with the simpler fusion strategies. Here, majority vote is

Table 1. Average inter modal dependencies of Washington and Corel collection and dependency found between the classifier outcomes calculated on each modality

	Washington			Corel		
	color-texture	color-text	texture-text	color-texture	color-text	texture-text
av	0.026	0.002	0.0008	0.003	$6.0e-05$	0.001
class	0.284	0.528	0.244	0.111	0.179	0.163

Table 2. Fusion experiments on Washington collection

in %	color	texture	text	hier SVM	concat SVM	averaging	weight sum	major vote
classification error	39.8	41.1	33.2	9.9	44.9	37.9	36.5	35.2
false alarm	9.4	32.8	1.5	23.9	14.6	4.6	3.4	5.6
miss	41.4	41.5	34.9	9.1	46.1	39.6	38.3	36.7

Table 3. Fusion experiments on Corel collection

in %	color	texture	text	hier SVM	concat SVM	averaging	weight sum	major vote
classification error	46.5	47.3	44.5	10.3	56.4	46.5	46.1	45.0
false alarm	34.0	35.3	19.0	58.9	26.9	20.9	18.5	24.5
miss	46.7	47.4	44.9	9.4	56.8	46.9	46.5	45.3

best in the overall classification, whereas weighted sum fusion performs best considering the false alarm rate. The experiment shows as well that the feature concatenation is really a weak fusion strategy and hence performs worst.

The observed results can be said to be ambiguous between the preference of learning and simple fusion approaches. Because the better performance of the simple fusion in discriminating the positive classes is in favor of information retrieval, where it would lead to more relevant documents in the result list. But this better performance compared to the learning approach is more than compensated by the performance in distinguishing the negative class. Here, more tests with improved classifier performance of the modalities should show, if this decreases the miss rate. Then simple fusion methods would be a very interesting approach for large scale problems, because of its low computational complexity.

In the overall performance the simple fusion strategies have unsurprisingly trouble to cope with the badly performing classifier results of the modalities. Text and color based classification work better than the texture based one, but in general they achieve only unreliable results especially for the negative class (miss). Up till now there is no over all successful strategy of fusing dependent, weak classifiers, even though more sophisticated score function approaches like bagging and boosting have been developed and applied with a certain success.

In the second experiment, we investigated how the usage of dependent, by means of correlation, and de-correlated features influences the performance. Since we did not want to search for more or less correlated input features, we created feature subsets for each modality with especially correlated or uncorrelated features. In order to find the correlated ones, we chose features, that have at least once a correlation coefficient with another feature larger than $C > \beta$. As uncorrelated features were chosen that have a maximum absolute correlation coefficient with another feature smaller than the threshold $|C| < \gamma$.

Table 4. Fusion of dependent and independent modalities on Washington collection

in %	color	texture	text	full	dependent	de-correlated
dep: $C > 0.85$ (8/166,58/120,80/338), de-cor: $|C| < 0.5$ (16/166, 1/120, 77/330)						
classification error	40.2	43.8	34.8	12.1	20.5	25.2
false alarm	10.4	35.1	5.3	22.5	29.1	36.5
miss	41.7	44.3	36.4	11.5	20.1	24.6
dep: $C > 0.75$ (58/166,71/120,186/338), de-cor: $|C| < 0.7$ (38/166, 26/120, 131/330)						
classification error	41.8	45.9	32.8	10.4	15.9	16.5
false alarm	10.3	30.4	4.8	24.3	27.1	30.1
miss	43.5	46.8	34.3	9.5	15.3	15.3

Table 5. Fusion of dependent and independent modalities on Corel collection

in %	color	texture	text	full	dependent	de-correlated
dep: $C > 0.75$ (11/166,65/120,176/1749), de-cor: $|C| < 0.5$ (16/166, 1/120, 232/1749)						
classification error	45.8	45.9	45.9	9.0	19.7	19.1
false alarm	32.9	40.6	22.2	60.9	59.3	60.1
miss	46.0	46.1	46.4	8.2	19.1	18.5

The tables 4 and 5 show the results for the Washington and Corel collection respectively, where the number of features selected for each modality (color, texture, text) is given in brackets. To make the results of the correlated and uncorrelated feature subset comparable, a near equality of the over all number of features was tried to achieve, since their number in determining the performance heavily.

The experiments above show a performance advantage for the correlated features in the experiments for the Washington collection. This can also be caused by the different number of features involved in each of the correlated and uncorrelated case. To investigate this further experiments are necessary. But in general both approaches are able to perform a strong dimensionality reduction using a different subset of features (subsets intersect in only up to 10 features). The result of experiment for the Corel collection is not this clear. Here both cases work equally good with a slight advantage for the uncorrelated features.

Concerning the Corel collection another point is interesting to see: the fusion based on the correlated and independent subsets performs in the false alarm rate better than the normal hierarchical SVM. This phenomenon was never observed for the Washington collection. For now we have not a satisfying explanation for this, but we will investigate this further in future.

More extensive tests with e.g. truly differently correlated input features or even artificially created data sets have to be done to prove the influence of correlation and independence to performance improvement of information fusion

Table 6. Correlation class dependent and uncorrelated fusion

in %	color	texture	text	full	dependent	uncorrelated
corel dep: $C > 0.75$, de-cor: $|C| < 0.5$ per cur class						
classification error	41.2	44.1	33.9	11.4	14.1	15.5
false alarm	14.7	33.1	3.7	26.5	38.5	40.8
miss	42.5	44.6	35.6	10.4	12.8	14.2

systems. Furthermore other measures of dependency such as mutual information and its influence on the fusion system result should be investigated. Finally fusion approaches that exploit more explicit the features dependencies like LSA and those that consider the accuracy of modalities will be interesting to compare when applied to this problem.

In the last experiment we changed the feature selection rule to chose the feature subsets not according to the correlation coefficients of the whole collection, but according to the correlation found in the currently to distinguish class. With this dynamic, class-dependent selection the feature subsets should contain those features, that are especially helpful in discriminating this class from the negative samples. The results for the Washington collection are presented in table 6.

As it can be seen the class-dependent features selection is not achieving a significant performance improvement, even though the theory presented in section 2 suggests this. We will still investigate this approach further by searching for more efficient and robust ways to adapt the features to the classes, since it is from the sound of theory an appealing approach.

4 Conclusions and Future Work

In retrieval, indexing and classification of multimedia data an efficient information fusion of the different modalities is essential for the system's overall performance. Since information fusion, its influence factors and performance improvement boundaries have been lively discussed in the last years in different research communities, our summarization of their findings will be helpful for all fusion system designers in future.

In our experiments we compared the utilization of correlated and uncorrelated features, because new findings in information theory advises that the better fusion performance can be achieved only with correlated feature. We were able to show that a correlated feature subset for this problem perform slightly better than explicitly de-correlated features. More extensive tests are necessary to underpin these preliminary results and the theoretical findings.

Another promising way to achieve better information fusion performance is to utilize class-dependent classifier settings. This helps in discriminating the positive from the negative classes. Our experiments for now have shown no real improvement in performance.

In general we like to experiment with artificial data where the correlation, diversity and accuracy of each modality as well of their contained features can be set. In this framework a better understanding of the influence factors to the fusion result could be obtained.

References

1. Benitez, A.B., Chang, S.F.: Multimedia knowledge integration, summarization and evaluation. In: Workshop on Multimedia Data Mining, pp. 23–26 (2002)
2. Ross, A., Jain, A.K.: Multimodal biometrics: An overview. In: EUSIPCO Proc. of 12th European Signal Processing Conference (EUSIPCO), pp. 1221–1224 (2004)
3. Fassinut-Mombot, B., Choquel, J.B.: A new probabilistic and entropy fusion approach for management of information sources. Information Fusion 5, 35–47 (2004)
4. Vogt, C.C., Cottrell, G.W.: Fusion via a linear combination of scores. Information Retrieval 1(3), 151–173 (1999)
5. Bruno, E., Moenne-Loccoz, N., Marchand-Maillet, S.: Design of multimodal dissimilarity spaces for retrieval of multimedia documents. IEEE Transaction on Pattern Analysis and Machine Intelligence (to appear, 2008)
6. Brown, G., Yao, X.: On the effectiveness of negative correlation learning. In: First UK Workshop on Computational Intelligence (UKCI 2001) (2001)
7. Chechik, G., Tishby, N.: Extracting relevant structures with side information. In: Advances in Neural Information Processing Systems, vol. 15 (2003)
8. Taylor, G., Kleeman, L.: Fusion of multimodal visual cues for model-based object tracking. In: Australasian Conference on Robotics and Automation (2003)
9. Barnard, K., Johnson, M.: Word sense disambiguation with pictures. Artificial Intelligence 167, 13–30 (2005)
10. Tumer, K., Gosh, J.: Linear order statistics combiners for pattern classification. Combining Artificial Neural Networks, 127–162 (1999)
11. Valet, L., Bolon, P., Mauris, G.: A statistical overview of recent literature in information fusion. In: Proceedings of the Third International Conference on Information Fusion, vol. 1, pp. MOC3/22 – MOC3/29 (2000)
12. Wu, L., Cohen, P.R., Oviatt, S.L.: From members to team to committee - a robust approach to gestural and multimodal recognition. Transactions on Neural Networks 13 (2002)
13. Llinas, J., Bowman, C., Rogova, G., Steinberg, A., Waltz, E., White, F.: Revisiting the jdl data fusion model II. Information Fusion, 1218–1230 (2004)
14. Kokar, M.M., Weyman, J., Tomasik, J.A.: Formalizing classes of information fusion systems. Information Fusion 5, 189–202 (2004)
15. Poh, N., Bengio, S.: How do correlation and variance of base-experts affect fusion in biometric authentication tasks? IEEE Transactions on Acoustics, Speech, and Signal Processing 53, 4384–4396 (2005)
16. Ueda, N., Nakano, R.: Generalization error of ensemble estimators. IEEE International Conference on Neural Networks 1, 90–95 (1996)
17. Koval, O., Pun, T., Voloshynovskiy, S.: Error exponent analysis of person identification based on fusion of dependent/independent modalities. In: Proceedings of SPIE-IS&T Electronic Imaging 2007, Security, Steganography, and Watermarking of Multimedia Contents IX (2007)
18. Aarabi, P., Dasarathy, B.V.: Robust speech processing using multi-sensor, multi-source information fusion - an overview of the state of the art. Information Fusion 5, 77–80 (2004)

19. Zhao, R., Grosky, W.I.: Narrowing the semantic gap - improved text-based web document retrieval using visual features. IEEE Transactions on Multimedia 4(2), 189–200 (2002)
20. Rosen, B.E.: Ensemble learning using decorrelated neural networks. Connections Science 8, 373–384 (1996)
21. Dass, S.C., Jain, A.K., Nandakumar, K.: A principled approach to score level fusion in multimodal biometric systems. In: Proceedings of Audio- and Video-based Biometric Person Authentication (AVBPA), pp. 1049–1058 (2005)
22. Beitzel, S.M., Chowdury, A., Jensen, E.C.: Disproving the fusion hypothesis: An analysis of data fusion via effective information retrieval strategies. In: ACM symposium on Applied computing, pp. 823–827 (2003)
23. Wu, S., McClean, S.: Performance prediction of data fusion for information retrieval. Information Processing and Management 42, 899–915 (2006)
24. Squire, D.M., Müller, W., Müller, H., Raki, J.: Content-based query of image databases, inspirations from text retrieval: inverted files, frequency-based weights and relevance feedback. Pattern Recognition Letters (Selected Papers from The 11th Scandinavian Conference on Image Analysis SCIA 1999) 21(13-14), 1193–1198 (2000)
25. Joachims, T., Shawe-Taylor, J., Cristianini, N.: Composite kernels for hypertext categorization, pp. 250–257. Morgan Kaufmann, San Francisco (2001)
26. Kolenda, T., Winther, O., Hansen, L.K., Larsen, J.: Independent component analysis for understanding multimedia content. Neural Networks for Signal Processing, 757–766 (2002)
27. Westerveld, T., de Vries, A.P.: Multimedia retrieval using multiple examples. In: Enser, P.G.B., Kompatsiaris, Y., O'Connor, N.E., Smeaton, A.F., Smeulders, A.W.M. (eds.) CIVR 2004. LNCS, vol. 3115, Springer, Heidelberg (2004)
28. Wu, Y., Chen-Chuan Chang, K., Chang, E.Y., Smith, J.R.: Optimal multimodal fusion for multimedia data analysis. In: MULTIMEDIA 2004: Proceedings of the 12th annual ACM international conference on Multimedia, pp. 572–579. ACM Press, New York (2004)
29. Yan, R., Hauptmann, A.G.: The combination limit in multimedia retrieval. In: MULTIMEDIA 2003: Proceedings of the eleventh ACM international conference on Multimedia, pp. 339–342. ACM Press, New York (2003)
30. Li, C., Biswas, G.: Unsupervised clustering with mixed numeric and nominal data - a new similarity based agglomerative system. In: International Workshop on AI and Statistics, pp. 327–346 (1997)

Multi-level Fusion for Semantic Video Content Indexing and Retrieval

Rachid Benmokhtar and Benoit Huet

Département Communications Multimédias
Institut Eurécom
2229, route des crêtes
06904 Sophia-Antipolis - France
{Rachid.Benmokhtar, Benoit.Huet}@eurecom.fr

Abstract. In this paper, we present the results of our work on the analysis of an automatic semantic video content indexing and retrieval system based on fusing various low level visual descriptors. Global MPEG-7 features extracted from video shots, are described via IVSM signature (Image Vector Space Model) in order to have a compact description of the content. Both static and dynamic feature fusion are introduced to obtain effective signatures. Support Vector Machines (SVMs) are employed to perform classification (One classifier per feature). The task of the classifiers is to detect the video semantic content. Then, classifier outputs are fused using a neural network based on evidence theory (NNET) in order to provide a decision on the content of each shot. The experimental results are conducted in the framework of the TRECVid feature extraction task.

1 Introduction

To respond to the increase in audiovisual information, various methods for indexing, classification and fusion have emerged. The need to analyze the content has appeared to facilitate understanding and contribute to a better automatic video content indexing and retrieval.

The retrieval of complex semantic concepts requires the analysis of many features per modalities. The task consisting of combining of all these different parameters is far from trivial. The fusion mechanism can take place at different levels of the classification process. Generally, it is either applied on signatures (Feature fusion) or on classifier outputs (Classifier fusion).

This paper presents our research conducted toward a semantic video content indexing and retrieval system aimed at the TRECVid high level feature detection task. It starts with a description of our automatic system architecture. We distinguish four steps: Feature extraction, feature fusion, classification and classifier fusion. The overall processing chain of our system is presented in Figure 1. The feature extraction step consists in creating a set of global MPEG-7 low level descriptors (based on color, texture and edges). Two feature fusion approaches are used: Static and dynamic. The static approach is based on simple operators

N. Boujemaa, M. Detyniecki, and A. Nürnberger (Eds.): AMR 2007, LNCS 4918, pp. 160–169, 2008.

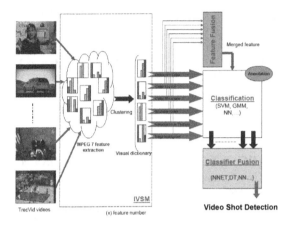

Fig. 1. General framework of the application

while the dynamic approach consist in reducing the data dimensionality using Principal Component Analysis (PCA). Both are implemented and evaluated with the aim to obtain effective signature for each shot. The classification step is used to estimate the video semantic content. Support Vector Machine (SVMs) are employed. In the final stage of our system, fusion of classifier outputs is performed thanks to a neural network based on evidence theory (NNET).

The experiments presented in this paper are conducted on the TRECVid collection, varying the automatic generation techniques and combination strategies. Finally, we examine the outcomes of our experiments, detail our continuing work on how dynamic feature fusion could be used to complement, rather than replace existing approaches.

2   System Architecture

The MPEG-7 standard defines a comprehensive, standardized set of audiovisual description tools for still images as well as movies. The aim of the standard is to facilitate quality access to content, which implies efficient storage, identification, filtering, searching and retrieval of media [?]. We have used the following still image features:

- **Dominant color (DC)** represents the most dominant colors,
- **Color layout (CL)** specifies a spatial distribution of colors. The image is divided into (8x8) blocks and the dominant colors are solved for each block in the YCbCr color system. Discrete Cosine Transform is applied to the dominant colors in each channel and the DCT coefficients are used as a descriptor.
- **Color structure (CS)** slides a structuring element over the image, the numbers of positions where the element contains each particular color is recorded and used as a descriptor.

Fig. 2. Example of key-frames illustrating three semantic concepts (*Person, airplane and car*)

- **Scalable color (SC)** is a 256-bin color histogram in HSV color space, which is encoded by a Haar transform.
- **Edge histogram (EH)** calculates the amount of vertical, horizontal, 45 degree, 135 degree and non-directional edges in 16 sub-images of the picture.
- **Homogeneous texture (HT)** descriptor filters the image with a bank of orientation and scale tuned filters that are modeled using Gabor functions. The first and second moments of the energy in the frequency domain in the corresponding sub-bands are then used as the components of the texture descriptor.

The obtained vectors over the complete database are clustered to find the N most representative elements. The clustering algorithm used in our experiments is the well-known k-means with the Euclidean distance. Representative elements are then used as visual keywords to describe video shot content. Then, the occurrence vector of the visual keywords in the shots are built and this vector is called the IVSM signature (Image Vector Space Model). The number of visual terms used in our experiments is 70.

2.1 Static Feature Fusion

In this work, experiments describe an automatic detection of semantic concepts. Four color descriptors, edges histogram and homogeneous texture descriptor are extracted from the visual content of a video shot. The main objective of feature fusion step is to reduce redundancy, uncertainty and ambiguity of signatures, in order to obtain a complete information of better quality, for take better decision and act.

Concatenation of Features. In the first fusion strategy, all global MPEG-7 descriptors are merged into a unique vector, that is called *merged fusion*(D_{merged}) as follow:

$$D_{merged} = [DC|CL|CS|SC|EH|HT] \tag{1}$$

All descriptors must have more or less the same numerical values to avoid scale effects [?].

Average of Features. This approach builds an average of the different descriptors. It requires no compilation of data, a simple normalization step is required before data can be added. It is interesting to give a weight or confidence level to each of the descriptors.

This method is commonly used, in particular in the automatic video concepts detection of the TRECVid project [?], where we observe the good contribution of the fusion operators as *Min* and average.

2.2 Dynamic Feature Fusion Using PCA

Many techniques for dimensionality reduction have been proposed in the literature. However, Principal Component Analysis (PCA), latent semantic analysis (LSA) [?] and recently Independent Component Analysis (ICA) are the most frequently used. PCA extracts the features as the projections on the principal subspace whose basis vectors correspond to the maximum variance directions in the original space, while discarding the complementary subspace as a noise subspace. In some cases, PCA can obtain satisfactory performance. However, no theory can prove the complementary subspace is useless for recognition, and, on the contrary, experiments show that using the complementary subspace properly may improve recognition performance [?,?]. In our work, the dimension $m \in [10, 450]$ evolve per step of 20.

2.3 Support Vector Machines Classification

SVMs were widely used in the past ten years and they have been proved efficient in many classification applications. They have the property to allow a non linear separation of classes with very good generalization capacities. They were first introduced by Vapnik [?] for the text recognition task. The main idea is similar to the concept of a neuron: separate classes with a hyperplane. However, samples are indirectly mapped into a high dimensional space thanks to a kernel function. To this end, the selected kernel denoted $\mathcal{K}(.)$ is a radial basis function which normalization parameter σ is chosen depending on the performance obtained on a validation set. The radial basis kernel is chosen for his good classification results comparing to polynomial and sigmoidal kernels [?].

$$\mathcal{K}_1(x, y) = \exp\left(\frac{-||x - y||^2}{\sigma}\right) \qquad (2)$$

2.4 Classifier Fusion: Neural Network Based on Evidence Theory (NNET)

Classifier fusion is a necessary step to efficiently classify the video semantic content from multiple cues. For this aim, an improved version of RBF neural network based on evidence theory [?] witch we call NNET is used [?], with one input layer L_{input}, two hidden layers L_2 and L_3 and one output layer L_{output} (Figure 3). Each layer corresponds to one step of the procedure described in following:

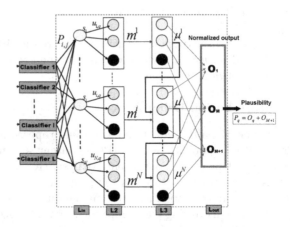

Fig. 3. Neural network based on evidence theory (NNET) classifier fusion structure

1. **Layer** L_{input}: Contains N units (prototypes). It is identical to the RBF network input layer with an exponential activation function ϕ and d a distance
   computed using training data. $\alpha \in [0, 1]$ is a weakening parameter associated
   to prototype i, where $\epsilon = 0$ at the initialization stage [?]:

$$\begin{cases} s^i = \alpha^i \phi(d^i) \\ \phi(d^i) = \exp\left(-\gamma^i (d^i)^2\right) \\ \alpha^i = \frac{1}{1+\exp(-\epsilon^i)} \end{cases} \tag{3}$$

   where γ^i is a positive parameter defining the receptive field size of prototype
   $i = \{1, ..., N\}$.

2. **Layer** L_2: Computes the belief masses m^i (Equ. 4) associated to each prototype. It is composed of N modules of $M+1$ units each (Equ. 5). The units
   of module i are connected to neuron i of the previous layer. Knowing that
   each image can belong to only one class (annotation clauses), we write:

$$\begin{cases} m^i(\{w_q\}) = \alpha^i u_q^i \phi(d^i) \\ m^i(\{\Omega\}) = 1 - \sum_{q=1}^{M} m^i(\{w_q\}) \end{cases} \tag{4}$$

   hence,

$$\begin{aligned} m^i &= (m^i(\{w_1\}), ..., m^i(\{w_{M+1}\})) \\ &= (u_1^i s^i, ..., u_M^i s^i, 1 - s^i) \end{aligned} \tag{5}$$

   where u_q^i is the membership degree to each class w_q, q class index $q = \{1, ..., M\}$.

3. **Layer** L_3: The Dempster-Shafer combination rule combines N different
   mass functions in one single mass. It's given by the following conjunctive
   combination:

$$m(A) = (m^1 \oplus ... \oplus m^N) = \sum_{B_1 \cap ... \cap B_N = A} \prod_{i=1}^{N} m^i(B_i) \qquad (6)$$

The N mass function m^i are composed of N modules of $M + 1$ units. The activations vector of modules i is defined as $\overrightarrow{\mu^i}$.

$$\begin{cases} \mu^i = \cap_{k=1}^{i} m^k = \mu^{i-1} \cap m^i \\ \mu^1 = m^1 \end{cases} \qquad (7)$$

The activation vectors for $i = \{2, ..., N\}$ can be recursively computed using the following formula:

$$\begin{cases} \mu_j^i = \mu_j^{i-1} m_j^i + \mu_j^{i-1} m_{M+1}^i + \mu_{M+1}^{i-1} m_j^i \\ \\ \mu_{M+1}^i = \mu_{M+1}^{i-1} m_{M+1}^i \end{cases} \qquad (8)$$

4. **Output Layer:** We build the normalized output O defined as:

$$O_j = \frac{\sum_{i=1}^{N} \mu_j^i}{\sum_{i=1}^{N} \sum_{j=1}^{M+1} \mu_j^i} \qquad (9)$$

The different parameters (Δu, $\Delta \gamma$, $\Delta \alpha$, ΔP, Δs) can be determined by gradient descent of output error for an input pattern x (more explanations see [?]). Finally, we compute the maximum of P_q (i.e the plausibility of each class w_q) as follow:

$$P_q = O_q + O_{M+1} \qquad (10)$$

3 Experiments

Experiments are conducted on TRECVid videos [?]. The main goal of TRECVid is to promote progress in content-based retrieval from digital video via open, metrics-based evaluation. TRECVid is a laboratory-style evaluation that attempts to model real world situations or significant component tasks involved in such situations. It will test on *news reports, science news, documentaries, educational programming, and archival video,* to see how well the technologies apply to new sorts of data. In this work, about 5 hours of video (4000 shots) are used to train the feature extraction system and 1 hour (800 shots) are used for evaluation purpose. The training set is divided into two subsets in order to train both classifiers and subsequently determine through learning the fusion parameters. Detection performance was measured using the standard precision and recall metrics. We are interested by the precision to have a measure of the ability of a system to present only relevant shots. Average precision is given in follow:

$$AP = \frac{\left(\frac{\text{Number of relevant shots retrieved}}{\text{Total number of shots retrieved}} \right)}{\text{Total number of relevant shots}} \qquad (11)$$

Table 1. key-frames distribution of the video key-frames in the various sets by semantic concepts. The relative quantity of every class is clarified to give an idea of the lower border of the performances to be obtained.

Id	Concepts	test	train
1	Sports	19	86
2	Outdoor	260	512
3	Building	90	205
4	Mountain	12	45
5	Waterscape	23	108
6	Maps	13	29

Table 2. Experiment systems

Id	System
1	System without feature fusion step (See Figure 1).
2	System with a concatenation feature fusion approach.
3	System with an average feature fusion approach.
4	System with PCA feature fusion approach.

The feature extraction task consists in retrieving video shots expressing one of the following six concepts (Sports, outdoor, building, mountain, waterscape, maps) among 36 proposed semantic concepts [?]. Table 1 provides some insight about the composition in terms of our selected semantic concepts.

We start the experimentations with the description of four system configurations (Table 2):

Figure 4 shows average precision results for the three distinct experiences. It can be seen that the *system 3* obtains better scores (4% improvement on MAP) comparing to *system 1*. Contrary to the *system 2*, that decreases precision.

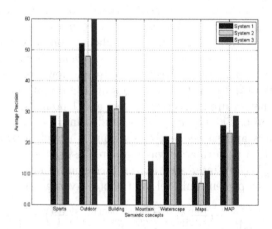

Fig. 4. Comparison of system configurations results

Table 3. Mean Average Precision (MAP) for different systems

Systems	Without Feature Fusion	Average Feature Fusion	PCA Feature Fusion
MAP	25.61%	29.16%	36.32%

The average precision $AP \in [8, 60\%]$, for exemple the semantic concept (*outdoor*) obtains $AP = 60\%$. This is can be explained by the high number of positive samples in the test set. Here, almost all positive samples are retrieved in the 100 first video shots returned by systems.

For semantic concepts (*mountain,maps*), the *system 3* obtains bad scores (14%, 11%). It can be explained per the low number of positive samples in the training and test sets.

On average, the MAP oscillates around 29% using average feature fusion step, which represents a good performance considering the video shots annotation complexity.

Figure 5 shows the variation of average precision results using PCA feature fusion *vs* dimension for each concept. The dimension $dim \in [10, 450]$ per step of 20. The *system 4* improves the precision of all concepts. The best $MAP = 36.32\%$ is obtained using $dim = 410$. In the test set, we have several monochrome video shots. We notice that the descriptors are highly redundant. This is not very surprising, because four of six investigated MPEG-7 descriptors are color descriptors.

So, smaller dimensions $dim \in [10, 170]$ lead to loss of information, and a high dimension raises the calculation time problem and also the relevance of our signatures. Observe that the stable dimension interval is $dim \in [190, 450]$.

Finally, the table 3 summarizes the mean average precision (MAP) for different systems. We notice that PCA feature fusion system obtain superior results to those obtained by the static feature fusion for all semantic concepts and to system without feature fusion step. This shows the importance of feature fusion.

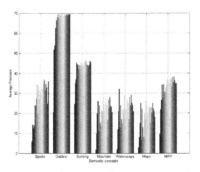 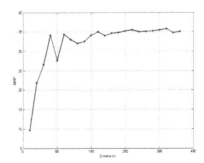

Fig. 5. NNET results using PCA feature fusion step. Mean Average Precision for PCA feature fusion, from 10 to 450 dimension by step of 20.

4 Conclusion

In this paper, both static and dynamic feature fusion approaches have been evaluated. Six global MPEG-7 visual descriptors are being employed for this difficult task. The aim of this feature fusion step is to provide a compact and effective representation for an SVM classifier which is trained to solve the challenging task of video content detection. A further classifier fusion step, featuring a neural network based on evidence theory, is also employed within the proposed system in order to combine in the most effective way the output of the SVMs.

We have demonstrated through empirical testing the potential of feature fusion, to be exploited in video shots retrieval. Our model, achieves respectable performance, particularly, for certain semantic concepts like outdoor and building, when the variety of the quality of features used is considered.

Of course, these small size of test set do not guarantee the usability of global MPEG-7 descriptors in the general case, but they imply that global MPEG-7 descriptors are worth experimenting with. We start to investigate the effect of TRECVid'07 data in our system (50 hours of videos) with new semantic concepts like (Person, face, car, explosion,...).

We believe that the dynamic feature fusion of different MPEG-7 descriptors based on dimensionality reduction has a positive impact on our system. Other statistical approaches, such as LDA and SOM are under investigation. In parallel, we are extending the global MPEG-7 descriptors used in this paper with local MPEG-7 descriptor in order to enrich the low level representation and to study the effect of their addition to a fusion system like ours.

Acknowledgment

The work presented here is supported by the European Commission under contract FP6-027026-K-SPACE. This work is the view of the authors but not necessarily the view of the community.

References

1. Mottaleb, M.A., Krishnamachari, S.: Multimedia descriptions based on MPEG-7: Extraction and applications. Proceeding of IEEE Multimedia 6, 459–468 (2004)
2. Spyrou, E., Leborgne, H., Mailis, T., Cooke, E., Avrithis, Y., O'Connor, N.: Fusing MPEG-7 visual descriptors for image classification. In: Duch, W., Kacprzyk, J., Oja, E., Zadrożny, S. (eds.) ICANN 2005. LNCS, vol. 3697, pp. 847–852. Springer, Heidelberg (2005)
3. Rautiainen, M., Seppanen, T.: Comparison of visual features and fusion techniques in automatic detection of concepts from news video based on gabor filters. In: Proceeding of ICME, pp. 932–935 (2005)
4. Souvannavong, F., Merialdo, B., Huet, B.: Latent semantic analysis for an effective region based video shot retrieval system. In: Proceedings of ACM MIR, pp. 243–250 (2004)
5. Jolliffe, I.: Principle component analysis. Springer, Heidelberg (1986)

6. Zhang, W., Shan, S., Gao, W., Chang, Y., Cao, B., Yang, P.: Information fusion in face identification. In: Proceedings of IEEE ICPR, vol. 3, pp. 950–953 (2004)

7. Vapnik, V.: The nature of statistical learning theory. Springer, Heidelberg (1995)

8. Shafer, G.: A mathematical theory of evidence. Princeton University Press, Princeton (1976)

9. Benmokhtar, R., Huet, B.: Neural network combining classifier based on Dempster-Shafer theory. In: Cham, T.-J., Cai, J., Dorai, C., Rajan, D., Chua, T.-S., Chia, L.-T. (eds.) MMM 2007. LNCS, vol. 4351, pp. 196–205. Springer, Heidelberg (2006)

10. TrecVid, Digital video retrieval at NIST,
    http://www-nlpir.nist.gov/projects/trecvid/

Image Data Source Selection Using Gaussian Mixture Models

Soufyane El Allali, Daniel Blank, Wolfgang Müller, and Andreas Henrich

University of Bamberg
Faculty of Information Systems and Computer Informatics
Chair of Media Informatics*
D-96045 Bamberg, Germany
soufyane.el-allali@wiai.uni-bamberg.de
http://www.uni-bamberg.de/wiai/minf

Abstract. In peer-to-peer (P2P) networks, computers with equal rights form a logical (overlay) network in order to provide a common service that lies beyond the capacity of every single participant. *Efficient similarity search* is generally recognized as a frontier in research about P2P systems. In literature, a variety of approaches exist. One of which is data source selection based approaches where peers summarize the data they contribute to the network, generating typically one summary per peer. When processing queries, these summaries are used to choose the peers (data sources) that are most likely to contribute to the query result. Only those data sources are contacted.

In this paper we use a Gaussian mixture model to generate peer summaries using the peers' local data. We compare this method to other local unsupervised clustering methods for generating peer summaries and show that a Gaussian mixture model is promising when it comes to locally generated summaries for peers without the need for a distributed summary computation that needs coordination between peers.

1 Introduction

Peer-to-peer (P2P) networks are made up of independently administered computers with equal rights (peers) that cooperate with each other. They form a logical overlay network in order to provide a common service that lies beyond the capabilities of each of its participants. P2P systems have shown their viability in a number of large-scale applications. Their success as means of large-scale data distribution in so-called file-sharing networks has motivated research in P2P data management. One focus of research is the search on stored data in a P2P network. Current research is spanning diverse areas such as efficient exact search (via distributed hash tables [19,17]), similarity search on text [20] and multimedia data [18,13], and semantic networks expressed via RDF [15].

The topic of this paper is similarity search for Information Retrieval (IR) and in particular Content-Based Image Retrieval (CBIR) in P2P networks. The basic

---

* This work is funded by the German Research Foundation DFG HE 2555/12-1.

N. Boujemaa, M. Detyniecki, and A. Nürnberger (Eds.): AMR 2007, LNCS 4918, pp. 170–181, 2008.

approach followed by our algorithm is that of probabilistic *source selection*: As each peer holds data, each peer is a potential source of interesting data. At query time, peers that are most probably a source of interesting data are selected. This selection is done based on *peer data summaries* that are maintained by the P2P network. The selected peers are queried, then their results are merged. This general approach that stems from classical Distributed IR [11,3] stands aside from many mainstream P2P approaches that use distributed indexing structures or the ones that try to improve the link structure in order to gain performance. We feel that the Distributed IR approach is not only promising in terms of performance, but also in terms of costs that have to be paid for maintaining such a network. For an overview on CBIR in P2P networks and their adaptivity properties we refer the reader to [14].

For our source selection mechanism, our approach builds Gaussian mixture models (GMM) based on peers' indexing data. We choose GMM because they allow adaptive multimedia retrieval. For instance, relevance feedback approaches have been proposed using GMM [16]. In our setting, every model corresponds to a peer summary that is shared with the other peers in our P2P network described in section 2.1. This allows us to reduce the costs of summary creation drastically given that the peers do not need to globally coordinate the creation of their summaries. We discuss next the cost associated with such an approach:

Joining the network: The cost of joining the network that has to be paid upfront is comparatively low. Typically, the summary of a joining peer has to be replicated once or multiple times within the network. Some approaches [6,13,12,5] allow flexible load balancing for distributing the cost of joining the network over multiple peers.

One peer summary usually has about the size of a very small number of index data items. So one can afford much replication before joining a summary-based network becomes as expensive as joining a distributed indexing structure based network.

Operation: The actual performance and cost of querying in a summary-based system depends on the *quality of the summaries employed* and the *quality of the peer ranking algorithm*. In literature successful summaries have been described for IR [6,1] and CBIR [13,9], however these approaches need global coordination between the peers in order to generate the peers' summaries. A task that we avoid when using our approach.

Leaving the network: When a peer leaves, the summaries need to be expired in the network. Depending on the architecture this task can be simple. Since each peer generates its summary locally, it becomes easy for the network to expire peers as no extra work is needed for the remaining peers to generate new summaries, all they need to do is to disable the leaving peer and its summary from their known peers' list. The networks considered here can perform expiry cheaply as part of their usual maintenance protocol.

The remainder of this paper is organized as follows: In section 2 we briefly describe our P2P environment and we present the source selection approach together with a description of the data source (*i.e.* the peer) summaries. Section 3.1

explains our experimental setup: the data acquisition and the performance measure used for evaluating the experiments. Our experimental results are shown in section 3.2. Section 4 finalizes our paper with a conclusion and an outlook on future work.

2   P2P Information Retrieval: A Summary-Based Network for Single-Hop Semantic Routing

We are looking for an approach that permits efficient indexing of documents without expensive replication of full indexing data. As indexing of high-dimensional vectors is hard, we choose a single-hop semantic routing approach, also known as source selection. We will seek to use summaries that are *simple to generate*, *cheap to distribute*, and *selective* by means of successfully permitting efficient source selection.

In a summary-based P2P network for single-hop semantic routing, the query processing consists of identifying peers that probably contain relevant data (*i.e.* ranking the peers), forwarding the query to them and afterwards collecting and merging the results. The advantage of this approach is that only summaries are distributed throughout the network (as opposed to full indexing data). And as mentioned before, the query performance is determined by the quality of the summaries and the peer selection method.

While our focus is rather on summary and selection quality, we give a short overview of the underlying P2P architecture.

2.1   The P2P Environment

Our considerations are based on PlanetP [6]. In PlanetP each peer knows the summary of every other single peer participating in the network. This makes routing simple and the network extremely robust. As a downside, this approach is not scalable. Depending on the churn rate (*i.e.* the number of peers arriving and leaving per minute related to the total number of peers in the network) and the type of summaries used, PlanetP starts to fail at a couple of thousands of peers. When the number of nodes in the network and the churn rate are too high, the peers are mainly busy forwarding summaries and the network is not able to process queries anymore.

As a solution to these scalability problems, a variant of PlanetP called Rumorama [13] has been proposed. Rumorama builds hierarchies of networks that are accessible by an efficient multicast. Its leaf networks behave like PlanetP. Therefore, while we examine ranking of peers and the effect of local clustering in PlanetP-like middle sized networks, our method can immediately be utilized (as is) in Rumorama-like networks.

The original PlanetP implementation is designed for text documents and summarizes each peer by a Bloom filter [2]. Bloom filters are lossy, efficient, and compact representations of sparse sets. Unfortunately, Bloom filters are not adapted to the indexing of densely populated high-dimensional vectors [14].

Within this paper we use Gaussian mixture models to generate peer data summaries using 36-dimensional indexing data as described in sections 2.2 and 3.1. Then, the summaries are distributed in the P2P network and the querying of documents is done based on the following scheme: rank the peers for a given query based on their summaries, contact them, receive their result sets, and merge them to obtain the top-N documents retrieved.

It is worth noting that our approach can also be used in super-peer networks [22] as a type of unstructured networks. In super-peer networks, some nodes take more responsibilities (*i.e.* load) than the average peer. In classical super-peer systems such as [22], super-peers hold *all* the indexing data present in the network. Queries are processed by looking only at the super-peers. However, super-peers can also be used in a summary-based context. Each (normal) peer transfers its *summary* to one super-peer. The super-peers then process the queries by source selection using the summaries stored in them. Since the super-peers contain all summaries of the peers that are attached to them, they are able to determine which peers in their sub-network are needed to be contacted. As a consequence, super-peers would obtain the same result as a PlanetP network, with roughly the same query cost. However, other networking properties would be much different from PlanetP and out of scope here. The botton line is that *also super-peer architectures could immediately be used with summaries proposed in this paper.*

Next we describe the probabilistic approach for P2P image retrieval.

2.2 Summaries for Efficient Source Selection: A Probabilistic Retrieval View

The probabilistic view of retrieval and similarity treats the image retrieval problem as a vector classification problem. We can define a mapping from images to image classes. It has been shown that this view is very flexible and successful [21]. In our case we try to find the best mapping between query images and peers in the network. This mapping maps a query image feature vector x to the peer $peer_\alpha$ that is most likely to contain similar feature vectors to x. In other words we choose the peer that maximizes the probability $p(peer_\alpha|x)$[1]. Using Bayes rule we can define this as follows:

$$g^*(x) = \operatorname*{argmax}_{peer_\alpha}\Big(p(peer_\alpha|x)\Big)$$

$$= \operatorname*{argmax}_{peer_\alpha}\Big(\frac{p(x|peer_\alpha)p(peer_\alpha)}{p(x)}\Big)$$

$$= \operatorname*{argmax}_{peer_\alpha}\Big(p(x|peer_\alpha)p(peer_\alpha)\Big) \text{ since } p(x) \text{ is constant}$$

---

[1] $p(peer_\alpha|x)$ in itself means only maximizing the probability of finding x in $peer_\alpha$. However, if we assume that the probability distribution over peers is smooth, $p(peer_\alpha|x)$ also means finding the peers that most probably contain similar documents to the query x.

where g is a mapping from indexing data $x \in X$ to the peers. $p(x|peer_\alpha)$ is the probability that x is found in $peer_\alpha$, and $p(peer_\alpha)$ is the prior probability of drawing the result for x from $peer_\alpha$ without any prior knowledge other than $peer_\alpha$'s size. $p(peer_\alpha)$ is proportional to the number of documents contained in $peer_\alpha$.

Now the goal is to find a representation for every peer in the netwok that enables the estimation of the probability to find a given data vector x within a given peer $peer_\alpha$. In order to achieve this, every peer generates its own model that we refer to as *peer model*, this model is then shared with other peers. Once a query is issued, the querying peer makes a ranking of peers to contact based on their models. The following are the criteria and the characteristics of our mechanism.

Simple to generate: Every peer generates its own model. This is done independently of other peers using the peers' local indexing data. In this paper we use a Gaussian mixture model (see section 2.3) to represent every peer and compare this model to models obtained through *k-means* and *linkage clustering*. In contrast to other methods that perform distributed clustering, for instance distributed *k-means* [8], locally generating a data model removes the costs induced by distributed clustering.

Cheap to distribute: On entering the P2P network, each peer needs to generate its model. After that, only this model's parameters need to be exchanged. The parameters' size need to be small and as such keep the distribution cheap. The cost of the summaries distribution process is proportional to the summary sizes. Section 3.2 describes the parameter sizes obtained by our approach. Furthermore, when a peer adds or removes data from its collection, all it needs to do is to generate a new Gaussian mixture model to describe its data representation and to let the other peers know its new peer model.

Selective: Based on the summaries, the peer issuing the query ranks the peers and contacts them based on this ranking. The efficiency of the ranking is summary specific. For example in the GMM case we rank the peers based on the maximum likelihood that a peer's summary/model generates for a particular query. In summary-based retrieval the query costs are proportional to the number of peers contacted.

2.3   Retrieval Using Compact Peer Descriptions

A Gaussian Mixture Approach: Every peer $peer_\alpha$ contains a set of indexing data $X_{peer_\alpha} = \{x_n | x_n \in \mathbb{R}^d, n \in [1, N_{peer_\alpha}]\}$, where N_{peer_α} is the number of indexing data items $peer_\alpha$ contains. The peer uses this indexing data to generate a Gaussian mixture model with parameters $\Theta_{peer_\alpha} = \{\theta_j = (\mu_j, \Sigma_j, p_j) | j \in [1, k_{peer_\alpha}]\}$ in order to represent its data distribution, where μ_j, Σ_j and p_j are the mean, covariance matrix and prior probability of every kernel (Gaussian) in the model. The generation of the model is initiated using a ten-fold cross validation in order to specify the number of clusters k_{peer_α}, where clusters correspond to kernels of the GMM. The probabilities p_j for each cluster $c_j \in C_{peer_\alpha}$ are determined using k-*means* to find $k_{peer_\alpha} = |C_{peer_\alpha}|$ that generates the minimum squared error for all clusters, where C_{peer_α} is the set of all clusters generated for $peer_\alpha$. We use the Expectation-Maximization (EM) algorithm [7] in order to estimate the Gaussian mixture models' parameters. For completeness we describe below the EM algorithm and its characteristics. In the following $\mathcal{N}(\boldsymbol{\mu}, \Sigma, \boldsymbol{x})$ is the multivariate normal distribution.

$$\mathcal{N}(\boldsymbol{\mu}, \Sigma, \boldsymbol{x}) = (2\pi)^{-d/2} |\Sigma|^{-1/2} exp\left(-\frac{1}{2}(\boldsymbol{x}-\boldsymbol{\mu})^T \Sigma^{-1}(\boldsymbol{x}-\boldsymbol{\mu})\right)$$

EM estimates a probability distribution for each indexing data item $\boldsymbol{x}_n$ given the set Θ_{peer_α}.

$$p(\boldsymbol{x}_n|\Theta_{peer_\alpha}) = \sum_{j=1}^{k_{peer_\alpha}} p_j \mathcal{N}(\boldsymbol{\mu}_j, \Sigma_j, \boldsymbol{x}_n)$$

The EM method determines Θ_{peer_α} that maximizes the log-likelihood L such that:

$$L(\Theta_{peer_\alpha}) = \sum_{n=1}^{N_{peer_\alpha}} ln(p(\boldsymbol{x}_n|\Theta_{peer_\alpha})) = \sum_{n=1}^{N_{peer_\alpha}} ln\left(\sum_{j=1}^{k_{peer_\alpha}} p_j \mathcal{N}(\boldsymbol{\mu}_j, \Sigma_j, \boldsymbol{x}_n)\right)$$

Θ_{peer_α}'s parameters are then computed in the following steps:

1. Choose initial parameter settings $\theta_j \; \forall j \in [1, k_{peer_\alpha}]$:
   - $\boldsymbol{\mu}_j \in X_{peer_\alpha}$ where $\boldsymbol{\mu}_j \neq \boldsymbol{\mu}_i \forall i \in [1, k_{peer_\alpha}]$
   - $\Sigma_j = (\boldsymbol{x}_n - \boldsymbol{\mu}_j)(\boldsymbol{x}_n - \boldsymbol{\mu}_j)^T$ where $\boldsymbol{x}_n$ is the nearest feature vector to $\boldsymbol{\mu}_j$
   - $p_j = \frac{|c_j|}{N_{peer_\alpha}}$
2. Repeat $\forall j \in [1, k_{peer_\alpha}]$ until likelihood convergence is reached:

M step: maximization

$$- \; \boldsymbol{\mu}_j = \frac{\sum\limits_{n=1}^{N_{peer_\alpha}} p(\theta_j|\boldsymbol{x}_n)\boldsymbol{x}_n}{\sum\limits_{n=1}^{N_{peer_\alpha}} p(\theta_j|\boldsymbol{x}_n)}$$

$$- \; \Sigma_j = \frac{\sum\limits_{n=1}^{N_{peer_\alpha}} p(\theta_j|\boldsymbol{x}_n)(\boldsymbol{x}_n-\boldsymbol{\mu}_j)(\boldsymbol{x}_n-\boldsymbol{\mu}_j)^T}{\sum\limits_{n=1}^{N_{peer_\alpha}} p(\theta_j|\boldsymbol{x}_n)}$$

$$- \; p_j = \frac{1}{N_{peer_\alpha}} \sum\limits_{n=1}^{N_{peer_\alpha}} p(\theta_j|\boldsymbol{x}_n)$$

E step: expectation

$$- \; p(\theta_j|\boldsymbol{x}_n) = \frac{p(\boldsymbol{x}_n|\theta_j^{old}) p(\theta_j^{old})}{\sum\limits_{i=1}^{k_{peer_\alpha}} p(\boldsymbol{x}_n|\theta_i^{old}) p(\theta_i^{old})} = \frac{\mathcal{N}(\boldsymbol{\mu}_j^{old}, \Sigma_j^{old}, \boldsymbol{x}_n) p_j^{old}}{\sum\limits_{i=1}^{k_{peer_\alpha}} \mathcal{N}(\boldsymbol{\mu}_i^{old}, \Sigma_i^{old}, \boldsymbol{x}_n) p_i^{old}}$$

Once the GMM parameter sets Θ are generated they are distributed in the PlanetP network in order for every $peer_\alpha$ to be able to reconstruct $peer_\beta$'s GMM given Θ_{peer_β}. This distribution process is taken care of by the PlanetP setup.

When a peer $peer_\alpha$ is given a query q all it needs to do is figure out which other peer's distribution in the network produces the maximum likelihood for $peer_\alpha$'s query. Hence, a ranking R of the peers is produced based on this likelihood such that:

$$p(peer_\alpha|q) \geq p(peer_\beta|q) \Rightarrow R(peer_\alpha) \geq R(peer_\beta) \ \forall \alpha \neq \beta$$

where $p(peer_\alpha|q)$ is the probability of a $peer_\alpha$ given a query q such that:

- $p(peer_\alpha|q) = p(q|peer_\alpha)p(peer_\alpha) = p\,(q|\Theta_{peer_\alpha})\,p(peer_\alpha)$
- Θ_{peer_α} is the GMM parameters set corresponding to $peer_\alpha$
- $p\,(q|\Theta_{peer_\alpha})$ is the probability of q given a model's parameter set Θ_{peer_α}

Therewith, we rank $peer_\alpha$ higher than $peer_\beta$ given a query q if the query has higher likelihood to come from $peer_\alpha$'s model than from $peer_\beta$'s one.

A Linkage Clustering Approach: We compare the previous approach to *k-means, complete link, average link* and *single link* [7] clusterings for the generation of peer summaries. Every peer locally clusters its data and sends the generated centroids to the other peers as a representation for its local data. We use seven centroids to represent a peer's data summary, this is a higher number than the average number of clusters in the GMM (see section 3.2), giving advantage to the linkage clustering approach with respect to the amount of summary data that can be shipped. Once a peer $peer_\alpha$ is given a query q, it determines a ranking R of the peers to contact based on the closest centroid to the query using the distance $dist_{euclid}$.

$$dist_{euclid}(q, C_{peer_\alpha}) \leq dist_{euclid}(q, C_{peer_\beta}) \Rightarrow R(peer_\alpha) \geq R(peer_\beta) \ \forall \alpha \neq \beta$$

where $C_{peer_\alpha} = \{c_1, c_2, ...c_k\}$ is the set of centroids of $peer_\alpha$'s clusters and $dist_{euclid}(q, C_{peer_\alpha})$ computes the minimum Euclidean distance of the query to all centroids $c_i \in C_{peer_\alpha}$.

3   Experiments

3.1   Experimental Setup

In the following we describe the data that our experiments are based on as well as the measure that is used for evaluating retrieval performance.

Data Acquisition: In our experimental setting we use a real world data set. The test data is a subset from a crawl of Flickr.com[2]. Flickr.com is a web-based

---

[2] Flickr, *http://www.flickr.com*

community portal to store, share and search images. Each user may store an arbitrary number of photographs and other pictures in his/her account. We take a randomly chosen subset of 2,623 user accounts so that the total number of images in these accounts is 50,000. We assign each user account to one peer to simulate Flickr.com in a P2P setting.

The feature set used to index the images is a 36-bin color histogram as used in [23,10] where the HSV color space is quantized into 36 intervals. The hue component is split into seven colors that correspond to the seven Chinese colors. The saturation/value components are split into six regions where for values of $V \leq 0,2$ only one bin is reserved for V independently from the S and H values. This results in $7 \cdot 5 + 1 = 36$ bins. Eight of the 36 colors are gray tones making the quantization suitable for both color and gray images. Every image is therefore represented as a single 36-dimensional real-valued vector.

Defining a Performance Measure: The main performance measure used in our experiments is the *fraction of peers contacted* on average to find a fraction out of the top-20 matches for a query. We concentrate on this measure since the processing cost for obtaining a GMM is not much of a problem for reasonable peer collection sizes. The top-20 matches are computed based on the global document collection. This is done prior to executing the query in the P2P network and can be seen as a baseline against which to compare the P2P retrieval system. We choose this measure since contacting other peers during query processing, sending the query and receiving the result sets of the other peers are the main query cost factors in our P2P information retrieval scheme. In our experiments the performance measure is averaged over 100 queries in order to minimize the influence of outliers on the results.

3.2   Empirical Results

Summary Sizes: The EM algorithm computes one GMM parameter set Θ_{peer_α} per $peer_\alpha$, as described in section 2.3. Each GMM approximates the true distribution of data points as a sum of k d-variate Gaussians with diagonal covariance matrices. The correlation of data points is expressed by the fact that the GMM is a mixture of *multiple* Gaussians. *Locally* the dimensions of the data points are independent of each other. Because of this independence assumption, Σ is a diagonal matrix *i.e.* the number of nonzero entries is equal to the dimension d of the indexing data. Otherwise there would be d^2 nonzero entries. This means that given d as the dimension of the indexing data (*i.e.* the feature vectors), the size of a single Gaussian θ_j is:

$$size(\theta_j) = size(\boldsymbol{\mu}_j) + size(\Sigma_j) + size(p_j)$$
$$= d + d + 1$$

where $d = 36$ in our case since we use a 36-dimensional indexing vector, and the covariance matrix can be reconstructed using its diagonal that is of size d. Therefore, the total summary size of a peer $peer_\alpha$ is $size(\Theta_{peer_\alpha}) = (2d + 1)k_{peer_\alpha}$,

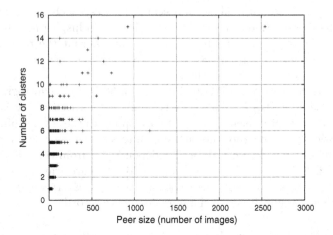

Fig. 1. Number of clusters k per peer vs. peer sizes. The average number of clusters per peer is 2. There are 2,623 points in the plot: one for every peer.

where k_{peer_α} is the number of clusters determined by cross validation. Hence, an important question arises: what is the number of clusters k_{peer_α} determined per peer in our P2P network?

Since we use cross validation to determine the number of clusters k_{peer_α}, it becomes necessary to have it constrained to a small range given that a big number is not applicable for data transfer between peers in a P2P network. In particular peer sizes can range from small sized peers with only few documents to very big peers with many documents. In our P2P network the peer size ranges from one document to 2,544 documents per peer. We plot the number of clusters determined per peer vs. the size of the peers (*i.e.* # of documents per peer) in figure 1.

From figure 1 we see that the maximum number of clusters determined for a peer is 15, and the average number of clusters is approximately 2 clusters per peer. This is a summary size that can easily be transferred in the network as part of its setup procedure. If we compare it to the local clustering techniques that distribute $\#centroids \times d \times \#bytes/float = 7 \times 36 \times 4 = 1008$ bytes per peer as summaries, we only distribute $size(\Theta_{peer_\alpha}) \times \#bytes/float = (2 \times 36+1) \times 2 \times 4 = 584$ bytes per peer on average while achieving a better retrieval performance as will be shown in the next section 3.2.

Retrieval Cost: Table 1 shows the effect of the GMM on the retrieval. We see that the fraction of peers contacted (10.5%) is relatively low when we need to retrieve 80% of the top-20 documents. And for the retrieval of all of the top-20 documents an increase of 113% is observed to reach 22.4% of the peers on average.

We compare in figure 2 the effect of the different approaches discussed in section 2. From this figure we see that the GMM performs better than the other

Table 1. Fraction of peers contacted to retrieve a fraction of the top-20 documents

top-20 [in %]	fraction of peers [in %]
10	0.4
20	1.1
30	1.8
40	3.0
50	4.0
60	5.6
70	7.8
80	10.5
90	14.5
100	22.4

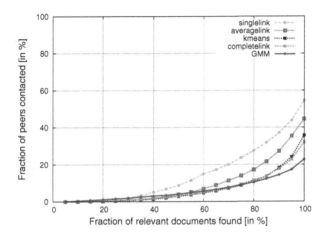

Fig. 2. Fraction of peers contacted vs. documents retrieved for *GMM*, *k-means*, *complete link*, *average link* and *single link*. Lower curves indicate lower retrieval cost for same retrieval performance.

clustering methods. Namely, in order to retrieve 100% of the top-20 documents the *GMM* approach contacts 22.4% of the peers whereas *single link*, *average link*, *k-means*, and *complete link* need to contact 54.6%, 44.6%, 35.7%, and 32% of the peers respectively in order to retrieve the top-20 documents. It is worth noting that *k-means*, *complete link* and the *GMM* approach have comparatively almost the same retrieval cost when retrieving 80% of the top-20 documents, however *GMM* starts to perform better than *k-means* and *complete link* as we retrieve all of the top-20 documents.

4   Conclusion

We have presented an approach to approximate peers' indexing data as Gaussian mixture models. In contrast to previous approaches [13,9], where for example distributed *k-means* is used to cluster the peers' indexing data, requiring thereof coordination between the peers, our new approach does not need coordination between peers. This approach has the advantage of representing the peers (*i.e.* data sources) using small and compact descriptions: *peer models*, which have little distribution cost in the network. These *peer models* allow a querying peer to determine the best peers to contact for its query in a probabilistic manner. We experimentally compared the Gaussian mixture approach to other unsupervised clustering algorithms and showed that on real-world data the *GMM* approach performs better than clustering-based approaches that also do not need coordination between peers.

For future work, our approach provides a basis where adaptive multimedia retrieval can be utilized, we can use *GMM*-based *relevance feedback* [21,16] in the context of CBIR for P2P networks.

We also see the approach presented here suitable as a basis for investigating the performance of more elaborate techniques, namely *meta-learning methods* (*e.g.* [4]). Here, the main idea is to have each PlanetP-peer combine the knowledge present in the summaries it holds in order to improve the peer ranking.

References

1. Bender, M., Michel, S., Triantafillou, P., Weikum, G., Zimmer, C.: Minerva: collaborative P2P search. In: VLDB 2005: Proc. of the 31st Intl. Conf. on Very large data bases. VLDB Endowment, pp. 1263–1266 (2005)
2. Bloom, B.H.: Space/time trade-offs in hash coding with allowable errors. Communications of the ACM 13(7) (1970)
3. Callan, J.P., Lu, Z., Croft, W.B.: Searching distributed collections with inference networks. In: Proc. 18th ACM SIGIR, Seattle, Washington (1995)
4. Chan, P.K.-W.: An extensible meta-learning approach for scalable and accurate inductive learning. PhD thesis, Sponsor-Salvatore J. Stolfo (1996)
5. Clarke, I., Sandberg, O., Wiley, B., Hong, T.W.: Freenet: A distributed anonymous information storage and retrieval system. In: Federrath, H. (ed.) Designing Privacy Enhancing Technologies. LNCS, vol. 2009. Springer, Heidelberg (2001)
6. Cuenca-Acuna, F.M., Nguyen, T.: Text-based content search and retrieval in ad hoc P2P communities. Technical Report DCS-TR-483, Department for Computer Science, Rutgers University (2002)
7. Duda, R.O., Hart, P.E., Stork, D.G.: Pattern classification. Wiley-Interscience (2001)
8. Eisenhardt, M., Müller, W., Henrich, A.: Classifying documents by distributed P2P clustering, 286–291 (2003)
9. Eisenhardt, M., Müller, W., Henrich, A., Blank, D., El Allali, S.: Clustering-based source selection for efficient image retrieval in peer-to-peer networks. In: IEEE MIPR 2007, pp. 823–830 (2006)
10. El Allali, S., Blank, D., Eisenhardt, M., Henrich, A., Müller, W.: Untersuchung des Einflusses verschiedener Bild-Features und Distanzmaße im inhaltsbasierten P2P Information Retrieval. In: BTW 2007, 12th GI-Fachtagung für Datenbanksysteme in Business, Technologie und Web (2007)
11. Gravano, L., García-Molina, H., Tomasic, A.: Gloss: text-source discovery over the internet. ACM Trans. Database Syst. 24(2), 229–264 (1999)

12. Kronfol, A.Z.: A Fault-tolerant, Adaptive, Scalable, Distributed Search Engine. Final Thesis, Princeton (May 2002),
    http://www.searchlore.org/library/kronfol_final_thesis.pdf
13. Müller, W., Eisenhardt, M., Henrich, A.: Scalable summary based retrieval in P2P networks. In: CIKM 2005: Proc. of the 14th ACM Intl. Conf. on Information and knowledge management, pp. 586–593. ACM Press, New York (2005)
14. Müller, W., Henrich, A., Eisenhardt, M.: Aspects of adaptivity in P2P information retrieval. In: The 4th International Workshop on Adaptive Multimedia Retrieval AMR 2006 (2006)
15. Nejdl, W., Wolpers, M., Siberski, W., Schmitz, C., Schlosser, M., Brunkhorst, I., Löser, A.: Super-peer-based routing and clustering strategies for rdf-based peer-to-peer networks. In: Proc. of the Intl. World Wide Web Conf. (2003)
16. Qian, F., Li, M., Zhang, L., Zhang, H.-J., Zhang, B.: Gaussian mixture model for relevance feedback in image retrieval. In: IEEE International Conference on Multimedia and Expo, 2002. ICME 2002 (2002)
17. Ratnasamy, S., Francis, P., Handley, M., Karp, R., Schenker, S.: A scalable content-addressable network. In: Proc. 2001 Conf. on applications, technologies, architectures, and protocols for computer communications, San Diego, CA, United States (2001)
18. Sahin, O.D., Gulbeden, A., Emekci, F., Agrawal, D., Abbadi, A.E.: PRISM: indexing multi-dimensional data in P2P networks using reference vectors. In: Proc. of the 13th annual ACM Intl. Conf. on Multimedia, pp. 946–955. ACM Press, New York (2005)
19. Stoica, I., Morris, R., Karger, D., Kaashoek, F., Balakrishnan, H.: Chord: A scalable Peer-To-Peer lookup service for internet applications. In: Proc. ACM SIGCOMM Conf., San Diego, CA, USA (2001)
20. Tang, C., Xu, Z., Mahalingam, M.: pSearch: Information retrieval in structured overlays. In: First Workshop on Hot Topics in Networks (HotNets-I). Princeton, NJ (2002)
21. Vasconcelos, N.: Bayesian Models for Visual Information Retrieval. PhD thesis, MIT (June 2000)
22. Yang, B., Garcia-Molina, H.: Designing a super-peer network. In: IEEE Intl. Conf. on Data Engineering (2003)
23. Zhang, L., Lin, F., Zhang, B.: A cbir method based on color-spatial feature. In: IEEE Region 10 Annual International Conference 1999, pp. 166–169 (1999)

Designing a Peer-to-Peer Architecture for Distributed Image Retrieval

Akrivi Vlachou, Christos Doulkeridis,
Dimitrios Mavroeidis, and Michalis Vazirgiannis

Department of Informatics
Univ. of Economics and Business
Athens, Greece
{avlachou, cdoulk, dmavr, mvazirg}@aueb.gr

Abstract. The World Wide Web provides an enormous amount of images easily accessible to everybody. The main challenge is to provide efficient search mechanisms for image content that are truly scalable and can support full coverage of web contents. In this paper, we present an architecture that adopts the peer-to-peer (P2P) paradigm for indexing, searching and ranking of image content. The ultimate goal of our architecture is to provide an adaptive search mechanism for image content, enhanced with learning, relying on image features, user-defined annotations and user feedback. Thus, we present PIRES, a scalable decentralized and distributed infrastructure for building a search engine for image content capitalizing on P2P technology. In the following, we first present the core scientific and technological objectives of PIRES, and then we present some preliminary experimental results of our prototype.

Keywords: Peer-to-peer, distributed search, image retrieval.

1 Introduction

The advent of the World Wide Web in conjunction with efficient centralized search engines like Google and Yahoo has made an enormous amount of information easily accessible to everybody. Search engines provide efficient ranking thus easing identification of important results. Image content is only partially covered by web search engines, although it is evident that there is a tremendous wealth of digital images available on computers or other devices around the world. This is probably due to the fact that image content induces further complicated problems regarding the search: current centralized image search facilities do not sufficiently support metadata management, semantics, advanced media querying etc.

The widespread use of digital image equipment enables end-users to capture and edit their own image content, sometimes of high intellectual or commercial value. The centralized character of Web search raises issues regarding royalties,

N. Boujemaa, M. Detyniecki, and A. Nürnberger (Eds.): AMR 2007, LNCS 4918, pp. 182–195, 2008.

in the case of protected content, censorship, and to some degree information monopoly. Moreover current tools for image retrieval are limited in query expressiveness and lack semantic capabilities.

The P2P paradigm for file sharing, and recently covering WWW content [10,3], is a challenging alternative to centralized search and ranking. In a large scale network of peers, the storage and access load requirements per peer are much lighter than for a centralized Google-like server farm; thus more powerful techniques from information retrieval, statistical learning, and ontological reasoning can be employed on each peer's local search engine towards boosting the quality of search results. In addition, the virtual monopoly of information imposed by centralized search engines calls for more efforts towards information sharing (in our case image content), where the participants enjoy similar capabilities at least at the structural level.

In this context, the objective of this paper is to research, design and prototype a distributed indexing and searching toolkit, for image content, that capitalizes on the P2P paradigm using the Web as dissemination means. The main characteristic of PIRES (P2P Image Retrieval System) is that both content and indexing information is distributed across a large scale network of peers willing to share resources. The PIRES scenario assumes that users are making available part of their image content to the wider community, in exchange for the ability to search and access other users' content. Image content is tagged/annotated by the users in a way that it is indexable and therefore searchable. PIRES provides the means to manage the features extracted from images, to organize and index metadata in a distributed manner, to provide efficient P2P search mechanisms, and to facilitate adaptive ranking based on user feedback. Users participating in PIRES have a rich query mechanism enabling mixed queries based on keywords, ontology-based classifications, image samples assisted by a personalization mechanism based on adaptive user feedback.

In this paper, we present the design of the overall P2P architecture of PIRES. We describe the requirements of our approach, the research challenges that we wish to address, and the specific system components we focus on, namely feature extraction and image annotation, P2P organization and indexing, P2P search and access, and P2P personalized ranking. Currently, we have implemented a prototype simulator to study the feasibility and performance of the proposed P2P architecture. A full implementation of PIRES as well as testing in a real setting is left for future work.

The rest of the paper is organized as follows: We present related work in Section 2, while in Section 3 we introduce the overall architecture and the main roles in the system. Afterwards, in Section 4, we briefly outline the individual modules that realize the proposed functionality. In Section 5 we describe the P2P organization and indexing, while P2P searching is presented in Section 6. Thereafter, in Section 7, we describe the adaptive P2P ranking employed in PIRES. In Section 8, we present some preliminary experimental results. Finally, we conclude in Section 9.

2   Related Work - State of the Art

The advent of image search engines, such as Google Image Search (`http://images.google.com/`), together with the popularity of photo sharing systems, like `flickr.com`, indicate that contemporary users show increasing interests in capturing, storing, sharing and searching digital image content. Numerous commercial systems are available online, making the task of successful retrieval of multimedia content particularly challenging. A non-exhaustive list of such systems includes: search engines, like AltaVista Image Search (`http://www.altavista.com/image/default`) and Riya (`www.riya.com`), content-based retrieval tools, like GIFT, the GNU Image-Finding Tool (`http://www.gnu.org/software/gift/`), and news/media portals, such as the REUTERS image library search and retrieval tool (`http://www.carydesign.co.uk/ril/`).

A number of EU research projects in relevant areas that have recently concluded or are under development imply the significance and increasing interest for multimedia (text, image, audio-visual content) search and retrieval. *MESH* (Multimedia Semantic Syndication for Enhanced News Services) (`http://www.mesh-ip.eu/`) intends to apply advanced multimedia analysis to provide personalized multimedia summaries and novel access mechanisms for news to end users. The *K-Space* network of excellence (`http://www.kspace-noe.net/`) also conducts research relevant to content-based image analysis. Projects related to advanced search technologies for digital audio-visual content are coordinated by the *CHORUS* coordination action. Two P2P-related projects, under this action, are *SAPIR* (`http://sysrun.haifa.il.ibm.com/sapir/`) and *Victory* (`http://www.victory-eu.org/`). *SAPIR* is the most similar research project to our work.

Distributed and peer-to-peer (P2P) image retrieval has attracted some research interest lately. In [6], a system called FuzzyPeer is presented for answering similarity queries in P2P networks, like *"find the top-k images which are similar to a given sketch"*. In [11], the authors argue against the appropriateness of structured P2P systems for queries based on image similarity metrics (such as color histograms). They investigate how unstructured P2P networks can be exploited to provide such enhanced searching facilities. Müller and Henrich also study P2P content-based image retrieval in unstructured P2P networks, based on compact summaries in [12]. They assume a small number (compared to the number of peers) of globally known clusters, so that queries can be directed to only a subset of peers with relevant content. In contrast, our approach does not make any assumptions about the distribution of peer contents, although better performance can be achieved if the data is clustered. In [7], the design and implementation of a system for P2P content-based multimedia retrieval is presented.

An overview of adaptivity features that a P2P image retrieval system should demonstrate is presented in [13]. A relevance feedback mechanism for P2P content-based image retrieval is proposed in [8]. Further, while there exists sufficient work on the issue of distributed ranking (top-k retrieval), there are only a few works that study the issue of P2P ranking, for example [1,9]. All these research papers are related to (parts of) the functionality that PIRES aims to provide.

In comparison to previous work in P2P image retrieval, our approach focuses mainly on scalability. We propose a feasible P2P system that encompasses and combines salient features, such as decentralization, high availability, fault-tolerance, relatively low response times as well as respect for peer autonomy. These features are hardly combined in existing research in the relevant literature.

3   Architecture

The PIRES architecture utilizes a P2P infrastructure for supporting the deployment of a scalable enhanced search engine for multimedia content, addressing (and particularly suitable to) future user needs and search requirements. A high-level abstraction of the PIRES architecture, showing the different participating entities (peers), their interconnections and functionality is shown in Figure 1. Collaborating peers in the PIRES search engine consist of: 1) *content providers* and 2) *information brokers*. These roles are not mutually exclusive. For instance, a media portal may utilize peers with substantial processing and storage capabilities as information brokers, which provide content as well as indexing and retrieval functionality at the same node. Other participants, such as mobile users running mobile client software on their personal computers may only act as content providers. Below we discuss these roles in more detail.

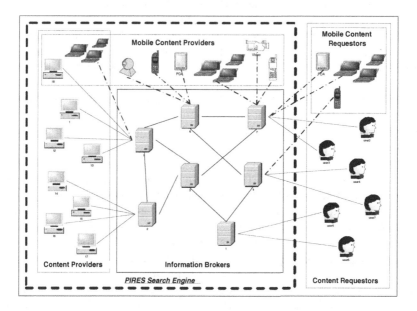

Fig. 1. High level view of the PIRES architecture

Content providers are nodes that produce or store images that they would like to publish. We stress here that only metadata is indexed and managed by PIRES; the actual content remains on the participating peers that own it. Using the PIRES client software, peers can register to a PIRES information broker peer and publish their content. This process involves manual annotation of the material to facilitate the indexing and retrieval potential of interested parties. One of the features of the PIRES client software is that it encapsulates a feature extraction functionality. Using this embedded service, a peer can automatically or semi-automatically extract a set of features for its local images.

Besides stationary content providers, PIRES supports mobile content providers, which are able to dynamically capture content and make it widely available. We envisage reporters or tourists as potential candidates for this role, allowing instant access to "fresh" multimedia content. Mobile content providers may additionally/optionally upload the actual multimedia content to dedicated servers – instead of only metadata – to ensure continuous availability.

Information brokers consist of more powerful and less volatile peers in the network. They realize a decentralized indexing service. In addition to the basic form of metadata that is generated by the content providers, information brokers may employ more sophisticated (and thus demanding) algorithms that could not be executed in lightweight peers, due to lack or processing power or lack of more widespread knowledge on the rest of the multimedia content in the network. By participating in PIRES, information brokers gain access to a wealth of "fresh" user-created multimedia content, which is organized and indexed in a way that allows more elaborate search facilities. We envisage news portals, agencies or third-party multimedia repositories as potential PIRES information brokers. With PIRES these entities increase the visibility of their content, but most importantly they enrich their content collection, by getting access to thousands or millions of independent and undiscovered multimedia sources (content providers).

Content requestors are not necessarily contributing content to PIRES search engine; however their role is crucial to the architecture, as they represent the users of the search engine. Moreover user feedback is exploited to provide improved ranking of results. Content requestors enjoy a rich repertoire of query and searching facilities seamlessly integrated in a simple/intuitive but powerful interface. PIRES supports a variety of different search modes and a mixture of them.

In more technical terms, PIRES relies on a super-peer architecture. Because super-peer infrastructures [15] harness the merits of both centralized and distributed architectures, we make a design choice of a super-peer architecture for the P2P network interconnection.

Content providers are simple peers (henceforth called peers) that keep multimedia content, usually generated on their own. Each peer joins the collaborative search engine, by connecting to one of the information brokers that act as super-peers, using the basic bootstrapping protocol. The information brokers are entities that maintain summaries/indexes of content/data that reside on content providers.

The choice of the proposed super-peer architecture is motivated and driven by our main requirement for scalability. Currently deployed super-peer networks, e.g. eMule (`www.emule-project.net`) and KaZaA (`www.kazaa.com`), support large number of users, demonstrating the appropriateness of super-peer architectures when scalability is required. In addition, peer autonomy is respected as the actual content/data remain on the owner peer, and only metadata is indexed and handled by the super-peer network.

In order to accommodate the proposed functionality, we identify the following main components of the proposed system:

- Feature extraction and image annotation
- P2P organization and indexing
- P2P search and access
- P2P personalized ranking

In the following, we provide a short overview of the system, and then we describe in more detail the individual components, their functionality, and how their collective combination realizes the proposed system.

4   System Overview

The overall objective of PIRES is to provide novel, dynamic and enhanced image retrieval services, over a P2P architecture of collaborative computers. For this purpose, a set of basic functionalities on each peer are required, varying from low level feature extraction and annotation of image data, to organizing, indexing and searching the extracted metadata in a distributed way.

4.1   Local Feature Extraction and Annotation

Content-based analysis and retrieval of multimedia documents requires methods for feature extraction. Features may include both text-based features (such as key words, annotations) and visual features (such as color, texture, shape, faces). Combing the low level features with the high level concepts of the keyword annotations bridges the gap between actual image content and the user's sense of similarity. There already exists rich literature on existing techniques of visual feature extraction [14]. However, finding an automatic transition from the low-level features to semantic entities or equivalently the automatic extraction of high-level characteristics is an extremely hard task [2].

For images, existing image segmentation and object recognition algorithms cannot yet reach a level of precision which would be adequate for automatic annotation. In PIRES, we aim to combine knowledge-driven image analysis and text-mining technologies, to support the user in the process of semantic annotation of the images and image-parts. This process is assisted by ontological information or some domain specific taxonomy, that enables annotation of images not only with keywords that can provide syntactic matching, but rather with semantic concepts that allow more enhanced semantic matching.

Reuse of already generated semantic metadata can be exploited to support automatic text-based and image-based methods also for other resources. Unfortunately, even with such a combined strategy it cannot be realistically expected that fully-automatic semantic metadata generation will always yield acceptable results. Therefore, we propose a semi-automatic approach, where users give feedback, correct and extend the results of image segmentation, image recognition and text mining algorithms. To achieve that, user-friendly annotation tools are needed, and they will be implemented in our future work.

4.2   Decentralized and Distributed Indexing of Image Content

The purpose of the advanced feature extraction mechanism is to feed a distributed indexing mechanism. Locally extracted metadata and user annotations are mapped to the global ontology, in order to: 1) create common semantics, and 2) enable more sophisticated retrieval mechanisms than exact matching.

Advanced P2P mechanisms will be designed to identify thematically coherent communities of participants and thus organize content in a way (we envisage semantic overlay networks [4] as a potential candidate) that enables efficient searching.

4.3   P2P Search and Access Mechanisms for Image Content

The search facilities in PIRES cover both spontaneous and subscription queries. The search is formulated based on a rich set of advanced features: keywords, metadata tags, semantics, media samples or a mixture of them. Additional parameters that will expand queries in the search process will be contextual attributes (i.e. location, time, device features, personal profiles). Furthermore, we envisage an advanced personalization process that will capitalize on mining query/usage logs and interaction histories. The combination of semantic/ontology methodologies and the statistical ones, will offer users the possibility to have a much more precise and to the point interaction with the distributed image content.

4.4   Peer-to-Peer Ranking

PIRES aims to use novel P2P ranking algorithms that assist users in their search. The issues to be taken into account in the ranking process deal with: 1) the limited knowledge of content any entity of PIRES has, and 2) how to incorporate user feedback in order to provide adaptive ranking of results.

Another issue that should be taken into account is the personalization of the rankings. This is due to the fact that different users could expect different results even when they provide the same query. In order to address this issue we employ a novel query expansion mechanism, based on relevance feedback that ensures the adaptiveness of the query ranking framework to the specific user needs.

In the next sections, we focus on the P2P aspects of the image content retrieval system, which justify its innovation and how PIRES enhances the state of the art, both from the scientific and technological point of view.

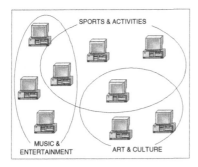

Fig. 2. The notion of semantic overlays in a P2P network

5   P2P Organization and Indexing

Users decide which features (metadata) to publish to the search engine, in order to make their content searchable. This is a deviation from the centralized search engine paradigm that relies on crawling: the user decides what meta-data information to publish and initiates the indexing phase. Thus the adopted model is push-based, similar to [3,4], compared to the traditional pull-based model for collecting web data. Furthermore, before making content and metadata publicly available, users may add annotations that enrich the expressiveness of their metadata, facilitating access by other users and increasing visibility. The client-software transmits to the information broker the instances and the mappings of the extracted features that will be appended on the appropriate representation file at the information broker. This reduces network traffic, as only changes to the file are communicated.

We stress here that the actual image content resides on the peers - only the metadata extracted are published (for instance for images only, a low-quality preview of the picture can be published as well). It should also be stressed, that digital rights management issues can be determined at this point, by having each user explicitly specify the access rights for its content. However, as such issues are out of the technical scope of this paper, they will not be consider further here.

5.1   Distributed Metadata Organization

A topic related to global indexing is the dynamic formation of interest-based communities in a transparent way to the end-user. In this manner, content is organized into thematic categories, with several advantages like more efficient query processing and creation of thematically focused groups. Towards this end, PIRES relies on the decentralized generation of Semantic Overlay Networks (SONs) as a scalable and efficient solution to P2P content organization and subsequent searching [3]. SONs (see also Fig. 2) have been proposed as a mechanism that reduces the cost of searching in large-scale P2P networks, while increasing the quality of the results, since queries are directed only to specific subsets of peers that hold relevant contents to the query [4]. Regarding the actual construction of these overlays, PIRES adopts P2P clustering and classification techniques either for a completely unsupervised scenario or for a semi-supervised setting respectively.

5.2   Distributed Indexing

Within the generated overlay networks, distributed indexing is required in order to serve requests for content. Information brokers accumulate metadata information that is published by the content providers. These metadata are used to populate local indices that describe the content of the connected peers. The precision/accuracy of these indices strongly depends on the quality of the feature extraction process.

In the distributed indexing phase, super-peers need to consolidate their local indices, in order to provide a global distributed index. This index needs to be distributed for several reasons: 1) scalability, 2) load-balancing, 3) fault-tolerance, 4) in order to avoid censoring phenomena. This exchange of local indices can be performed by broadcasting, in the absence of more sophisticated dissemination mechanisms.

Ontologies influence the global index too, since they provide information of the keywords and the topics of the material that is indexed at a super-peer and can be retrieved from its peers. For instance, we can use them to quickly discard super-peers that can not contribute to the final result, thus decreasing communication costs.

Our prototype implementation uses distributed indexing based on clustering over the features extracted by the images to support the retrieval of similar based on content images.

6   P2P Search and Access

Search requests (henceforth also termed queries) for image content are initiated by content requestors that wish to retrieve and exploit fresh content. Notice that the role of content requestors can correspond to end users, content providers and information brokers. By utilizing its P2P indexing scheme, PIRES supports not only most of the conventional query models, but also provides a flexible infrastructure, where future user requirements or more human-centric query interfaces (that resemble more the way human requests are posed in the real world) can be accommodated. PIRES supports the following non-conventional query/search models:

Semantic Keyword-Based Queries. The user provides a set of keywords that are transparently associated with parts of the ontology to exploit semantic inferences. This query type differs from the traditional keyword-based search, since it goes beyond exact matching techniques supporting semantic relationships. We also consider queries expressing semantic or knowledge based relationships.

Query by Thematic Category. In addition to providing keywords, users belonging to specific communities and interested in particular topics may issue queries within specific thematic areas (i.e. in terms of taxonomy paths), in order to increase the search precision. In this case, a generic query that would normally have low precision can be targeted to a specific thematic category, thus increasing the probability of high quality results and at the same time decreasing the incurred processing cost. The choice of thematic category implies some data organization (manual or semi-automatic), e.g. into a globally known taxonomy (such as DMOZ), so that the user is supplied with a list of categories at query time.

Similarity-Based Queries. Instead of traditional text based requests an object is given by the user and similar objects based on a given image are retrieved. These queries belong to the Query by Example (QBE) category and are evaluated based on the feature space in which the images are represented. Each image is represented by a high-dimensional vector and the closest images to the given image are retrieved.

Mixed Queries. A combination of keyword-based, thematic category and query by example. Mixed queries aim to enhance the expressiveness of the query interface by combining the aforementioned query types. These queries are particularly useful when users cannot explicitly specify what they seek in terms of (for example) keywords only. Nevertheless, it is often the case that users know other parts of information that can help shaping a more specific query, for example the thematic category corresponding to the query. This facility is usually missing from current search engines.

Subscription-Based Queries. PIRES also supports subscription-based queries. Rather than having clients explicitly requesting the information they need, data is sent to them as soon as it is available. Clients submit a subscription to receive updates on new image content that is published based on a variety of criteria (similar to pull-based queries) and then disconnect.

From the aspect of the Information Brokers, the design of the indexing and organization of the metadata takes into account the efficient query processing of all mentioned types of queries. Based on the distributed organization, when a query is posed to a super-peer (initiator super-peer) the initiator must propagate the query to those peers (based on the global index) that influence the result set. After all queried super-peers respond, the initiator super-peer has to merge the result into a global result set, which are returned to the content requestor that had submitted the query.

7 Ranking the Retrieved Image Metadata

Searching in a large-scale environment is practically useless in the absence of efficient ranking. According to the experience from traditional search engines, users seldom browse through the entire list of results, they rather focus on the first few results only. It is therefore crucial to provide ranking of the retrieved images and this brings up several challenging research questions, i.e., how to rank image content? A trivial ranking is based on media-specific information, e.g. image resolution, size, date. On the other hand, it would be advantageous to contemplate a quality metric for ranking the results using the annotations. This metric can be based on (for example) how often a keyword occurs.

The user interface also provides certain extensions to make ranking more flexible and thus useful to the user. For example, the user can rank the retrieved results according to location, time, etc., which can be particularly useful when searching for nearby or "fresh" content. Thus, we identify at this stage, the following ranking criteria: 1) Semantic-based, 2) Context-based (Location-based, Time-aware, Media-specific).

Another interesting extension is to use **query feedback** to better rank matching data for future queries. This functionality is provided at the screens that depict the query results in the client software and can be used to fine-tune the local indexes and also enable the provisions of personalized rankings.

We observe that the practical appropriateness of the ranking of results depends heavily on the utilization of a "good" similarity measure. A "good" similarity measure should be able to identify conceptually similar objects, thus helping users to retrieve relevant images based on their queries. Many researchers have argued that instead of trying to define a "global" similarity measure systems should be adaptive, exploiting the feedback provided by the users.

As we have mentioned in Section 6, we aim to use semantic relations/concepts that are provided by an ontology/hierarchical taxonomy to improve the effectiveness of input queries. In the interest of creating personalized rankings, the framework includes a personalization mechanism that learns locally (at peer level) the weights of ontology concepts based on relevance feedback. Since peers utilize the ontology relations for enhancing queries with semantics, the local weight learning process results into a personalized ranking for each peer, thus adapting the query results based on the personalized needs of each peer.

Accessing image content. The query result set that is displayed to the user that posed a query contains only the metadata of the actual object, such as description and a thumbnail. The original (high quality) image file is hosted by the content provider in general. In PIRES, mechanisms will be implemented to support mechanisms that supervise the transactions of files. The content requestors access the original files hosted by the content providers, through the client software and the information broker infrastructure.

Navigating. The query result set containing the metadata of the actual objects is displayed to the user that posed a query as a list, where each row of the list contains a thumbnail and media-specific features, such as size and date. The user may navigate through the list and choose (by clicking) any object he is interested in. Then a more detailed description of the object is displayed where the thematic and semantic categories based on the ontology are represented. The user may navigate through all associated categories or request objects similar to the object based on the displayed semantics.

8   Experimental Results

We have implemented a prototype simulator of the proposed system, in order to study experimentally its properties and test whether PIRES satisfies its design requirements. In our prototype, a super-peer architecture is implemented, and

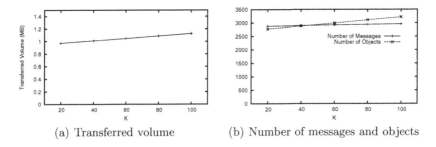

(a) Transferred volume   (b) Number of messages and objects

Fig. 3. Transferred volume, number of messages and objects transmitted during search

peers store image content described by feature extracted by the images. In particular, we use the VEC dataset, which consists of 1M 45-dimensional vectors of color image features. The algorithms used in the experiments are described in [5].

The P2P network topology used in the experiments consists of 200 interconnected super-peers in a random graph topology, built using the GT-ITM topology generator[1], with average connectivity degree equal to 4. Each super-peer is assigned 10 peers, making a total of 2000 peers in the system. At this stage, we study only queries by example based on the image feature space, i.e. given an n-dimensional query object, retrieve the top-k most similar objects to the query. This can also be expressed as retrieval of those objects that are similar to the query with a certain similarity threshold. Similarity is based on a distance function and in this set of experiments we use the Euclidean distance. All simulations run on 3.8GHz Dual Core AMD processors with 2GB RAM, and in all cases we show the average values over all queries.

At first, we measure the volume transferred through the network, for answering a query. Note that this volume corresponds only to the volume of the features values. In Fig. 3(a), we see that the volume is in the order of 1MB, for different number of requested results. Given the size of the simulated network, this is considered quite tolerable for our network. The value k on the x-axis denotes the number of results requested by the user, i.e. the top-20 to top-100 most similar images to the query.

Next, the number of required messages and the number of objects transferred in the network is measured. In Fig. 3(b), we show these numbers again for varying values of k. The increasing tension in both curves is due to the increasing k values. Also, it is important to notice that the number of messages increases very slowly with the number of results, which is a sign in favor of the scalability of the approach with number of results. The number of objects retrieved increases faster, but this is expected and due to its explicit relationship with the k value.

Finally, Fig. 4 depicts the response time of the system for varying network transfer times. As response time, we mean the time required to retrieve the

---

[1] Available at: http://www.cc.gatech.edu/projects/gtitm/

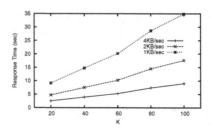

Fig. 4. Response time

number of results specified by the user. Notice that we use very modest transfer times, 1-4KB/sec, that resemble the speed of dial-up connections. In reality, connections between super-peers or peers will be much faster, so we study here a worst case scenario of poor communication, in terms of bandwidth. Even for this setup, for example in the case of 4KB/sec and 20 results, the response time is approx. 2.5 seconds. In general, the response time increases with k, as more results require more time to reach the user.

9   Conclusions

In this paper, we presented an P2P architecture for efficient search mechanism for the image content that is scalable and supports coverage of the web contents. We outlined the requirements for indexing, searching and ranking of image content in a decentralized and distributed environment. Relying on a super-peer architecture, we presented the overall architecture of the PIRES framework and presented the initial results of our prototype implementation. In our future work, we plan to implement and deploy our system, in order to test it in a real network platform like PlanetLab[2].

References

1. Balke, W.-T., Nejdl, W., Siberski, W., Thaden, U.: Progressive distributed top-k retrieval in peer-to-peer networks. In: Proceedings of ICDE, pp. 174–185 (2005)
2. Chang, S.: The holy grail of content-based media analysis. IEEE Multimedia 9(2), 6–10 (2002)
3. Doulkeridis, C., Nørvåg, K., Vazirgiannis, M.: The SOWES approach to P2P web search using semantic overlays. In: Proceedings of WWW, pp. 1027–1028 (2006)
4. Doulkeridis, C., Nørvåg, K., Vazirgiannis, M.: DESENT: Decentralized and distributed semantic overlay generation in P2P networks. IEEE Journal on Selected Areas in Communications (J-SAC) 25(1), 25–34 (2007)
5. Doulkeridis, C., Vlachou, A., Kotidis, Y., Vazirgiannis, M.: Peer-to-peer similarity search in metric spaces. In: Proceedings of VLDB 2007, pp. 986–997 (2007)

---

[2] https://www.planet-lab.org/

6. Kalnis, P., Ng, W.S., Ooi, B.C., Tan, K.-L.: Answering similarity queries in peer-to-peer networks. Inf. Syst. 31(1), 57–72 (2006)
7. King, I., Ng, C.H., Sia, K.C.: Distributed content-based visual information retrieval system on peer-to-peer networks. ACM Trans. Inf. Syst. 22(3), 477–501 (2004)
8. Lee, I., Guan, L.: Content-based image retrieval with automated relevance feedback over distributed peer-to-peer network. In: Proceedings of ISCAS, pp. 5–8 (2004)
9. Michel, S., Triantafillou, P., Weikum, G.: Klee: A framework for distributed top-k query algorithms. In: Proceedings of VLDB, pp. 637–648 (2005)
10. Michel, S., Triantafillou, P., Weikum, G.: Minerva∞: A scalable efficient peer-to-peer search engine. In: Middleware, pp. 60–81 (2005)
11. Müller, W., Boykin, P.O., Sarshar, N., Roychowdhury, V.P.: Comparison of image similarity queries in P2P systems. In: Proceedings of P2P, pp. 98–105 (2006)
12. Müller, W., Henrich, A.: Fast retrieval of high-dimensional feature vectors in P2P networks using compact peer data summaries. In: Proceedings of MIR, pp. 79–86 (2003)
13. Müller, W., Henrich, A., Eisenhardt, M.: Aspects of adaptivity in P2P information retrieval. In: Proceedings of AMR, pp. 1–15 (2005)
14. Rui, Y., Huang, T., Chang, S.: Image retrieval: current techniques, promising directions and open issues. Journal of Visual Communication and Image Representation 10(4), 39–62 (1999)
15. Yang, B., Garcia-Molina, H.: Designing a super-peer network. In: Proceedings of ICDE 2003, p. 49 (2003)

Comparison of Dimension Reduction Methods for Database-Adaptive 3D Model Retrieval

Ryutarou Ohbuchi, Jun Kobayashi[1], Akihiro Yamamoto[2], and Toshiya Shimizu

[1] NEC Corp., [2] Fujitsu Corp.
4-3-11 Takeda, Kofu-shi, Yamanashi-ken, 400-8511, Japan
`ohbuchi@yamanashi.ac.jp`, `jun066@quartz.ocn.ne.jp`,
`yama.akihiro@jp.fujitsu.com`, `g06mk009@Yamanashi.ac.jp`

Abstract. Distance measures, along with shape features, are the most critical components in a shape-based 3D model retrieval system. Given a shape feature, an optimal distance measure will vary per query, per user, or per database. No single, fixed distance measure would be satisfactory all the time. This paper focuses on a method to adapt distance measure to the database to be queried by using learning-based dimension reduction algorithms. We experimentally compare six such dimension reduction algorithms, both linear and non-linear, for their efficacy in the context of shape-based 3D model retrieval. We tested the efficacy of these methods by applying them to five global shape features. Among the dimension reduction methods we tested, non-linear manifold learning algorithms performed better than the other, e.g. linear algorithms such as principal component analysis. Performance of the best performing combination is roughly the same as the top finisher in the SHREC 2006 contest.

1 Introduction

Research on shape-based retrieval of 3D models [24, 13, 26] has recently gained attention. A shape-based 3D model retrieval system retrieves, given a query, a set of shape models ranked by their shape-based similarity to the query. The query may be texts, 2D sketches, 3D sketches, or 3D models. In this paper, we assume the query is a 3D model defined, for example, as a set of polygons and that the system retrieves 3D models similar in their shape to the query.

Two of the most significant technical challenges for shape-based retrieval of 3D models are feature extraction and distance computation. We first have to device a compact yet expressive shape feature that can be extracted and compared with reasonable computational cost. In feature extraction, compatibility of the shape feature with various shape representations, e.g., polygon soup and voxel enumeration solid, is an important factor to be considered. Then, distance, or dissimilarity among a pair of models to be compared must be computed. It is desirable that the feature and distance measure be adaptive to a database, to a user, or even to a specific query. For example, a combination of feature and distance metric that works well for comparing human face models may be sub-optimal for comparing screws. Or, the bunny model I wanted yesterday may be different from a bunny model I want today. So-called "curse of

N. Boujemaa, M. Detyniecki, and A. Nürnberger (Eds.): AMR 2007, LNCS 4918, pp. 196–210, 2008.
© Springer-Verlag Berlin Heidelberg 2008

dimensionality", which discourages higher dimensional shape feature vectors, also comes into play as the dimensionality of 3D shape feature tend to be quite high.

In our previous work [20], we adopted Xhaofei He's approach [12] for a significant gain in retrieval performance. Instead of the distance in the original feature (or input) space, the method uses geodesic distance on a *subspace*, or a *manifold*, spanned by the features of 3D models in a database. He used the *Laplacian Eigenmaps* [3] for learning a manifold from the set of features for learning-based dimension reduction.

Our previous work [20] has several limitations, however. The experimental results are derived using only one non-linear dimension reduction algorithm, LE. And the LE is combined with only two shape features, the AAD [19] and SPRH [28]. Also, the training set size in our previous work [20] was limited to about 4000 samples, mostly due to memory space limitation.

In this paper, we try to experimentally explore the approach further in the following three aspects;

1. How do various subspace learning methods compare?
2. How well does the approach work when it is applied to various shape features?
3. What is the impact of the number of learning samples?

To answer the first question, we compared five dimension reduction methods, all of which are based on unsupervised subspace learning. The set of dimension reduction methods we compared are the *Principal Component Analysis* (*PCA*), *Kernel PCA* (*KPCA*) [10], *Locality Preserving Projections* (*LPP*) [11], *Laplacian Eigenmaps* (LE) [3], *Locally Linear Embedding* (*LLE*) [21], and *Isometric feature mapping* (*Isomap*) [25]. To answer the second question, we experimented with five shape features and their respective multiresolution variations [18]. The five features we compared are; the *Ray-based Spherical Harmonics* (*RSH*) [27], *Exponentially-decaying EDT* (*ED-EDT*) [27], *Spherical Harmonics* (SH) [14], *Absolute Angle-Distance histogram* (AAD) [19], and the *Surflet-Pair Relation Histogram* (SPRH) [28]. We also applied the multiresolution shape feature extraction approach by Ohbuchi et al [18] on these shape features; all in all, we experimented with 16 different shape features. To answer the third question, we increased the number of training samples from 4,000~6,000 to 10,000, by using CPU, OS, and application codes that support 64bit addressing.

Measured using the PSB [22] test set, the original, single-resolution (SR-) SPRH, which uses *Kullback-Leibler divergence* for its distance, has R-Precision of 37.4%, while its multiresolution SPRH has R-Precision of 42.5%. After the dimension reduction using the LLE, *multi-resolution* (*MR*) SPRH clicked in at 49.3% for R-Precision, a 12% overall increase in performance from the original. The best performing combination we have experimented with, the MR-SPRH feature dimension reduced by using the LLE trained by 10,000 samples, tied with the best performer in the SHREC 2006 contest, the method by Makadia et al. [26].

This paper is organized as follows. In the following section, we will review learning-based approach to 3D model retrieval. In Section 3, our algorithm is described. In Section 4, we will report on the results of experimental evaluations. We conclude the paper in Section 5 with some remarks on future work.

2 Previous Work

Learning based approach to similarity retrieval can be classified into on-line learning and off-line learning. The on-line learning approach tries to learn human intentions interactively, e.g., through iterative relevance feedback or by interactive grouping of examples. An advantage of this approach is its capability to adapt to personal preference or even to changes in personal preference over time or occasion. The off-line learning approach learns from a prescribed training database prior to actual retrieval. The learning may be unsupervised to learn the structure of subspace on which the measured features exist. Or, the learning may be supervised, e.g., by using a pre-categorized database.

Relatively small number of work exploiting learning has so far been published for shape-based 3D model retrieval. Interactive relevance feedback, a form of on-line interactive learning, has been explored by several re-searchers for 3D model retrieval [8, 1, 15, 16]. Elad et al. is among the first to apply *Support Vector Machines (SVM)* learning in an on-line learning setting to improve 3D model retrieval [8]. Leifman et al. [15] performed *Kernel Principal Component Analysis (Kernel PCA)* [10] for an unsupervised learning of a feature subspace before applying a relevance feedback technique that employs *Biased Discriminant Analysis* (BDA) or *Linear Discriminant Analysis* (LDA) on the learned subspace. Novotni et al. [16] compared several learning methods, SVM, BDA, and *Kernel-BDA*, for their retrieval performance in a relevance feedback setting. Unlike relevance feedback, unsupervised off-line learning has seen very little attention in 3D model retrieval. The Kernel-PCA employed by Leifman et al. [15] is an example. The purity proposed by Bustos et al. [5] can also be considered as a weak form of unsupervised off-line learning. Purity is an estimate of the performance of a shape descriptor determined by using a pre-classified training database. Bustos used the purity to weight distance obtained from multiple shape descriptors.

Classical methods for unsupervised learning of sub-space includes Principal Component Analysis (PCA) and Multi-Dimensional Scaling (MDS), both of which are quite effective if the feature points lie on or near a linear sub-space of the input space. However, if the subspace is non-linear, these methods do not work well. Many non-linear methods have been proposed for unsupervised learning of subspace; *Self-Organizing Map* (SOM) and Kernel-PCA are some of the well-known examples [10]. Recently, a class of geometrically inspired non-linear methods, called "manifold learning" has been proposed for learning the m-manifold of measured feature vectors.

Some of the examples of non-linear manifold learning algorithms are *Isomap* [25], *Locally Linear Embedding (LLE)* [21], *Laplacian Eigenmaps (LE)* [3], and *Local Tangent Space Alignment (LTSA)* [29].

Manifold learning algorithms aim at preserving their own metric for spatial distortion. The LLE, LE, and LTSA are classified as a "local" approach, which tries to preserve local geometry of the feature space in the learned manifold. These methods might not preserve global geometric shape of the original feature space in the lower dimensional embedding. However, they tend to preserve local metric structure better than a "global" approach such as the *Isometric feature mapping (Isomap)* [25]. "Global" approaches, such as Isomap tries to preserve metric at both global and local spatial scales. In doing so, however, Isomap may incur more local distortions. Also,

Isomap could only be applied to flat manifold, e.g., a cylinder, embedded in a higher-dimensional space.

For our purpose, which is to rank 3D shape features based on their similarity, we expect the locality preserving nature of the LLE, the LE, or the LTSA is preferable to global approaches. What we want are good matches in the top k retrievals, whose features must be positioned close to the feature of the query on the manifold. A property (drawback) of the LE, the LLE, and the Isomap is that the mapping they produce is defined only at the feature vectors in the training set. To query a 3D model outside of the training set, however, its feature vector must have an image on the manifold. In a 2D image retrieval setting, He et al [12] solved this problem by using *Radial Basis Function* (RBF) network [10] for a continuous approximation of the manifold.

3   The Method

The method employed in this paper is essentially that of Xhaofei He's approach for 2D image retrieval [12] with some modifications. The method first learns, unsupervised, the subspace spanned by the 3D shape features computed from the models in the training database. The subspace is then used for dimension reduction of the features in the database, to be used for distance computation at the retrieval step. (See Fig. 1.) As mentioned before, we compared the total of six dimension reduction algorithms based on subspace, or manifold learning, linear and non-linear, for their effectiveness. In case of the LE, LLE, and the Isomap, the manifolds learned by using these methods are defined only at the input samples. As we need the manifold defined at an out-of-sample (i.e., out-of-training-set) query models, the learned manifold is approximated continuously and smoothly by using RBF network [10] as in [12].

The following explains the steps the method uses for 3D model retrieval;

Learning

(1) **Extract feature:** Extract n-dimensional feature vectors from the K models in the training database (i.e., corpus).
(2) **Select training samples:** To reduce computational costs, sub-sample, if necessary, the training set down to L ($L \leq K$) feature vectors.
(3) **Learn the manifold:** Perform unsupervised learning of the m-manifold ($m \leq n$) from the n-dimensional training samples by using a manifold learning algorithm. Certain learning algorithms, e.g., LE and LLE, produce a manifold defined only at the set of training samples. In such a case, to handle queries outside of the training set, continuously approximate the manifold by using RBF network [6].

Database Pre-Processing

(1) **Extract feature:** Extract an n-dimensional feature vector from all the models in the database to be retrieved.
(2) **Reduce dimension of features of the database models:** Project features of all the models in the database onto the m-manifold (or its approximation), and store the resulting m-dimensional feature together with the corresponding 3D models.

The Retrieval Phase

(1) **Extract feature:** Extract an n-dimensional feature vector from the query model.
(2) **Reduce dimension:** Project the n-dimensional vector of the query's feature onto the (approximated) m-manifold to obtain a dimension reduced feature of the query.
(3) **Compute distances on the manifold:** Compute distances from the query model to all the models in the database using the dimension reduced features.
(4) **Retrieve top p matches:** Retrieve the models in the database having the p-smallest distances from the query model, and present the result to the user.

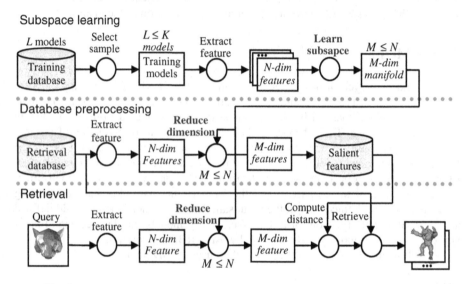

Fig. 1. An unsupervised learning approach to database-adaptive 3D model retrieval

We used the following five dimension reduction algorithms, all of which are based on unsupervised learning; (1) *PCA*, (2) *LE* [3], (3) *LPP* [11], (4) *LLE* [21], (5) *Isomap* [25], and (5) *KPCA* [10]. The PCA and LPP learn linear subspaces, while the others learn globally non-linear subspaces. The LLE, LE, and Isomap are sometimes called *graph-based algorithms*, for their computation starts with the construction of a graph that connects feature points in the input m-dimensional space. The LLE and LE are local methods that try to preserve local distance. The *Isomap* is a global method, which tries to preserve global distance as well. While LLE and LE produces a sparse connectivity graph, Isomap produces a dense one. The Isomap thus incur a higher computational cost than the others.

Fig. 2 and Fig. 3 show examples of dimension reduction using the LE, LLE, and Isomap. Data points are synthetic 3D points sampled on 2D surfaces embedded in 3D space. Points have colours to depict the embeddings that resulted. In Figure 2, the PCA failed to dissolve four classes in the subspace. All three manifold learning methods, LE, LLE, and Isomap, mapped the data points so that the four colours do not overlap. Globally, the Isomap appears to produce the best result without distortion, albeit an increased computational cost. However, local distance metric of the Isomap may have suffered compared to the other two, in order to satisfy global geometric constraints. In Figure 3, the original data points are distributed on a non-manifold surface that has no "correct" 2D embedding. As expected, all three methods failed to represent one of the colours (brown) properly in their 2D embeddings. Representation of the remaining three colours appears about the same among the three methods. The efficacies of these methods applied to higher dimensional data are not obvious from these simple, low-dimensional examples.

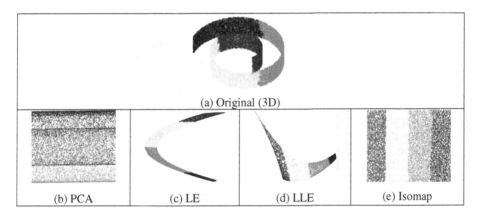

Fig. 2. A toy example for dimension reduction from a 2D manifold "Swiss roll" embedded in 3D space. The LE, LLE, and the Isomap successfully found a 2D manifold. The PCA failed, whose result shows points from different parts of the "Swiss roll" manifold overlapped.

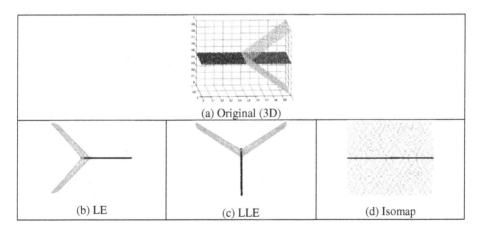

Fig. 3. Another toy example for dimension reduction from a non-manifold surface embedded in 3D space. Finding a flat 2D manifold may be quite difficult or impossible in such a case.

We paired these five dimension reduction algorithms with the five features, the EDEDT [27], RSH [27], SH [14], AAD [19], and SPRH [28]. We also applied the multiresolution shape feature extraction approach by Ohbuchi et al [18] on these shape features. All in all, we experimented with 10 different shape features, which are, five single-resolution (SR) features and five multi-resolution (MR) features. The multiresolution shape comparison method [18] will be explained in the next section.

3.1 Multiresolution Shape Comparison Method

A better shape comparison may be possible if shapes are compared at multiple scales. For example, for some queries, trees should be compared with each other by their overall shape, not by the shapes of their leaves or branches. Ohbuchi et al proposed an approach [18] for 3D shape similarity comparison that uses a mathematical morphology-like multiresolution (MR) representation (See Fig. 4). The approach first creates a set of 3D MR shape models by using 3D alpha shapes algorithm. The L alpha values for an L-level MR representation is computed from the diameter of the model. Once the MR set of 3D models is obtained, appropriate (single resolution) shape feature is extracted at each resolution level for an L-level MR feature.

Dimension reduction may be applied to an MR set of features in several different ways, e.g., independently at each resolution level, or to a big feature vector created by concatenating feature vectors from all the resolution levels. In the experiment reported in this paper, a dimension reduction method is applied separately at each resolution level. That is, if the MR representation has L resolution levels, L unsupervised learning and then L dimension reductions are performed independently at each level. To compare a pair of 3D models, each having a set of L-level MR features, a distance

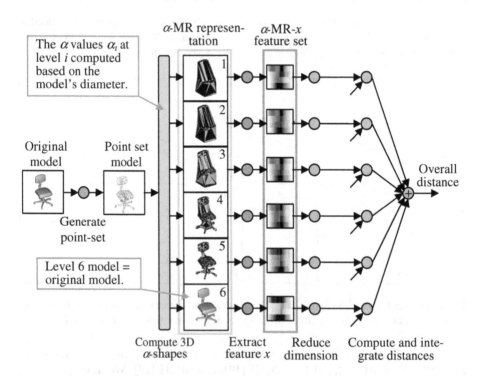

Fig. 4. Multiresolution shape comparison using morphological hierarchy

is calculated at each of the L levels of the MR representation. The L distance values are then combined into an overall distance among the pair of models by using a fixed-weight linear combination of distances. In the experiments described in this paper, all the weights are fixed at 1.0.

4   Experiments and Results

We conducted experiments (1) to evaluate the effectiveness of the six dimension reduction methods, and (2) to find the best performing pair of the feature and the dimension reduction method.

The experiments use 3D model databases for two purposes; (1) to train dimension reduction algorithms, and (2) to be queried, e.g., for performance evaluation. To train learning-based dimension reduction algorithms, we used the union of the training set of the *Princeton Shape Benchmark* (PSB) database [22] containing 907 models and the *National Taiwan University 3D Model Database* (NTU) ver. 1.0 containing 10,911 models [17]. The NTU database does not have any labels. The labels in the PSB training set are simply ignored. By using *Niederreiter* sequence, we sub-sampled the union (12,775 models) down to 4,000, 5,000, and 10,000 models to make the learning tractable. We used the SHREC 2006 benchmark [26] protocol as well as its set of tools for computing performance indices for the experiments. Thus, the database to be queried is the union of the PSB training set and the PSB test set as specified in the SHREC 2006. The 30 queries are out-of-database models. While the SHREC 2006 computes six different performance figures, we show only a subset of them in the following.

We computed five shape features using our own code and executables available on the Internet by the original authors of the methods [14, 19, 27]. Codes are also available on the Internet for some of the learning-based dimension reduction algorithms, such as LE, LLE, and Isomap. We wrote our own set of codes in C++ and *MatLab* for retrieval and a part of performance evaluation.

Table 1. Features and their parameters for the learning-based dimension reduction

Learning algorithms	feature	Original feature dimension n	Reduced feature dimension m	Neighborhood size k (%)	RBF kernel size σ
LE	AAD	256	220	0.30	0.6
	SPRH	625	500	1.00	1.2
	RSH	130	90	0.55	5.5
	EDEDT	544	200	0.75	8.0
	SH	544	200	0.40	9.0
LLE	AAD	256	220	2.00	0.3
	SPRH	625	400	2.00	0.9
	RSH	130	90	1.00	5.5
	EDEDT	544	200	0.67	8.0
	SH	544	300	0.67	9.0
Isomap	AAD	256	60	1.30	0.6
	RSH	130	90	1.30	5.5

Some of the learning-based dimension reduction algorithms have parameters, e.g., number of output dimensions m, neighborhoods size k for manifold reconstruction, and spreads of RBF kernels σ for the RBF-network approximation. We chose, through experiments, the numbers listed in Table 1 for the experiments below.

4.1 Effectiveness of Various Learning-Based Dimension Reduction Methods

We first compare the effectiveness of the six learning-based dimension reduction algorithms. Due to space limitation, we show the results for two features only, the AAD (Fig. 5) and the RSH (Fig. 6). Both single-resolution (SR) and multi-resolution (MR) versions of the features are shown in the graphs. For the PCA, we employed the manifold dimensions that resulted in the contribution of 99%, which are listed in Table 2.

Several observations can be made. First, effectiveness of learning methods clearly depends on the feature. The AAD and the RSH behaved differently when dimension reduction methods are applied. For example, LLE method improved the performance of AAD by 4% for the SR case and 6% for the MR case. However, for the RSH, dimension reduction using LLE actually lowered the performance score, while KPCA produced small performance gain. Second, with or without dimension reduction, multiresolution shape features are better than single resolution shape features. Also, learning based dimension reduction methods seem to work better for multi-resolution features. For example, in the case of the RSH, the performance often drops after dimension

Table 2. Dimensions N of the manifold that resulted in 99% contribution for PCA

Features	Single resolution	Multi-resolution
AAD	62~58	168~151
RSH	79~78	314~311

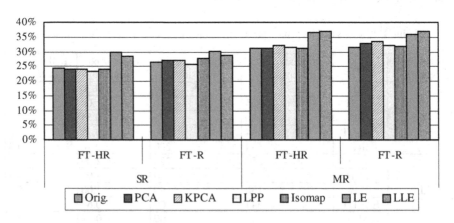

Fig. 5. Dimension reduction methods and retrieval performance for the SR-AAD feature

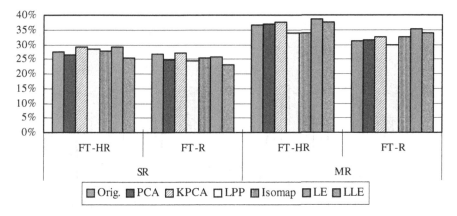

Fig. 6. Dimension reduction methods and retrieval performance for the SR-RSH feature

reduction in case of the single resolution features. However, for the multiresolution features, the performance improves after dimension reduction using the LLE and LE, non-linear, local dimension reduction methods.

Overall, the LE and the LLE, which are local, non-linear dimension reduction methods, produced better performance than the other dimension reduction methods. This tendency is more apparent for the multiresolution cases. Global non-linear methods such as Isomap, and global linear methods such as PCA and LPP did not perform well.

4.2 Effectiveness of the LE and LLE Methods on Five Shape Features

In this section, we compare the five shape features processed by using two of the most successful dimension reduction methods, the LE and the LLE. The results are shown in Fig. 7 for the single resolution features and in Fig. 8 for the multi-resolution features.

Gain in retrieval performance depends on the shape feature. For the single resolution cases, all but one feature gained performance by applying dimension reduction using the LE or LLE method. An exception is the RSH feature, in which the dimension reduction produced small degradation in performance. For the multiresolution cases, all the features including the RSH gained performance after dimension reduction using the manifold estimated by using LE or LLE. There appears to be a synergistic relationship between the LE (or LLE) and the multiresolution shape comparison approach [18].

Among the features, before the dimension reduction, and for SR features, the SH and the EDEDT performed the best. Comparing among the MR features without dimension reduction, the RSH and the SPRH almost caught up with the EDEDT and the SH in retrieval performance. After the dimension reduction, the MR version of the SPRH somehow outperformed the rest of the features. The reason is unclear, but it is possible that structure of the subspace produced by the SPRH feature was easier to estimate using the LE or the LLE than those produced by the EDEDT and SH.

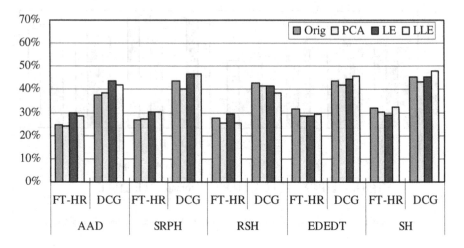

Fig. 7. Retrieval performances in FT-HR [%] of various single-resolution (SR) features after dimension reduction using LE and LLE

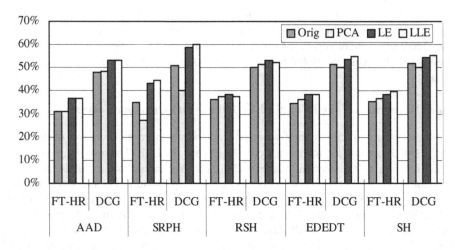

Fig. 8. Retrieval performances in FT-HR [%] of various multi-resolution (MR) features after dimension reduction using LE and LLE

4.3 Number of Training Samples and Retrieval Performance

In our previous paper [20], we used LE to estimate the manifold spanned by AAD and SPRH features having the number of samples up to 5,000 samples. The experiment showed that the unsupervised learning of the manifold for dimension reduction becomes effective if the number of training samples exceeded about 1,500 samples. The performance kept increasing up to 5,000 samples, which was at the time the maximum number of sample we were able to process using the LE running on the *MatLab*.

Table 3. Performance of the EDEDT and SPRH features trained by using 5,000 and 10,000 training samples

Learning methods	SR/MR	Learned models	AP-HR	FT-HR [%]	DAR	NCG @25	NDCG @25
EDEDT							
-	SR	-	0.3250	31.46	0.4027	0.3862	0.4377
	MR	-	0.3724	34.68	0.4604	0.4692	0.5135
PCA	SR	5,000	0.3030	28.00	0.3733	0.3749	0.4167
		10,000	0.3049	28.55	0.3755	0.3739	0.4198
	MR	5,000	0.3697	36.11	0.4515	0.461	0.5005
		10,000	0.3707	35.64	0.4529	0.4627	0.5022
LE	SR	5,000	0.2949	28.10	0.3722	0.3832	0.4273
		10,000	0.3004	28.42	0.3817	0.3948	0.4437
	MR	5,000	0.3817	38.55	0.4768	0.4955	0.535
		10,000	0.3785	37.28	0.4763	0.5003	0.5363
LLE	SR	5,000	0.3168	29.54	0.3891	0.4083	0.4573
		10,000	0.3088	29.14	0.3877	0.3816	0.4359
	MR	5,000	0.3988	38.49	0.4861	0.5043	0.5442
		10,000	0.3978	37.57	0.4836	0.5098	0.5469
SPRH							
no	SR	-	0.2886	26.68	0.3990	0.3920	0.4384
no	MR	-	0.3761	34.93	0.4631	0.4519	0.5101
PCA	SR	5,000	0.2726	27.20	0.3722	0.3560	0.4035
		10,000	0.2726	26.61	0.3718	0.3560	0.4037
	MR	5,000	0.2726	27.20	0.3722	0.3560	0.4035
		10,000	0.2726	26.61	0.3718	0.3560	0.4037
LE	SR	5,000	0.2958	28.89	0.3819	0.4131	0.4423
		10,000	0.3234	30.27	0.4116	0.4275	0.4647
	MR	5,000	0.4490	43.29	0.5177	0.5377	0.5759
		10,000	0.4586	42.24	0.5250	0.5421	0.5867
LLE	SR	5,000	0.2810	29.64	0.3768	0.3889	0.4295
		10,000	0.3097	30.32	0.4047	0.4294	0.4658
	MR	5,000	0.4614	44.46	0.5341	0.5604	0.5966
		10,000	0.4747	44.44	0.5382	0.5584	0.6013
SHREC 2006 top 2 results (excerpts).							
Makadia (run 2)			0.4869	44.77	0.5499	0.5498	0.5906
Daras (run 1)			0.4475	42.75	0.5242	0.5246	0.5791
Other methods							
LFD [7]			0.4014	38.48	0.4867	0.4889	0.5426
Hybrid [27]			0.4499	44.13	0.5136	0.5032	0.5626

AP-HR: Mean Average Precision (Highly Relevant)
FT-HR: Mean First Tier (Highly Relevant)
DAR: Mean Dynamic Average Recall
NCG @25: Mean Normalized Cumulated Gain @25
NDCG @25: Mean Normlized Discounted Cumulated Gain @25

Here we compare the performance of the features processed using LE and LLE that are trained by using 5,000 as well as 10,000 training samples. We used the *MatLab*

2006b having 64bit address space for the experiments below using 10,000 training samples.

Table 3 shows the results of a pair of features processed by using LE and LLE dimension reduction methods and 5,000 as well as 10,000 training samples. Due to space limitations, only the results for the EDEDT and the SPRH features could be included. In case of the PCA, the number of training sample has had essentially no effect. In cases of the LE and LLE applied to the SPRH feature, the increase in the number of training samples from 5,000 to 10,000 increased the retrieval performance. In the case of the EDEDT feature, however, the increase in the number of training samples from 5,000 to 10,000 often resulted in a small but consistent performance loss.

Table 3 also shows the performance of the 1st and 2nd finishers for the SHREC 2006 [26]. The best performing of our methods is the multiresolution SPRH trained by using LLE and 10,000 samples. It performed on a par with the 1st finisher in the SHREC 2006, and outperformed other powerful methods such as LFD [7] and Hybrid [27]. (We have conducted the experiments that produced SHREC 2006 based performance figures for the LFD and the Hybrid (HBD) features.)

Note that, in the table (and also in Fig. 5 and Fig. 6.) the performance of the SPRH feature is the same for its SR and MR versions. This is not an editorial error, but because the trained MR version actually ended up using only the highest resolution level (Level 6). At all the other levels, i.e., from Level 1 to Level 5, the PCA subspace collapsed due to numerical instability. Subspace learning failures also happened when we tried to use LE or LLE to learn subspace of the Hybrid (HBD) [27], Depth-buffer (DB) [27], and Silhouette features (SHL) [27]. While the exact cause is not known, we suspect that the pose normalization, i.e., normalization of orientation, position, and size, of 3D models employed in all these three features may be related. Imperfect pose normalization, especially in terms of orientation, may have created feature distribution that is quite difficult to learn.

5   Conclusion and Future Work

Effective retrieval of 3D models based on their shape similarity requires a salient and compact shape feature as well as a good distance measure. In our previous paper, we adopted, for shape-based 3D model retrieval, the approach originally proposed by He et al [12] for 2D image retrieval. The idea is to learn, unsupervised, the subspace, or manifold of features spanned by the set of models in the database, and to use the manifold for dimension reduction. A distance computed using the dimension reduced features is database-adaptive, improving the retrieval performance. Our previous paper showed that the approach using Laplacian Eigenmaps (LE) [3] for manifold learning improved 3D model retrieval performance. However, the feature we tried was limited to two, and the dimension reduction algorithm was limited to the LE only.

In this paper, we explored the approach more comprehensively by comparing six learning-based dimension reduction methods, namely, Principal Component Analysis (PCA), Kernel-PCA (KPCA), Locality Preserving Projections (LPP), Locally Linear Embedding (LLE), Isometric feature mapping (Isomap), and the Laplacian Eigenmaps (LE). We applied these six dimension reduction methods to five shape features to find a best performing pair. The experimental evaluation showed that two local, non-linear methods, the LE and LLE, produced significant gains in retrieval performance for many of the shape features we tested. A learning based dimension reduction appears to be especially effective if it is combined with the multiresolution shape comparison approach we have previously proposed [19]. The linear, global methods such as PCA and LPP did not significantly improve retrieval performance.

Several avenues of future exploration exist. We would like to see if the off-line unsupervised learning approach used in this paper could be combined effectively with an on-line supervised learning approach based on relevance feedback, or with a supervised learning of pre-defined categories. Such a combination would exploit either short-term, local knowledge or long-term, universal knowledge for more effective shape-based 3D model retrieval. We would also like to explore the ways to effectively combine heterogeneous features by using, again, a learning-based approach. Such a combination would produce a very powerful shape comparison and retrieval method.

Acknowledgements

The authors would like to thank those who created benchmark databases, those who made available codes for their shape features, and those who made available codes for various learning algorithms. This research has been funded in parts by the Ministry of Education, Culture, Sports, Sciences, and Technology of Japan (No. 17500066 and No. 18300068).

References

1. Atmosukarto, I., Leow, W.K., Huang, Z.: Feature Combination and Relevance Feedback for 3D Model Retrieval. In: Proc. MMM 2005, pp. 334–339 (2005)
2. Baeza-Yates, R., Ribiero-Neto, B.: Modern information retrieval. Addison-Wesley, Reading (1999)
3. Belkin, M., Niyogi, P.: Laplacian eigenmaps for dimensionality reduction and data representation. Neural Computation 15, 1373–1396 (2003)
4. Bratley, P., Fox, B.L., Niederreiter, H.: Algorithm 738: Programs to Generate Niederreiter's Low-discrepancy Sequences. ACM TOMS Algorithm 738
5. Bustos, B., Keim, D., Saupe, D., Schreck, T., Vranić, D.: Automatic Selection and Combination of Descriptors for Effective 3D Similarity Search. In: Proc. IEEE MCBAR 2004, pp. 514–521 (2004)
6. Chen, S., Cowan, C.F.N., Grant, P.M.: Orthogonal Least Squares Learning Algorithm for Radial Basis Function Networks. IEEE Trans. on Neural Networks 2(2), 302–309 (1991)
7. Chen, D.-Y., Tian, X.-P., Shen, Y.-T., Ouhyoung, M.: On Visual Similarity Based 3D Model Retrieval. Computer Graphics Forum 22(3), 223–232 (2003)
8. Elad, M., Tal, A., Ar, S.: Content based retrieval of vrml objects – an iterative and interactive approach. In: Proc. EG Multimedia, vol. 39, pp. 97–108 (2001)
9. Funkhouser, T., Min, P., Kazhdan, M., Chen, J., Halderman, A., Dobkin, D., Jacobs, D.: A Search Engine for 3D Models. ACM TOG 22(1), 83–105 (2003)
10. Haykin, S.: Neural network a comprehensive foundation, 2nd edn. Prentice-Hall, Englewood Cliffs (1999)

11. He, X., Niyogi, P.: Locality Preserving Projections. In: Advances in Neural Information Processing Systems, Vancouver, Canada, vol. 16 (2003), http://people.cs.uchicago.edu/~xiaofei/LPP.html

12. He, X., Ma, W.-Y., Zhang, H.-J.: Learning an Image Manifold for Retrieval. In: Proc. ACM Multimedia 2004, pp. 17–23 (2004)

13. Iyer, M., Jayanti, S., Lou, K., Kalyanaraman, Y., Ramani, K.: Three Dimensional Shape Searching: State-of-the-art Review and Future Trends. Computer Aided Design 5(15), 509–530 (2005)

14. Kazhdan, M., Funkhouser, T., Rusinkiewicz, S.: Rotation Invariant Spherical Harmonics Representation of 3D Shape Descriptors. In: Proc. Symposium of Geometry Processing 2003, pp. 167–175 (2003), http://www.cs.jhu.edu/~misha/

15. Leifman, G., Meir, R., Tal, A.: Semantic-oriented 3d shape retrieval using relevance feedback. The Visual Computer (Pacific Graphics) 21(8-10), 865–875 (2005)

16. Novotni, M., Park, G.-J., Wessel, R., Klein R.: Evaluation of Kernel Based Methods for Relevance Feedback in 3D Shape Retrieval. In: Proc. The Fourth International Workshop on Content-Based Multimedia Indexing (CBMI 2005) (2005)

17. NTU 3D Model Database ver.1, http://3d.csie.ntu.edu.tw/

18. Ohbuchi, R., Takei, T.: Shape-Similarity Comparison of 3D Shapes Using Alpha Shapes. In: Proc. Pacific Graphics 2003, pp. 293–302 (2003)

19. Ohbuchi, R., Minamitani, T., Takei, T.: Shape-similarity search of 3D models by using enhanced shape functions. IJCAT 23(3/4/5), 70–85 (2005)

20. Ohbuchi, R., Kobayashi, J.: Unsupervised Learning from a Corpus for Shape-Based 3D Model Retrieval. In: Proc. ACM MIR 2006, pp. 163–172 (2006)

21. Roweis, S.T., Saul, L.K.: Nonlinear Dimensionality Reduction by Locally Linear Embedding. Science 290(5500), 2323–2326 (2000)

22. Shilane, P., Min, P., Kazhdan, M., Funkhouser, T.: The Princeton Shape Benchmark. In: Proc. SMI 2004, pp. 167–178 (2004), http://shape.cs.princeton.edu/search.html

23. Statistical Pattern Recognition Toolbox for Matlab, http://cmp.felk.cvut.cz/cmp/software/stprtool/index.html

24. Tangelder, J., Veltkamp, R.C.: A Survey of Content Based 3D Shape Retrieval Methods. In: Proc. SMI 2004, pp. 145–156 (2004)

25. Tanenbaum, J.B., de Silva, V., Langford, J.C.: A Global Geometric Framework for Nonlinear Dimensionality Reduction. Science 290(5500), 2319–2323 (2000)

26. Veltkamp, R.C., Ruijsenaars, R., Spagnuolo, M., Van Zwol, R., ter Haar, F.: SHREC, 3D Shape Retrieval Contest, Utrecht University Dept. Information and Computing Sciences. Technical Report UU-CS-2006-030 (2006), http://give-lab.cs.uu.nl/shrec/shrec2006/index.html, ISSN: 0924-3275

27. Vranić, D.V.: 3D Model Retrieval, Ph.D. Thesis, University of Leipzig (2004), http://merkur01.inf.uni-konstanz.de/CCCC/

28. Wahl, E., Hillenbrand, U., Hirzinger, G.: Surflet-Pair-Relation Histograms: A Statistical 3D-Shape Representation for Rapid Classification. In: Proc. 3DIM 2003, pp. 474–481 (2003)

29. Zhang, Z., Zha, H.: Principal manifolds and nonlinear dimension reduction via local tangent space alignment. SIAM Journal of Scientific Computing 26(1), 313–338 (2004)

Smart Photo Sticking

Sebastiano Battiato[1], Gianluigi Ciocca[2], Francesca Gasparini[2],
Giovanni Puglisi[1], and Raimondo Schettini[2]

[1] Dipartimento di Matematica ed Informatica
Università di Catania
viale A. Doria 6, 95125 Catania, Italy
[2] DISCo, Dipartimento di Informatica Sistemistica e Comunicazione
Università degli Studi di Milano-Bicocca,
via Bicocca degli Arcimboldi 8, 20126 Milano, Italy
{battiato, puglisi}@dmi.unict.it,
{ciocca, gasparini, schettini}@disco.unimib.it

Abstract. Smart photo sticking is a novel strategy to automatically arrange a collection of photos in a pleasant collage. The proposed approach improves previous solutions both considering a self-adaptive image cropping algorithm, exploiting visual and semantic information, and introducing an optimization process based on a genetic algorithm. Preliminary results confirm the effectiveness of the proposed strategy on a heterogeneous collection of non professional photos.

Keywords: Image summarization, saliency region, genetic algorithm.

1 Introduction

Images are playing a more and more important role in sharing, expressing and exchanging information in our daily lives. Now we all can easily capture and share personal photos anywhere and anytime.

Generating a collage that summarizes a group of pictures could be trivial if realized manually 1, but developing an automatic tool is intrinsically difficult. A simple technique for image arrangement is page layout 2 that tries to cover the canvas area with no overlap without considering (or distinguishing) the relevant regions of each input image. On the other hand most previous image summarization works are mainly based on content based techniques (3, 4) to provide a high-level description of a set of images. The CeWe colourbook album software 5, does a lot of cropping, salience recognition and collaging; it detects snapshots which are out of focus and also those which are over-exposed, under-exposed or double, though on photo album and not on poster. A different approach for image summarization is presented in (9, 10) where the collage is assembled joining subsets of each picture together by using ad-hoc techniques (i.e. Poisson Editing, etc.) to hide the joins between input images. An other interesting way of viewing photos on a computer is Microsoft Photosynth 11; it takes a large collection of partially overlapping photos of a place or an object, analyzes them for similarities, and then displays them in a three-dimensional space. Some further approaches (6,7,8) have been recently proposed by obtaining impres-

N. Boujemaa, M. Detyniecki, and A. Nürnberger (Eds.): AMR 2007, LNCS 4918, pp. 211–223, 2008.

sive results just considering ad-hoc heuristics for both image analysis and layout positioning.

One of the most successful attempt to manage this kind of situation is Picture Collage described in 12, where the authors propose a system to arrange groups of pictures inside a canvas with possible overlay, minimizing the occlusion of salient regions of each involved image. In 12 the image arrangement is formulated as a Maximum a Posterior (MAP) problem such that the output picture collage shows as many visible salient regions (without being overlaid by others) from all images as possible. Moreover, a classic Markov chain Monte Carlo (MCMC) method is designed for the optimization.

We propose two different improvements with respect to the work presented in 12. First of all, the detection of the saliency region has been performed by applying a novel self-adaptive image cropping algorithm which exploits both semantic and visual information. Semantic information relates to the automatically assigned image categories (landscape, close-ups, ...) and to the detection of face and skin regions, while visual information is obtained by a visual attention model 13 that has been developed in order to find a salient image region to be cropped, and visualized on small displays. In this work, the cropping area is used to drive the photo sticking.

The second improvement is related to the different optimization criterion used. We have implemented a genetic algorithm able to capture the different constraints derived directly from the typical good layout that a collage of photos must satisfy. Preliminary results confirm that the fitness we have designed is able to reach a good solution in almost all cases.

The paper is organized as follows. Next Section briefly summarizes the self-adaptive cropping system used to locate the saliency region inside each image. Section 3 is devoted to describing the main underlying ideas of the proposed genetic algorithm. Preliminary results are presented in the next Section while Section 5 closes the paper tracking directions for future works and research.

2 Self-Adaptive Image Cropping

As stated before, we use a self-adaptive image cropping algorithm to detect the relevant region within an image. This information is then fed to the algorithm responsible for the photo arrangement. Most of the approaches for adapting images only focused on compressing the whole image in order to reduce the data transmitted. Few other methods use an auto-cropping technique to reduce the size of the image transmitted 14, 15. These methods decompose the image into a set of spatial information elements (saliency regions) which are then displayed serially to help users' browse or search through the whole image. These methods are heavily based on a visual attention model technique that is used to identify the saliency regions to be cropped.

Figure 1 shows the flow diagram of the algorithm we have developed. The images are first classified into three broad classes, that is, "landscape", "close-up", and "other". The classification is based on the use of ensembles of decision trees, called decision forests. The trees of the forests are constructed according to CART (Classification and Regression Trees) methodology 16. The features used in this classification process are related to color, texture, edge and composition of the image 17, 18. Then, an ad-hoc cropping strategy is applied for each image class.

The detection of the relevant region depends on the image content. The three broad classes have been chosen so that they cover the main groups of images that we may find in any collection of photos. The classification of the images allows us to build a detection strategy specific for each image class. The effectiveness of the strategy is maximized by taking into account the properties of the image and focusing our attention to some objects in the image instead of others. A landscape image, for example, due to its lack of specific focus elements, is not processed at all: the image is regarded as being wholly relevant. A close up image, generally, shows only a single object or subject in the foreground, and thus, the relevant region should take into account only this, discarding any region that can be considered as background. In the case of an image belonging to the other class, we are concerned if whether it contains people or not: the cropping strategy should prioritize the selection of regions containing people.

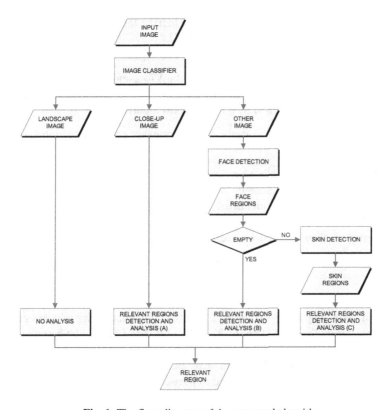

Fig. 1. The flow diagram of the proposed algorithm

Landscape images. In the case of landscape images, no cropping is performed. We adopt this strategy because landscape images usually do not present a specific subject to be focalized. Examples of landscape images are reported in Fig. 2.

Fig. 2. Examples of "Landscape" images

Close-up images. For close-up images here we define a new procedure which we called "Relevant regions detection and analysis (A)" in Fig. 1:

a. A saliency map is generated based on the Itti-Koch visual attention model 19. Visual attention facilitates the processing of the portion of the input associated with the relevant information, suppressing the remaining information.
b. The saliency map is automatically binarized in order to identify saliency regions. The regions with areas smaller than a threshold which are a function of the area of the larger region are discarded.
c. A single relevant region is obtained, considering the bounding box that includes all the saliency regions previously identified.
d. The image is then cropped with respect to this region.

Other images. A face detector inspired by the Viola and Jones one 20 is applied to distinguish between images with and without faces. The detector is composed of a chain of weak classifiers trained by the Ada-boost algorithm.

For images without faces we designed the "relevant region detection and analysis (B)" strategy:

a. Same as point a. of the close-up case.
b. Same as point b. of the close-up case.
c. The most salient region identified in point b. is now considered as the relevant region.
d. The image is then cropped with respect to this region.

For images with faces, we designed the "relevant region detection and analysis (C)" strategy:

a. Same as point a. of the close-up case.
b. A skin color map is also computed. For the skin detector we adopted an explicit skin cluster method based on the YCbCr color space, where the boundaries of the color skin cluster were chosen to offer high recall in pixel classification 21.
c. The saliency map, the skin color map and the face regions are then combined together to form a global map, used to locate the most relevant region.
d. The image is then cropped with respect to this region.

For both *close-up* and *other* images, the borders of the final cropped region are enlarged to include the relevant area better.

In Figures 3-5 examples of the final crop region for these different classes of images are reported.

Fig. 3. Relevant regions selected within some of the "close-up" images

Fig. 4. Relevant regions selected within some of the "Other" images. No faces are present or detected.

Fig. 5. Relevant regions selected within some of the "Other" images containing faces

3 Photo Arrangement

In order to obtain a good photo sticky the following properties should be considered 12:

- salience maximization, to show in the canvas as many important region as possible;
- blank space minimization, to use all the canvas without holes;
- salience ratio balance, to reach a stable ratio balance (percentage of visible salient region).

To satisfy these properties the problem can be formulated as an optimization problem but, due to its complexity (NP complete), only an advanced (smart) solution has to be designed. For this reason we have chosen a genetic algorithm: an optimization and search technique based on the principle of genetics and natural selection. An initial population, usually randomly selected, of possible solutions evolves toward a better solution. In each step some population elements are stochastically selected based on their fitness (the function to be optimized), and new elements are created through some techniques inspired by evolutionary biology (mutation, crossover). Genetic algorithms have found application in many fields 22: computer science, engineering, economics, chemistry, physics, etc.

Given N input images I_i $i=1, ..., N$ and the corresponding saliency maps s_i $i=1, ...,$ N the final goal is devoted to arrange such pictures in a canvas C. The canvas is rectangular (with the classic aspect ratio set to 4/3) and its size is set to that its area is about half of the total area of all input images. Each image I_i, in the picture collage, can be labelled as a triplets $\{c_i, o_i, l_i\}$ where c_i is the 2D spatial coordinate of the center, o_i is the orientation angle and l_i is the placement order of the image in canvas.

In order to properly encode salience maximization, blank space minimization and salience ratio balance, we have modelled the fitness function (to be minimized) as follows:

$$Fitness(\overline{A_{occ}}, \overline{B}, V) = e^{(\overline{A_{occ}} + \overline{B} + V)} \ .$$

(1)

where:

- $\overline{A_{occ}}$ is the normalized sum of occluded saliency regions defined as:

$$\overline{A_{occ}} = \frac{A_{occ}}{A_{max}} \ .$$

(2)

$$A_{occ} = A_{max} - A_{vis} \ .$$

(3)

$$A_{vis} = \sum_i s_i^{vis} \text{ where } s_i^{vis} \text{ is the visible part of the saliency region } s_i \ .$$

(4)

$$A_{max} = \sum_i s_i \ .$$

(5)

- $\overline{B}$ is the normalized sum of canvas uncovered regions defined as:

$$\overline{B} = \frac{Area(B)}{Area(R_c)} \ .$$

(6)

$$B = R_c - \bigcup_i R_i \ .$$

(7)

where R_i is the bounding rectangle of picture I_i and R_c is the canvas bounding rectangle

- V is the variance of saliency ratios:

$$V = \frac{1}{N} \sum_i (r_i - \bar{r})^2 \text{ where } r_i = \frac{s_i^{vis}}{s_i} \text{ and } \bar{r} \text{ is the } r_i \text{ mean value .} \tag{8}$$

Standard crossover and mutation operators cannot be used directly because each layer order is a permutation: an unique layer index must be assigned to each image. To simplify the problem we initially fix, a layer order $\{l_1, l_2, ..., l_n\}$ $l_i \neq l_j$ $i \neq j$, based on the following consideration:

- Let $ns_i = Area(I_i)$- s_i be the not saliency region of image I_i. Some saliency region occlusions can be avoided positioning the pictures with high ns_i values just below images with low ns values. The ns_i regions can occlude saliency regions and hence they slow function optimization.

The initial layer order is assigned by sorting the input images according to the ns_i values in descending order. In order to speed-up the overall process, the initial population is defined as follows:

- divide the canvas into N* rectangles (with N*>N);
- select N centers c_i* of rectangular blocks;
- sample c_i from a normal distribution with mean c_i* and variance 1/6 of rectangular width and height respectively;
- sample o_i (image orientation) from a normal distribution with zero mean and variance $\pi/27$.

Genetic optimization is realized by using standard approaches in the field. In particular we have used default crossover and mutation algorithms provided by Genetic Toolbox functions of MATLAB 7.

4 Experimental Results

In order to test our solution we have used some image databases obtained by typical consumer usage. In particular, we present preliminary results obtained by considering two different experiments involving 9 and 10 images respectively. The image resolution is about 5MPixel. In both experiments we set the population size to 20 and the generation number to 200.

Figure 6 reports the values of the fitness function with respect to the number of involved generation.

Figures 7 to 10 show the final output by showing also the overall results in terms of saliency region occlusion with respect to the considered layer ordering, canvas usage and image cropping. The final results are promising, in both cases the sum of visible saliency region is about 90% and the overall covered canvas regions are around 99%

of the total. Table 1 reports the final values of $\overline{A_{occ}}$, $\overline{B}$ and V after the optimization process. The timing performances of the system can generate picture collage in about 3 minutes; in this phase we are mainly interested in the effective convergence of the iterative process.

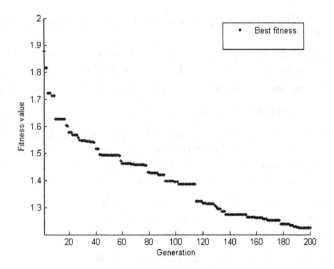

Fig. 6. *Test1* best fitness function

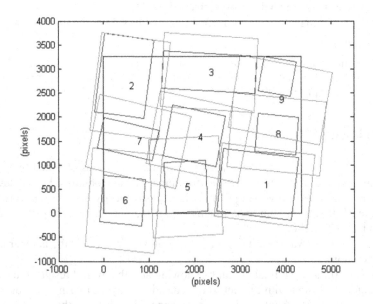

Fig. 7. *Test1* final output in terms of saliency regions *(red)*, image borders *(green)*, layer order and canvas *(blue)*

Fig. 8. *Test1* picture collage

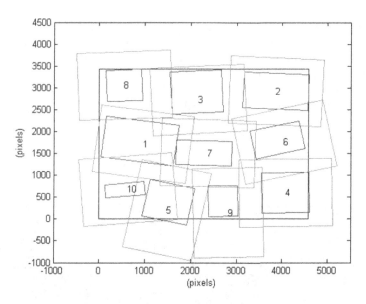

Fig. 9. *Test2* final output in terms of saliency regions *(red)*, image borders (green), layer order and canvas *(blue)*

Our approach works very well for collages of medium size (10-12 photos) finding good solutions quickly. However it lack of scalability in terms of execution time; especially for large collages, the number of needed generation could be very high.

Fig. 10. *Test2* picture collage

Figure 11 shows a comparison between a photo collage which uses the saliency regions detected by the auto cropping algorithm and a photo collage which does not. As can be seen, the disposition of the photos where the saliency regions are used, is more appealing since all the photos are clearly visible and the relevant information is retained in the collage. On the contrary, without the saliency regions, several photos are totally or partially hidden by others and subjects are cut out from the collage. Figure 12 shows a collage which includes images from the landscape class. Since images belonging to this class are considered wholly relevant, they are shown in the foreground forcing the disposition of the other images around them. In order to create a more appealing collage, we plan to introduce rules to cope with landscape images.

Fig. 11. Picture collage comparison, with (left) and without (right) saliency regions

Figure 13 shows a first result where we have forced landscape images to appear in the background instead of the foreground. The improvement is clearly visible.

Fig. 12. Picture collage containing images from the "landscape" class

Fig. 13. Picture collage containing images from the "landscape" class. A rule has been introduced to force these images to appear in the background.

Table 1. Final values of $\overline{A_{occ}}$, $\overline{B}$ and V for *test1* (9 pictures) and *test2* (10 pictures)

	$\overline{A_{occ}}$	$\overline{B}$	V
Test1(9 pictures)	0.1713	0.0081	0.0308
Test2(10 pictures)	0.0412	0.00001	0.0076

5 Conclusion and Future Works

In this paper we have presented a novel approach for photo sticking able to realize an effective image summarization of a set of pictures. Existing approaches require user assistance or change the relative appearance of each picture 9. The original work presented in 12 has been modified by making use of a self-adaptive image cropping algorithm, exploiting visual and semantic information together with an optimization process based on a genetic algorithm. Preliminary results confirm the ability of the proposed method to generate sub-optimal results. The evaluation is mainly based on saliency region occlusion, layer ordering, canvas usage and image cropping. Future works will be devoted to designing further optimization strategies to improve overall robustness also capable of speeding up the overall process. We also plan to introduce compositional rules aimed to cope with the landscape images. Furthermore, we will investigate a quantitative methodology to evaluate collage results by conducting some subjective tests.

References

1. Agarwala, A., Dontcheva, M., Agrawala, M., Drucker, S., Colburn, A., Curless, B., Salesin, D., Cohen, M.F.: Interactive digital photomontage. ACM Trans. Graph. 23(3), 294–302 (2004)
2. Atkins, C.B.: Adaptive photo collection page layout. In: ICIP, pp. 2897–2900 (2004)
3. Carson, C., Belongie, S., Greenspan, H., Malik, J.: Blobworld: Image segmentation using expectation-maximization and its application to image querying. IEEE Trans. Pattern Anal. Mach. Intell. 24(8), 1026–1038 (2002)
4. Fei-Fei, L., Fergus, R., Perona, P.: A bayesian approach to unsupervised one-shot learning of object categories. In: ICCV, pp. 1134–1141 (2003)
5. http://fotoinsight.co.uk/book/
6. Chen, J., Chu, W., Kuo, J., Weng, C., Wu, J.: Tiling Slideshow. In: Proceedings of ACM Multimedia Conference, pp. 25–34 (2006)
7. Diakopoulos, N., Essa, I.: Mediating photo collage authoring. In: Proceedings of the 18th Annual ACM Symposium on User interface Software and Technology (2005)
8. Girgensohn, A., Chiu, P.: Stained Glass Photo Collages. In: Proceedings of UIST 2004 Companion, October 24, 2004, pp. 13–14 (2004)
9. Rother, C., Kumar, S., Kolmogorov, V., Blake, A.: Digital tapestry. In: Proceedings of CVPR 2005 Computer Vision and Pattern Recognition, vol. 2005(1), pp. 589–596 (2005)
10. Rother, C., Bordeaux, L., Hamadi, Y., Blake, A.: AutoCollage. ACM Transactions on Graphics 25, 847–852 (2006)

11. Snavely, N., Seitz, S.M., Szeliski, R.: Photo Tourism: Exploring photo collections in 3D. ACM Transactions on Graphics 25(3) (August 2006)
12. Wang, J., Sun, J., Quan, L., Tang, X., Shum, H.Y.: Picture Collage. In: Proceedings of CVPR 2006 – Computer Vision and Pattern Recognition, pp. 347–354 (2006)
13. Ciocca, G., Cusano, C., Gasparini, F., Schettini, R.: Self- Adaptive Image Cropping for Small Displays. In: Proceedings of IEEE ICCE 2007 - International Conference on Consumer Electronics (2007)
14. Chen, L., Xie, X., Fan, X., Ma, W., Zhang, H.J., Zhou, H.Q.: A visual attention model for adapting images on small displays. Multimedia Systems 9, 353–364 (2003)
15. Suh, B., Ling, H., Bederson, B.B., Jacobs, D.W.: Automatic Thumbnail Cropping and its Effectiveness. In: Proc. UIST 2003, pp. 95–104 (2003)
16. Breiman, L., Friedman, J.H., Olshen, R.A., Stone, C.J.: Classification and Regression Trees. Wadsworth and Brooks/Cole (1984)
17. Schettini, R., Brambilla, C., Cusano, C., Ciocca, G.: Automatic classification of digital photographs based on decision forests. IJPRAI 18(5), 819–846 (2004)
18. De Ponti, M., Schettini, R., Brambilla, C., Valsasna, A., Ciocca, G.: Content-Based Digital-Image Classification Method. European Patent no. EP1102180 (2001)
19. Itti, L., Koch, C.: A model of saliency based visual attention of rapid scene analysis. IEEE Trans. on PAMI 20, 1254–1259 (1998)
20. Viola, P., Jones, M.J.: Robust real-time face detection. International Journal of Computer Vision 57, 137–154 (2004)
21. Gasparini, F., Corchs, S., Schettini, R.: Recall or precision oriented strategies for binary classification of skin pixels. Pattern Recognition (submitted, 2006)
22. Haupt, R.L., Haupt, S.E.: Practical Genetic Algorithms, 2nd edn. John Wiley & Sons, Hoboken, New Jersey (2004)

How to Use SIFT Vectors to Analyze an Image with Database Templates

Adrien Auclair[1], Laurent D. Cohen[2], and Nicole Vincent[1]

[1] CRIP5-SIP, University Paris-Descartes,
45 rue des Saint-Pères, 75006 Paris, France
{adrien.auclair,nicole.vincent}@math-info.univ-paris5.fr
[2] CEREMADE, University Paris-Dauphine,
Place du Maréchal De Lattre De Tassigny 75775 PARIS, France
cohen@ceremade.dauphine.fr

Abstract. During last years, local image descriptors have received much attention because of their efficiency for several computer vision tasks such as image retrieval, image comparison, features matching for 3D reconstruction... Recent surveys have shown that Scale Invariant Features Transform (SIFT) vectors are the most efficient for several criteria. In this article, we use these descriptors to analyze how a large input image can be decomposed by small template images contained in a database. Affine transformations from database images onto the input image are found as described in [16]. The large image is thus covered by small patches like a jigsaw puzzle. We introduce a filtering step to ensure that found images do not overlap themselves when warped on the input image. A typical new application is to retrieve which products are proposed on a supermarket shelf. This is achieved using only a large picture of the shelf and a database of all products available in the supermarket. Because the database can be large and the analysis should ideally be done in a few seconds, we compare the performances of two state of the art algorithms to search SIFT correspondences: Best-Bin-First algorithm on Kd-Tree and Locality Sensitive Hashing. We also introduce a modification in the LSH algorithm to adapt it to SIFT vectors.

1 Introduction

In this article, we are concerned about the problem of analyzing how a large input image can be described by small template images contained in a database. Our goal is to provide a working solution for this problem but we also want it to be as fast as possible. The large input image is expected to be covered by a set of small patches which are found in the database. Examples of images to analyze are shown on figures 2.(a) and 2.(b). A typical application is to analyze a picture of a supermarket shelf. The input is a large image of the shelf taken in the supermarket. The database contains images of all the available products. The output is a list of products contained in the image with their corresponding positions. Products in database and products on the supermarket shelf can be slightly different. For example, a price sticker or a discount sticker can be added.

N. Boujemaa, M. Detyniecki, and A. Nürnberger (Eds.): AMR 2007, LNCS 4918, pp. 224–236, 2008.

Or the product can be partly hidden (e.g., by the shelf itself, by a discount or any decorative item). For these reasons, local descriptors matching is a natural method for this problem.

During last years, Scale Invariant Features Transform (SIFT) features [16] have received much attention. It has been shown in a recent survey ([17]) that it leads to the best results compared to other local descriptors. Several minor modifications of the initial SIFT features have also been presented (PCA-SIFT [12], or Gloh-SIFT [17]), but the gain is not obvious in all experiments. Thus, we will only focus on the original SIFT descriptors in this article.

These SIFT features will be used to compute several affine transformations between products in database and the input image. An important remark is that some products in database can be very similar. For example, a brand icon will appear on a large number of images in database. Thus, if the input image contains a single product with this brand icon, all the database images having this icon will be found by affine matching. We will thus need a filtering step that will keep only a small subset among all found affine transformations. This filter will use the fact that found templates images cannot overlap themselves too much in the input image.

Because the database can be large and the analysis should ideally be done in a few seconds, we compare two state of the art optimization methods to search for SIFT correspondences. These algorithms are related to the problem of finding approximate nearest neighbors in high dimensional space. The first one is based on Kd-Tree: Best-Bin-First algorithm of [2]. The second one is using hash table: Locality Sensitive Hashing of [9]. We also introduce a modification in the LSH algorithm to adapt it to SIFT vectors.

Used Databases. Our researches were motivated by applying the described method to an actual private database. It contains 440 images of supermarket products. These images are compressed in JPEG. The image size approximately varies from 100x100 pixels to 500x500 pixels. Images of database lead to more than 270.000 descriptors, each one being in $\Re^{128}$. We call this database DB_{440}.

We also tested our algorithm on the publicly available Amsterdam Library of Object Images [8]. We picked the dataset where the illumination direction changes, using the gray-value images of size 384x288 pixels. Within this dataset, we used the 1000 pictures that were taken from light position number 4 and camera number 3. This database generates 170.000 local descriptors. Figure 1 shows some images of this database, noted ALOI.

Fig. 1. Four images from the ALOI database

In the following section, we first recall the SIFT construction algorithm and the classical method we used to robustly compute affine transformations from SIFT correspondences. Then, in section 3 we introduce a filtering step to keep only valid matchings. Eventually, in section 4 we compare two optimization methods and introduce a modification in LSH algorithm.

2   Using SIFT for Affine Matching

In this part, we introduce the first building blocks of our method: SIFT descriptors and robust affine matching. More details about these two steps can be found in [16].

2.1   SIFT Descriptors

Like any local descriptor algorithm, it can be split in two distinct steps. The first one is to detect points of interest where to compute the local descriptors. The second one is to actually compute these local descriptors. The first stage is achieved by finding scale-space extrema in the difference of Gaussian pyramid. A point is said extremum if it is below or above its 8 neighbors at same scale and the 9 neighbors at up and down scales. Thus, a point of interest is found at a given scale. Its major orientation is computed as the major direction of a patch of pixels around its position. Then, the descriptor vector is computed at the feature scale. It is a vector of 16 histograms of gradient. Each histogram contains 8 bins, leading to a 128 dimensional descriptor.

Due to their construction, SIFT vectors are invariant by scale change and rotation. And experiences show that they are also robust to small viewpoint changes or illumination variations. This is particularly adapted to our problem as our images (both input and database images) are taken from a frontal point of view and templates from database can be rotated and scaled in the image to analyze.

2.2   Finding Affine Matchings

As a pre-process step, SIFT vectors are computed from the input image, and noted $SIFT_{IN}$. All the descriptors from the database images have also been extracted offline and are noted $SIFT_{DB}$. Features of the ith database image are noted $SIFT_{DB}^i$. The first step is to identify correspondences between $SIFT_{IN}$ and $SIFT_{DB}$.

Linear Search. Each feature from $SIFT_{IN}$ is compared to each feature from $SIFT_{DB}$ and only correspondences whose L^2 distance is lower than a threshold ϵ are kept. For a query feature q of $SIFT_{IN}$, this can be seen as finding the $\epsilon - neighborhood$ of q in $SIFT_{DB}$. Once we have obtained for each descriptor of $SIFT_{IN}$ a list of its neighbors in $SIFT_{DB}$, these correspondences are fitted to affine transformations. The goal of this fitting step is twofold. First, it is needed to remove outliers from the correspondences. Then, it gives the mapping of database images onto the input image.

Affine Fitting. In our experiments, database images and input images are taken from a frontal point of view. The affine model is thus well adapted. An affine matrix transforms a point $p1 = (x_1, y_1)$ in the first image, to a point p_2 in the second image:

$$p_2 = \begin{bmatrix} a & b & t_x \\ c & d & t_y \end{bmatrix} \cdot \begin{bmatrix} x_1 \\ y_1 \\ 1 \end{bmatrix}$$

Fitting is achieved independently for each database image. For the ith image in database, we consider correspondences between $SIFT_{IN}$ and $SIFT_{DB}^i$. These correspondences are fitted by several affine matrices corresponding to the multiple occurrences of this database image within the input image.

As introduced in [16], all the correspondences are clusterized. Each correspondence c between feature $f1$ in $SIFT_{IN}$ and feature $f2$ in $SIFT_{DB}^i$ can be seen as a four dimensional point: $c(\theta, \eta, x, y)$ where θ is the rotation between the orientations of $f1$ and $f2$, η is the scale ratio between $f1$ and $f2$, and (x, y) is the coordinates of $f1$ in the input image. Each correspondence is projected in a 4D grid. For being less sensitive to the grid tile sizes, each point is projected on its two closest tiles on each dimension. Thus, a correspondence is projected in 16 tiles. Eventually, every cluster with at least 3 correspondences can be fitted by an affine transformation and can be seen as a potential product match.

Estimating an affine matrix from a cluster of correspondences requires robust method as outliers are common. We used a RANSAC [6] for this task. The affine matrix needs only 3 samples (i.e., correspondences) to be estimated. Once the matrix with the major consensus is obtained, it is optimized by least square.

3   Filtering Potential Images Occurrences

Eventually, we obtain a list of potential template images occurrences. Each one can be seen as a triplet:

$$\langle i, A, n \rangle$$

where i is the index of the database image, A is the found affine matrix and n is the number of SIFT correspondences that agree with this matrix.

Because several products of the database are very close (e.g., same brand icons), some potential occurrences are incorrect. Some of them are also overlapping and a few ones are completely wrong. These wrong product matchings are mostly due to affine matrices which were fitted with only 3 or 4 correspondences. Our solution to filter these results is to set up a spatial checking. Product matches are sorted according to the number of points supporting their affine transformation, in decreasing order. Then, they are iteratively pasted in this order on the large image only if their underlying pixels have not already been reached by other products. Using this method, correct product matchings with many SIFT correspondences are pasted first and are accepted while wrong ones with few

Table 1. Computation time for linear search of SIFT correspondences

number of products in database	time to compute correspondences
10	30 seconds
100	5 minutes
450	22 minutes

correspondences cannot be pasted and are discarded. The final result is a list of the product matchings that do not overlap themselves too much when warped on the input image. In practice, a product is accepted if it does not recover more than a certain percentage of the surface of an already accepted product (20% in our tests).

The figure 2 shows the result of the previous algorithm on two input images. Image 2.(a) contains twelve templates of 3 distinct products. Some of them are partially hidden by their corresponding price stickers. The database contains 440 products. Image 2.(b) is made up manually from images of the ALOI database. Some templates were pasted on a flower background, and partially occluded by painting on it. Then a gaussian blur was applied. Found images are shown in figures 2.(c) and 2.(d). In figures 2.(e) and 2.(f), these found products are warped at their found positions on the input image. In both examples, database images are retrieved and their positions are correct.

The problem of this approach is it slowness. In the example of the figure 2.a, the input image contains 6475 descriptors and the DB_{440} database contains 274.587 descriptors thus there are more than one milliard of euclidean distances to compute. The table 1 shows the running time on our machine (Pentium 1.7GHz) for the linear search. The time is of course linear in the number of SIFT vectors in the database. For convenience, table 1 uses the number of products in database (using an average value of 600 descriptors per database image). It clearly shows that running times are far from acceptable for any interactive application as soon as the database contains more than 10 products. The two other steps of robustly computing affine transformations and checking the spatial coherence are insignificant in time compared to the search of SIFT neighbors. This is why in the next section, we present and compare two optimization methods for searching nearest neighbors in high dimensional space.

4   Optimization Methods

The previous algorithm is very slow because of the time needed to search for SIFT correspondences. This is due to the large amount of 128 dimensional euclidean distances to be computed. An idea explored in [12] was to reduce the dimension of local descriptors using PCA. Changing from a 128 dimensional vector to a 36 dimensional vector is an interesting gain but still not enough to get to interactive applications. Moreover, PCA-SIFT is a little less efficient in term of quality (see [17]), thus we will not use this method. In [7], the authors prune a large amount of the descriptors for each database image. But they say this

Fig. 2. (a): A supermarket shelf image to analyze, using DB_{440}. (b): A test image made up manually from images of the ALOI database. Green painting added by us is for being more challenging. (c): The three database images found on image (a). (d): The five database images found on image (b). (e) and (f): Found database images are warped on their found locations on input image. Backgrounds of these result images are input images with lowered intensity.

approach is only efficient for near-duplicate image detection. In our case, input image and database images can have different lighting for example because of a photographer using a flash on reflective surface. Images can be blurred because of a bad focus. Thus, pruning many descriptors would lead to miss database images with low quality. This is confirmed by our results as the number of SIFT descriptors is sometime less than 10 for a correct affine matrix. Thus, pruning a large amount of SIFT vectors would lead to miss some products.

Instead, we concentrate more on optimization algorithm for searching neighbors in high dimensional spaces. Methods have been proposed in the literature for exact nearest neighbors computation (one can find a review of this problem in [4]). Tree based methods include Kd-Trees [3], Metric-Trees [18] or SR-Trees [11]. Kd-Tree hierarchically divide the space along one dimension at a time, choosing the median value along this dimension as the pivot. Metric Trees use the same concept but hyperplanes are not aligned with axis. SR-Trees merge the concepts of rectangles trees (R*-Trees [1]) and similarity search trees that uses englobing spheres (SS-Tree [19]).

In [15], the authors compare these tree-based exact nearest neighbors algorithms. The metric-Tree method gives the best results. But even this algorithm has a little gain compared to an exhaustive search. The results obtained in [15] are not better than one order of magnitude in dimension 64. In fact, if the problem is to look for exact neighbors, there is no method that can optimize much the linear one presented in 2.2. This is especially true in high dimensional space (i.e., with more than 20 dimensions). This particularity is known as the 'curse of dimensionality'. Thus, we will focus on another class of algorithms which are looking for approximate nearest neighbors (so called ANN problem).

4.1   Approximate Nearest Neighbors Problem

We restrict ourselves to two classes of algorithm: tree-based methods (hierarchical split of the space) and hashing methods. In the next sections, we will test two state of the art algorithms, one of each class. The first one uses a Kd-Tree coupled with the Best-Bin-First algorithm presented in [2]. The second one is the Locality Sensitive Hashing method of [9]. Another method not presented here uses Hilbert Curve to map the high dimensional space to a one-dimensional data space. The search is then achieved in this space ([14]). One can then restrict the search on some portions of the curve to find neighbors as done in [10] in a video retrieval system.

Before presenting the tested methods, we need to define how accuracy will be measured. The goal of these algorithms is to find for each query feature q its $\epsilon - neighborhood(q)$ (i.e., all database features whose distance from q is below a threshold ϵ). The ground truth is found by a linear search. Then, for a given *epsilon* and for a query feature q, the optimized algorithm will give its $\epsilon - neighborhood_{approx}(q)$. Points further than ϵ from the query point are removed to have no false neighbor and thus we have:

$$\epsilon - neighborhood_{approx}(q) \subseteq \epsilon - neighborhood(q).$$

The quality of an algorithm will be function of its time of execution and of its ability to retrieve most of the correct neighborhoods of query points. This second property is measured by the recall:

$$recall = \frac{\text{number of points found}}{\text{number of points to be found}} = \frac{\sum_q \# \{\epsilon - neighborhood_{approx}(q)\}}{\sum_q \# \{\epsilon - neighborhood(q)\}}.$$

In our tests, some products are detected with only a few correspondences. This is why it is important to keep a high recall on this step of the algorithm.

4.2   Using Best-Bin-First with Kd-Trees

Kd-Trees have been introduced in [3]. They are successful for searching exact nearest neighbors when the dimensionality is small. In higher dimensional spaces, this is not anymore true. In our case (i.e., dimension 128), it can only be used for approximate nearest neighbors using the Best-Bin-First algorithm ([2]).

A Kd-Tree is constructed with all the features from the whole database. Each node splits its point cloud into two parts according to a split plane. Each split plane is perpendicular to a single axis and positioned at the median value along this axis. Eventually, each leaf node contains one point. For exact search, a depth first search is used to initialize the closest neighbor. Backtracking is then achieved on a limited number of sub-branches that can have a point closer than the current closest one.

The Best-Bin-First algorithm does not achieve a complete backtracking. To limit its search, it keeps a list of nodes where search has already been done. This list is sorted according to the distance between the query point and the split plane of the given node. Then, instead of full backtracking from the initial leaf found by the depth first search, backtracking is done on a limited number of branches. The next branch to visit is the one at the head of the sorted list of nodes. The user can then decide the number of branches to visit. We will call this parameter E_{max}. When reducing its value, the user increases speed but more neighbors are missed by the algorithm. Results are presented in section 4.5.

4.3   Using Locality Sensitive Hashing

This hashing has been introduced in [9]. It has been successfully used on image retrieval in very large database [13]. The idea is that if two points are close, they will be hashed with high probability in the same bucket of an hash table. And if they are far, they will be hashed with low probability in the same bucket. Because of the uncertainty of this method, points are hashed in several hash tables using several hash functions.

More formally, points are hashed by l different hash functions g_i, leading to store points in l different hash tables. The hash functions are parametrized by the number of hashed dimensions k. Each g_i function is parametrized by two vectors: $D_i = \langle D_0^i, D_1^i \dots D_{k-1}^i \rangle$ and $T_i = \langle t_0^i, t_1^i \dots t_{k-1}^i \rangle$. Values of D_i are randomly drawn with replacement in $[0...127]$. Thresholds of T_i are drawn in $[0...C]$, where C is the maximum value of the vectors along one dimension. Each g_i maps $\Re^{128}$ to $[0...2^k - 1]$. $g_i(p)$ is computed as a $k - bits$ string $b_0^i, b_1^i \ldots b_{k-1}^i$ such that:

$$b_j^i = 0 \ \ if \ \ \left(p(D_j^i) < t_j^i\right) \ \ else \ 1.$$

This $k - bits$ string is the hash index for the point p in the ith hash table. To search for neighbors of a query point q, it is hashed by the l functions. Then, the corresponding l buckets are linearly tested for points closer than the given threshold ϵ. Modifying both l and k allows to tune the algorithm for speed or accuracy. Because k can be chosen high (e.g., above 32), the destination space of the hash functions can be too large. This is why a second hash function is added to project the result of g_i functions to an actual bucket index whose domain is smaller. Because this will add collisions in the table, a third hash function computes a checksum from the bit string. When going through the linked list of a bucket, only points with the same checksum than the query point are tested. After tuning, we choose to use $l = 20$ hash tables and to adjust k to choose performance or efficiency. The algorithm is benchmarked in section 4.5.

4.4   Adapting LSH to the SIFT Vectors

In the literature, some authors adapted nearest neighbor algorithms for non uniform data distribution. BOND algorithm of [5] is a natural method for such data. But the exact search method proposed in this article leads to a gain below one order of magnitude that are not enough for our application. In [20], the authors claim that LSH is not adapted for non uniform distribution and thus create a hierarchical version of LSH.

Figure 3 shows the distribution of the coordinates of SIFT vectors on three chosen directions. These figures were obtained from the 170.000 SIFT descriptors from the ALOI database. But we obtained similar histograms using the DB_{440}. Histograms of figures 3.a and 3.b are almost representative of all the 128 histograms. Just a few ones are different (e.g., 3.c). These different distribution are a consequence of the SIFT vectors construction. As explained in 2.1, each dimension is a bin where local gradients of a given direction are accumulated. This direction is measured relatively to the major direction of the SIFT descriptor. Thus, local bins which represent gradient of the same direction as the major one

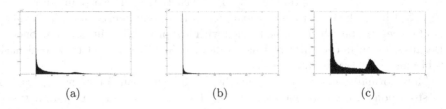

(a)   (b)   (c)

Fig. 3. Histograms of SIFT vectors values along several dimensions: (a) SIFT coordinate 0 (b) SIFT coordinate 10 (c) SIFT coordinate 48

Table 2. LSH probabilities of collisions

range to draw LSH thresholds	$P_{close \rightarrow same}$	$P_{far \rightarrow same}$
$[0...C]$	0.001	0.0002
$[60...120]$	0.008	0.0005

are naturally the largest. Histogram of 3.c corresponds to dimension 48 which accumulated gradient in a direction equal to the major one. But excepted a few dimensions with this type of distribution, most of the histograms looks like 3.a or 3.b.

The consequence is that coordinates of the 128 dimensional descriptors which are very low are much more common than those with high values. Thus, when the LSH threshold on one dimension is low, a large amount of points will be projected in different buckets even if they are close. Accepting low thresholds will thus lead to bad hash functions. For this reason, we tried to choose the thresholds vectors T_i of the LSH hash functions in the range $[min, max]$ where min is much higher than zero. Experimentally, we tuned this range and found that $[60, 120]$ gives the best results.

We can analyze this modification by measuring the probability of collisions for close points. We say two points are close if their distance is below the threshold $\epsilon = 260$. The probability of two close points to be projected by a hash function in the same bucket is noted $P_{close \rightarrow same}$. The probability of two points which are not close to arrive in the same bucket is noted $P_{far \rightarrow same}$. A family of hash function is efficient if $P_{close \rightarrow same}$ is relatively high and $P_{far \rightarrow same}$ is relatively low. These probabilities are experimentally measured, averaging the obtained values over the 20 used hash functions. Results are shown in table 2.

Using the range $[60...120]$ multiplies $P_{close \rightarrow same}$ by 8 while only multiplying $P_{far \rightarrow same}$ by 2.5. This confirms the fact that restricting the interval of hashing thresholds leads to better hash functions. In the next paragraph, we will call this method *adaptedLSH* and compare its performance to standard LSH.

4.5   Results

We benchmarked the three presented algorithms: BBF on Kd-Tree, LSH and *adaptedLSH*. Tests were achieved on the two presented databases to ensure being independent of the images. These databases contain respectively 270.000 and 170.000 SIFT vectors.

Figure 4 shows the speed gain of each optimized method, according to the obtained accuracy. BBF algorithm on Kd-Tree is outperformed by both methods based upon LSH. Obtaining a ratio of 70% (i.e.: recall of 0.7) with this algorithm on the DB_{440} database is almost no faster than using a linear search. If the requirement is to be 100 times faster than linear search on the ALOI database, the LSH algorithm still finds 70% of the neighborhoods, while the *adaptedLSH* method finds 90% of the points. If the need is to find 80% of the points, *adaptedLSH* is twice faster than LSH.

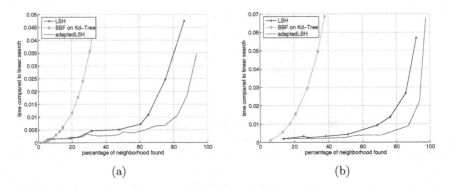

Fig. 4. Results for Kd-Tree, LSH and *adaptedLSH*, using $\epsilon = 260$ on (a): *DB*440 and (b): ALOI

With the first input image, linear search time is around 21 minutes on our machine. A gain of two orders of magnitude means the same computation is achieved in 13 seconds, while finding around 80% of the points. This quality is good enough so that all the products found by the exact linear search are also found by this approximate method. For an application that would require only 20% of the correspondences, the required time for a query could be divided by a factor 500 relatively to the linear search.

5   Conclusion

The contributions of this article are twofold. First we proposed a complete algorithm to analyze an input image using database template images. This work uses the initial SIFT matching algorithm of [16]. It adds a filtering step to ensure that found images do not overlap themselves when warped on the input image. Our second contribution concerns speed limitations. We compared two optimization algorithm for the approximate nearest neighbors problem. In these tests, LSH outperforms the BBF-Kd-Tree algorithm. We also introduce a modification in the LSH algorithm to adapt it to the SIFT distributions. If the quality requirement is to find 80% of the correspondences, this modified LSH is at least twice faster than standard LSH. Comparatively to a linear search, the gain is of two orders of magnitude. Being able to keep a high percentage of the correspondences is a major advantage for our application as it can be sensitive to missing points because some templates matchings are based only on a few points. In the tested images, result are encouraging as we exactly find all the database images at their correct location. For these experiments, we tuned the parameters of the optimization algorithm to find 80% of the SIFT correspondences. We plan to investigate performances of the overall algorithm in terms of recall-precision when modifying the parameters of the LSH algorithm. Moreover, we believe that the criteria we used to filter the matchings (i.e., the number of points validating the found affine transformation) is not optimal.

References

1. Beckmann, N., Kriegel, H.-P., Schneider, R., Seeger, B.: The r*-tree: an efficient and robust access method for points and rectangles. In: SIGMOD 1990: Proceedings of the 1990 ACM SIGMOD international conference on Management of data, pp. 322–331. ACM Press, New York (1990)
2. Beis, J.S., Lowe, D.G.: Shape indexing using approximate nearest-neighbour search in high-dimensional spaces. In: CVPR 1997: Proceedings of the 1997 Conference on Computer Vision and Pattern Recognition (CVPR 1997), p. 1000. IEEE Computer Society Press, Washington, DC, USA (1997)
3. Bentley, J.L.: Multidimensional binary search trees used for associative searching. Commun. ACM 18(9), 509–517 (1975)
4. Böhm, C., Berchtold, S., Keim, D.A.: Searching in high-dimensional spaces: Index structures for improving the performance of multimedia databases. ACM Comput. Surv. 33(3), 322–373 (2001)
5. de Vries, A.P., Mamoulis, N., Nes, N., Kersten, M.: Efficient k-nn search on vertically decomposed data. In: SIGMOD 2002: Proceedings of the 2002 ACM SIGMOD international conference on Management of data, pp. 322–333. ACM Press, New York (2002)
6. Fischler, M.A., Bolles, R.C.: Random sample consensus: A paradigm for model fitting with applications to image analysis and automated cartography. Communications of the ACM 24(6), 381–395 (1981)
7. Foo, J.J., Sinha, R.: Pruning sift for scalable near-duplicate image matching. In: Bailey, J., Fekete, A. (eds.) Eighteenth Australasian Database Conference (ADC 2007), Ballarat, Australia. CRPIT, vol. 63, pp. 63–71. ACS (2007)
8. Geusebroek, J.-M., Burghouts, G.J., Smeulders, A.W.M.: The Amsterdam library of object images. Int. J. Comput. Vision 61(1), 103–112 (2005)
9. Gionis, A., Indyk, P., Motwani, R.: Similarity search in high dimensions via hashing. The VLDB Journal, 518–529 (1999)
10. Joly, A., Frélicot, C., Buisson, O.: Feature statistical retrieval applied to content-based copy identification. In: ICIP, pp. 681–684 (2004)
11. Katayama, N., Satoh, S.: The sr-tree: an index structure for high-dimensional nearest neighbor queries. In: SIGMOD 1997: Proceedings of the 1997 ACM SIGMOD international conference on Management of data, pp. 369–380. ACM Press, New York (1997)
12. Ke, Y., Sukthankar, R.: Pca-sift: A more distinctive representation for local image descriptors. In: CVPR (2), pp. 506–513 (2004)
13. Ke, Y., Sukthankar, R., Huston, L.: An efficient parts-based near-duplicate and sub-image retrieval system. In: MULTIMEDIA 2004: Proceedings of the 12th annual ACM international conference on Multimedia, pp. 869–876. ACM Press, New York (2004)
14. Lawder, J.K., King, P.J.H.: Querying multi-dimensional data indexed using the hilbert space-filling curve. SIGMOD Record 30(1), 19–24 (2001)
15. Liu, T., Moore, A.W., Gray, A.G., Yang, K.: An investigation of practical approximate nearest neighbor algorithms. In: NIPS (2004)
16. Lowe, D.G.: Distinctive image features from scale-invariant keypoints. International Journal of Computer Vision 20, 91–110 (2004)
17. Mikolajczyk, K., Schmid, C.: A performance evaluation of local descriptors. IEEE Trans. Pattern Anal. Mach. Intell. 27(10), 1615–1630 (2005)

18. Uhlmann, J.K.: Satisfying general proximity/similarity queries with metric trees. Inf. Process. Lett. 40(4), 175–179 (1991)
19. White, D.A., Jain, R.: Similarity indexing with the ss-tree. In: ICDE 1996: Proceedings of the Twelfth International Conference on Data Engineering, pp. 516–523. IEEE Computer Society, Los Alamitos (1996)
20. Yang, Z., Ooi, W.T., Sun, Q.: Hierarchical, non-uniform locality sensitive hashing and its application to video identification. In: ICME, pp. 743–746 (2004)

Video Semantic Content Analysis Framework Based on Ontology Combined MPEG-7

Liang Bai[1,2], Songyang Lao[1], Weiming Zhang[1],
Gareth J.F. Jones[2], and Alan F. Smeaton[2]

[1] School of Information System & Management,
National University of Defense Technology,
ChangSha, China, 410073
lbai@computing.dcu.ie, laosongyang@vip.sina.com,
wmzhang@nudt.edu.cn
[2]Centre for Digital Video Processing, Dublin City University, Glasnevin, Dublin 9, Ireland
{gjones, asmeaton}@computing.dcu.ie

Abstract. The rapid increase in the available amount of video data is creating a growing demand for efficient methods for understanding and managing it at the semantic level. New multimedia standard, MPEG-7, provides the rich functionalities to enable the generation of audiovisual descriptions and is expressed solely in XML Schema which provides little support for expressing semantic knowledge. In this paper, a video semantic content analysis framework based on ontology combined MPEG-7 is presented. Domain ontology is used to define high level semantic concepts and their relations in the context of the examined domain. MPEG-7 metadata terms of audiovisual descriptions and video content analysis algorithms are expressed in this ontology to enrich video semantic analysis. OWL is used for the ontology description. Rules in Description Logic are defined to describe how low-level features and algorithms for video analysis should be applied according to different perception content. Temporal Description Logic is used to describe the semantic events, and a reasoning algorithm is proposed for events detection. The proposed framework is demonstrated in sports video domain and shows promising results.

Keywords: Video Semantic Content, MPEG-7, Ontology, OWL, Description Logic, Temporal Description Logic.

1 Introduction

Audiovisual resources in the form of image, video, audio play more and more pervasive role in our lives. Especially, the rapid increase of the available amount in video data has revealed an urgent need to develop intelligent methods for understanding, storing, indexing and retrieval of video data at the semantic level [1]. This means the need to enable uniform semantic description, computational interpretation and processing of such resources.

The main challenge, often referred to as the semantic gap, is mapping high-level semantic concepts into low-level spatiotemporal features that can be automatically

N. Boujemaa, M. Detyniecki, and A. Nürnberger (Eds.): AMR 2007, LNCS 4918, pp. 237–250, 2008.

extracted from video data. Feature extraction, shot detection and object recognition are important phases in developing general purpose video content analysis [2] [3]. Significant results have been reported in the literature for the last two decades, with several successful prototypes [4] [5]. However, the lack of precise models and formats for video semantic content representation and the high complexity of video processing algorithms make the development of fully automatic video semantic content analysis and management a challenging task. And, the mapping rules often are written into program code. This causes the existing approach and systems to be too inflexible and can't satisfy the need of video applications at the semantic level. So the use of domain knowledge is very necessary to enable higher level semantics to be integrated into the techniques that capture the semantics through automatic parsing.

Ontology is formal, explicit specifications of domain knowledge: it consists of concepts, concept properties, and relationships between concepts and is typically represented using linguistic terms, and has been used in many fields as a knowledge management and representation approach. At the same time, several standard description languages for the expression of concepts and relations in ontology have been defined. Among these the important are: Resource Description Framework (RDF) [6], Resource Description Framework Schema (RDFS), Web Ontology Language (OWL) [7] and, for multimedia, the XML Schema in MPEG-7.

Many automatic semantic content analysis systems have been presented recently in [8] [9] and [10]. In all these systems, low-level based semantic content analysis is not associated with any formal representation of the domain.

The formalization of ontology is based on linguistic terms. Domain specific linguistic ontology with multimedia lexicons and possibility of cross document merging has instead been presented in [11]. In [12], concepts are expressed in keywords and are mapped in object ontology, a shot ontology and a semantic ontology for the representation of the results of video segmentation. However, although linguistic terms are appropriate to distinguish event and object categories in a special domain, it is a challenge to use them for describing low-level features, video content analysis and the relationships between them.

An extending linguistic ontology with multimedia ontology was presented in [13] to support video understanding. Multimedia ontology is constructed manually in [14]. M.Bertini et al., in [15], present algorithms and techniques that employ an enriched ontology for video annotation and retrieval. In [16], perceptual knowledge is discovered grouping images into clusters based on their visual and text features and semantic knowledge is extracted by disambiguating the senses of words in annotations using WordNet. In [17], an approach for knowledge assisted semantic analysis and annotation of video content, based on an ontology infrastructure is presented. Semantic Web technologies are used for knowledge representation in RDF/RDFS. In [18], an object ontology, coupled with a relevance feedback mechanism, is introduced to facilitate the mapping of low-level to high-level features and allow the definition of relations between pieces of multimedia information.

Multimedia standards, MPEG-7 [19], provide a rich set of standardized tools to enable the generation of audiovisual descriptions which can be understood by machines as well as humans and to enable the fast efficient retrieval from digital archives as well as filtering of streamed audiovisual broadcasts on the Internet. But MPEG-7 is expressed solely in XML Schema and can not provide enough support for expressing semantic knowledge, while most of video content is out of the scope of the standard at a semantic level. So a machine-understandable and uniform representation of the semantics associated with MPEG-7 metadata terms is needed to enable the interoperability and integration of MPGE-7 with metadata descriptions from different domain. Web ontology language (OWL) can be used to do this, which is an accepted language of the semantic web due to its ability to express semantics and semantic relationships through class a property hierarchies. Some new metadata initiatives such as TV-Anytime [20], MPEG-21 [21], NewsML [22] have tried to combine MPEG-7 multimedia descriptions with new and existing metadata standards for resource discovery, rights management, geospatial and educational.

In this paper, a framework for video semantic content analysis based on ontology combined MPEG-7 is presented. In the proposed video semantic content analysis framework, video analysis ontology is developed to formally describe the detection process of the video semantic content, in which the low-level visual and audio descriptions part of MPEG-7 is combined and expressed in OWL. This idea drives the work to investigate the feasibility of expressed MPEG-7 terms in OWL and how to express. Semantic concepts within the context of the examined domain area are defined in domain ontology. Rules in Description Logic are defined which describe how features and algorithms for video analysis should be applied according to different perception content and low-level features. Temporal Description Logic is used to describe the semantic events, and a reasoning algorithm is proposed for events detection. OWL language is used for ontology representation. By exploiting the domain knowledge modeled in the ontology, semantic content of the examined videos is analyzed to provide a semantic level annotation and event detection.

2   Framework of Video Semantic Content Analysis

The proposed video semantic content analysis framework is shown in Fig.1. According to the available knowledge for video analysis, a video analysis ontology is developed which describes the key elements in video content analysis and supports the detection process of the corresponding domain specific semantic content. The visual and aural descriptions of MPEG-7 are combined into this ontology expressed in OWL. Semantic concepts within the context of the examined domain are defined in domain ontology, enriched with qualitative attributes of the semantic content. OWL language is used for knowledge representation for video analysis ontology and domain ontology. DL is used to describe how video processing methods and low-level features should be applied according to different semantic content, aiming at the detection of special semantic objects and sequences corresponding to the high-level semantic concepts defined in the ontology. TDL can model temporal relationships and define semantically important events in the domain. Reasoning based DL and TDL can carry out object, sequence and event detection automatically.

Based on this framework, video semantic content analysis depends on the knowledge base of the system. This framework can easily be applied to different domains provided that the knowledge base is enriched with the respective domain ontology. OWL semantic definitions for MPEG-7 terms provide rich low-level visual and aural descriptions and importantly a common understanding of these descriptions for different domains. Further, the ontology-based approach and the utilization of OWL language ensure that semantic web services and applications have a greater chance of discovering and exploiting the information and knowledge in the video data.

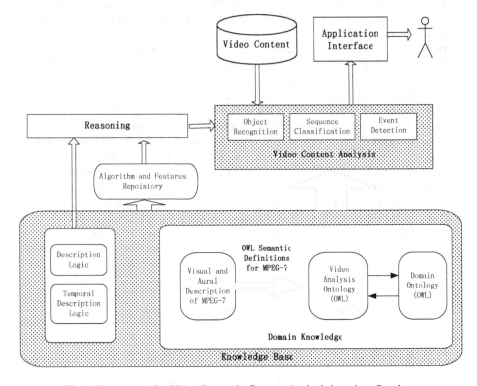

Fig. 1. Framework for Video Semantic Content Analysis based on Ontology

3 Video Analysis Ontology Development

3.1 The Definition for Video Analysis Ontology

In order to realize the knowledge-based and automatic video semantic content analysis explained in section 2, the knowledge for video analysis is abstracted and a video analysis ontology is constructed. In general, video content detection, such as objects, considers the utilization of content characteristic features in order to apply the appropriate detection algorithms for the analysis process in form of algorithms and features. So all elements for the video content analysis, including content, features, algorithms and necessary restrictions, must be described clearly in a video analysis ontology. The audio track in video data, including aural sequences and objects, is important information for video semantic content analysis. The development of the proposed video analysis ontology deals with the following concepts (OWL classes) and their corresponding properties, as illustrated in Fig. 2. The classes defined above are expressed in OWL language in our work.

- Class **Sequence**: the subclass and instance of the super-class "Sequence", all video sequences can be classified through the analysis process at shot level, such as: long-view shot or tight-view shot in sports video. It is sub-classed to **Visual-Sequence** and **AuralSequence**. Each sequence instance is related to appropriate feature instances by the **hasFeature** property and to appropriate detection algorithm instances by the **useAlgorithm** property.

- Class **Object**: the subclass and instance of the super-class "Object", all video objects can be detected through the analysis process at frame level. It is sub-classed to **VisualObject** and **AuralObject**. Each object instance is related to appropriate feature instances by the **hasFeature** property and to appropriate detection algorithm instances by the **useAlgorithm** property.

- Class **Feature**: the super-class of video low-level features associated with each sequence and object. It is linked to the instances of **FeatureParameter** class through the **hasFeatureParameter** property.

- Class **FeatureParameter**: denotes the actual qualitative descriptions of each corresponding feature. It is sub-classed according to the defined features. It is linked to the instances of **pRange** class through **hasRange** property

- Class **pRange**: is sub-classed to Minimum and Maximum and allows the definition of value restriction to the different feature parameters.

- Class **Algorithm**: the super-class of the available processing algorithms to be used during the analysis procedure. It is linked to the instances of **Feature-Parameter** class through the **useFeatureParameter** property.

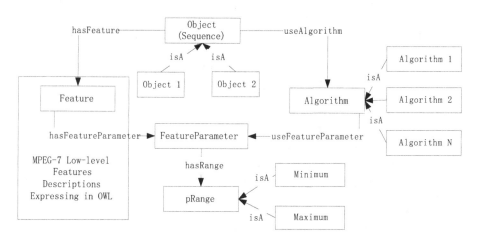

Fig. 2. Classes and Properties in Video Analysis Ontology

3.2 Expressing MPEG-7 in OWL

In this paper, we try to combine the low-level visual and aural descriptions of MPEG-7 into video analysis ontology for constructing a common understanding low-level features description for different video content. In the same way, we can combine other parts of MPEG-7 into an OWL ontology.

The set of features or properties which is specific to the visual entities defined in MPEG-7 include: Color, Texture, Motion and Shape. Each of these features can be represented by a choice of descriptors. Similarly there is a set of audio features which is applicable to MPEG-7 entities containing audio: Silence, Timbre, Speech and Melody.

Taking the visual feature descriptor "Color" as an example, we demonstrate in Figure 3, how MPEG-7 descriptions are combined into video analysis ontology with OWL definitions.

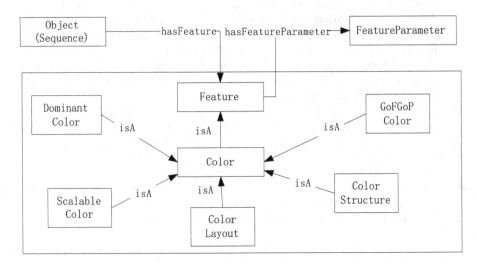

Fig. 3. Definitions of MPEG-7 Color Descriptor in Video Analysis Ontology

An example of color descriptor expressed in OWL is shown in List 1.

List 1. Example of Color Descriptor Expressing in OWL

```
...
<owl:Class rdf:ID = "Color"/ >
    <rdfs:label>Color</rdfs:label>
    <rdfs:subClassOf rdf:resource="#Feature"/>
</owl:class>
<owl:Class rdf:ID = "DominantColor">
    <rdfs:label>DominantColor</rdfs:label>
    <rdfs:subClassOf rdf:resource="#Color"/>
</owl:class>
<owl:Class rdf:ID = "ScalableColor">
    <rdfs:label> ScalableColor </rdfs:label>
    <rdfs:subClassOf rdf:resource="#Color"/>
</owl:class>
...
```

4 Rules in Description Logic Construction

The choice of algorithm employed for the detection of sequences and objects is directly dependent on its available characteristic features which directly depend on the domain that the sequences and objects involve. So this association should be considered based on video analysis knowledge and domain knowledge, and is useful for automatic and precise detection. In our work, the association is described by a set of properly defined rules represented in DL.

The rules for detection of sequences and objects are: rules to define the mapping between sequence (or object) and features, rules to define the mapping between sequence (or object) and algorithm, and rules to determine algorithms input feature parameters. The rules are represented in DL as follows:

- An sequence 'S' has features F_1, F_2, ..., F_n: $\exists hasFeature(S, F_1, F_2, ..., F_n)$

- An sequence 'S' detection use algorithms A_1, A_2, ..., A_n :

  $\exists useA\lg orithm(S, A_1, A_2, ..., A_n)$

- An object 'O' has features F_1, F_2, ..., F_n: $\exists hasFeature(O, F_1, F_2, ..., F_n)$

- An object 'O' detection uses algorithms A_1, A_2, ..., A_n :

  $\exists useA\lg orithm(O, A_1, A_2, ..., A_n)$

- An algorithm 'A' uses features parameters FP_1, FP_2, ..., FP_n :

  $\exists useFeatureParameter(A, FP_1, FP_2, ..., FP_n)$

- If $S \cap (\exists hasFeature.F \cap \exists hasA\lg orithm.A)$

  Then $\exists useFeatureParameter(A, FP)$ *(FP is the parameter values of F.)*

- If $O \cap (\exists hasFeature.F \cap \exists hasA\lg orithm.A)$

  Then $\exists useFeatureParameter(A, FP)$ *(FP is the parameter values of F.)*

In the next section, a sports ontology is constructed which provides the vocabulary and domain knowledge. In the context of video content analysis the domain ontology maps to the important objects, their qualitative and quantitative attributes and their interrelation.

In videos events are very important semantic entities. Events are composed of special objects and sequences and their temporal relationships. A general domain ontology is appropriate to describe events using linguistic terms. It is inadequate when it must describe the temporal patterns of events. Basic DL lacks of constructors which can express temporal semantics. So in this paper, Temporal Description Logic (TDL) is used to describe the temporal patterns of semantic events based on detected sequences and objects. TDL is based on temporal extensions of DL, involving the combination of a rather expressive DL with the basis tense modal logic over a linear, unbounded, and discrete temporal structure. $\mathcal{TL}$-$\mathcal{F}$ is the basic logic considered in this paper. This language is composed of the temporal logic $\mathcal{TL}$, which is able to express interval temporal networks, and the non-temporal Feature Description Logic $\mathcal{F}$ [23].

The basic temporal interval relations in $\mathcal{TL}\text{-}\mathcal{F}$ are: before (b), meets (m), during (d), overlaps (o), starts (s), finishes (f), equal (e), after(a), met-by (mi), contains (di), overlapped-by (oi), started-by (si), finished-by (fi).

Objects and sequences in soccer videos can be detected based on video analysis ontology. Events can be described by means of the occurrence of the objects and sequences, and the temporal relationships between them. The events description and reasoning algorithm for event detection are introduced in next section.

5 Sports Domain Ontology

As previously mentioned, for the demonstration of our framework an application in the sports domain is proposed. The detection of semantically significant sequences and objects, such as close-up shots, players and referees, is important for understanding and extracting video semantic content, and modeling and detecting the events in the sports video. The features associated with each sequence and object comprise their definitions in terms of low-level features as used in the context of video analysis. The category of sequences and objects and the selection of features are based on domain knowledge. A sports domain ontology is constructed and the definitions used for this ontology are described in this section.

5.1 Objects

Only a limited number of object types are observed in sports videos. Visual objects include: ball, player, referee, coach, captions, goalposts in soccer, basket in basketball and so on (see figure 4).

In general, in a sports match there are two kinds of important audio: whistle and cheers. So the individuals of aural object class are: whistle and cheers.

Fig. 4. Objects in Sports Videos

5.2 Sequences

In sports videos we observe just three distinct visual sequence classes: Loose View, Medium View and Tight View. The loose view and medium view share analogical visual features and are often associated with one shot zooming action, so they can be defined as one visual sequence style named Normal View. When some highlights occur, the camera often captures something interesting in the arena, called Out-of-field. Important semantic events are often replayed in slow motion immediately after they occur. So individuals of visual sequence class are: Normal View (NV), Tight View (TV), Out-of-field (OOF) and Slow-motion-replay (SMR). (For example in soccer, see Figure 5).

Fig. 5. Sequences in Soccer Game

5.3 Features and Algorithms

In section 3.2, we have combined MPEG-7 visual and aural descriptions into video analysis ontology expressed in OWL. The definitions of these visual and aural features are used for the detections of the sequences and objects defined in the sports domain ontology.

In our previous work [24], HMM was used for distinguishing different visual sequences, Sobel edge detection algorithm and Hough transform are used to detect "Goalposts" object, and image cluster algorithm based on color features have been proved to be effective in the soccer videos content analysis domain. The pixel-wise mean square difference of the intensity of every two subsequent frames and RGB color histogram of each frame can be used in a HMM model for slow-motion-replay detection [25]. For detection of aural objects, frequency energy can be used in SVM model for detection of "Cheers"[26], "Whistles" can be detected according to peak frequencies which fall within a threshold range [27].

5.4 Events Description and Detection

It is possible to detect events in sports videos by means of reasoning on TDL once all the sequence and objects defined above are detected with the video content analysis ontology. In order to do this we have observed some temporal patterns in soccer videos in terms of series of detected sequences and objects. For instance, if an attack leads to a scored goal, cheers from audience occurs immediately, then sequences are from "Goal Area" to "Player Tight View", "Out-of-Field", "Slow Motion Replay", and another player "Tight View", and finally returning to "Normal View", then a "Caption" is shown. Essentially these temporal patterns are the basic truth existing in sports domain which characterize the semantic events in sports videos and can be used to formally describe the events and detect them automatically. TDL is used for descriptions of the events. And the necessary syntaxes in TDL are listed as follows:
x, y denote the temporal intervals;

◊ is the temporal existential quantifier for introducing the temporal intervals, for example: $◊(x, y)$;

@ is called bindable, and appears in the left hand side of a temporal interval. A bindable variable is said to be bound in a concept if it is declared at the nearest temporal quantifier in the body of which it occurs.

For example, the description of goal scored event in soccer event is as follows:

$$Scoredgoal = ◊\left(d_{goal}, d_{whistle}, d_{cheers}, d_{caption}, d_{GA}, d_{TV}, d_{OOF}, d_{SMR}\right)$$
$$\left(d_{goal} \ f \ d_{GA}\right)\left(d_{whistle} \ d \ d_{GA}\right)\left(d_{GA} \ o \ d_{cheers}\right)\left(d_{caption} \ e \ d_{TV}\right)$$
$$\left(d_{cheers} \ e \ d_{TV}\right)\left(d_{GA} \ m \ d_{TV}\right)\left(d_{TV} \ m \ d_{OOF}\right)\left(d_{OOF} \ m \ d_{MSR}\right).$$
$$(goal @ d_{goal} \cap whistle @ d_{whistle} \cap cheers @ d_{cheers} \cap caption @ d_{caption} \cap$$
$$GA @ d_{GA} \cap TV @ d_{TV} \cap OOF @ d_{OOF} \cap SMR @ d_{SMR})$$

$d_{goal}, d_{whistle}, d_{cheers}, d_{caption}, d_{GA}, d_{TV}, d_{OOF}, d_{SMR}$ represent the temporal intervals of responding objects and sequences.

Based on the descriptions of event in TDL, reasoning on event detection can be designed. After detection of sequences and objects in a sports video, every sequence and object can be described as formal in TDL as: $◊x( ).C @ x$. C is the individual of sequence or object; x is the temporal interval of C. $()$ denotes C dose not any temporal relationship with itself. So the reasoning algorithm is described as follows:

Suppose: $\{S_0, S_1, ..., S_{n-1}, S_n\}$ is a sequence individuals set from detection results of a soccer video. Each element S_i in $\{S_0, S_1, ..., S_{n-1}, S_n\}$ can be represented as follows:

$$S_i = ◊x_i ( ).S_i @ x_i$$

The definition of $\{S_0, S_1, ..., S_{n-1}, S_n\}$ includes a latent temporal constraint: $x_i \ m \ x_{i+1}, i = 0, 1, ..., n-1$ which denotes two consecutive sequences in $\{S_0, S_1, ..., S_{n-1}, S_n\}$ are consecutive in the temporal axis of the video.

$\{O_0, O_1, ..., O_{m-1}, O_m\}$ is object individuals set from detection results of a soccer video. Each element O_i in $\{O_0, O_1, ..., O_{m-1}, O_m\}$ can be represented as follows:

$$O_i = ◊y_i ( ).O_i @ y_i$$

Reasoning algorithm for goal scored event in soccer video:

Step 1. Select the subsets in $\{S_0, S_1, ..., S_{n-1}, S_n\}$ which are composed of consecutive sequences individuals GA->TV->OOF->MSR. Each of the subsets is a candidate goal scored event E_{Ck}.

$$E_{Ck} = \{GA_k, TV_{k+1}, OOF_{k+2}, MSR_{k+3}\}$$

where k is the subscript mark of the current NV of the current candidate event in $\{S_0, S_1, ..., S_{n-1}, S_n\}$.

Step 2. For each candidate event E_{Ck}, Search goal objects O_{goal}, $O_{whistle}$, O_{cheers}, $O_{caption}$ in $\{O_0, O_1, ..., O_{m-1}, O_m\}$, they have corresponding temporal intervals y_{goal}, $y_{whistle}$, y_{cheers}, $y_{caption}$, and satisfy corresponding temporal constrains y_{goal} f GA_k, $y_{whistle}$ d GA_k, GA_k o y_{cheers}, $y_{caption}$ e TV_{k+1}, y_{cheers} e TV_{k+1}. If all of such objects exist, E_{Ck} is a goal scored event.

Other events can be detected using same reasoning algorithm. We just need to adjust the definition of candidate event subset and searched objects. A particular strength of the proposed reasoning algorithm for events description and detection in TDF based on domain ontology is that the user can define and describe different events, and use different description in TDL for the same event based on their domain knowledge.

6 Experiment and Results

The proposed framework was tested in the sports domain. In this paper we focus on developing the framework for video content analysis based on ontology and demonstrating the validity of the proposed reasoning algorithm in TDL for event detection. So the experiments described here used a manually annotated data set of objects and sequences in sports videos. Experiments were carried out using five soccer games and three basketball games recordings captured from 4:2:2 YUV PAL tapes which were saved as MPEG-1 format. The soccer videos are from two broadcasters, ITV and BBC Sport, and are taken from the 2006 World Cup, taking a total of 7hs 53mins28s. The basketball videos are NBA games recorded from ESPN, FOX Sports and CCTV5 taking a total of 6hs 47mins 18s.

For soccer videos we defined Goal Scored, Foul in Soccer and Yellow (or Red) Card events. And Highlight Attack and Foul events are defined and detected in basketball videos. Table 1 shows "Precision" and "Recall" for detection of the semantic events. "Actual Num" is the actual number of events in entire matches, which are recognized manually; "True Num" is the number of detected correct matches, and "False Num" is the number of false matches.

From Table 1, it can be seen that the precision results of event detection are higher than 89%, but the recall results are relatively low. This is because the description in TDL is very strict in logic and do not allow any difference between the definition of events and the occurrence of events to be detected, thus the reasoning algorithm for event detection can ensure high precision, but it may lose some correct results. If we define different descriptions in TDL for the same event which has different composition of objects, sequences and temporal relationship, high recall can be obtained.

Table 1. Precision and recall for five soccer and basketball semantics

semantic	Actual Num	True Num	False Num	Precision (%)	Recall (%)
Goal Scored	10	8	0	100	80
Foul in Soccer	193	141	11	92.8	73.1
Yellow (or Red) Card	26	22	2	91.7	84.6
Highlight Attack	45	36	4	90.0	80.0
Foul in Basketball	131	106	12	89.8	80.9

We also compared the proposed approach with other approaches. In our previous work, a Petri-Net (PN) model is used for video semantic content description and detection [28]. HMM is a popular model for video event detection. In our experiments, we use the PN based approach and HMM based approach proposed in [24] to detect semantic content using same video data set. The results are shown in Table 2.

Table 2. Results based on PN and HMM Approach

semantic		Goal Scored	Foul in Soccer	Yellow(Red) Card	Highlight Attack	Foul in Basketball
PN	Pre(%)	85.2	86.6	91.7	85.8	84.5
	Rec(%)	100	84.1	97.5	91.6	90.3
HMM	Pre(%)	75.4	63.8	77.6	61.5	59.2
	Rec(%)	80.1	72.5	83.1	64.9	67.3

From Table 2, we can find the precision and recall of PN based approach is almost equivalent with the proposed approach. It is because both of these approaches detect high-level semantic events based on middle semantics, objects and sequences. Low precision and recall are shown in the experimental results of HMM based approach, in which low-level features are extracted to training different HMM models for different semantic content. This approach maps low-level features to high-level semantic directly, which can capture perception feature pattern well but not be effective to model and detect spatiotemporal relationship between different semantic content.

Based on the above experimental results, we believe that the proposed framework for video content analysis and event detection method based on TDL have considerable potential. We are currently conducting a more thorough experimental investigation using a larger set of independent videos and utilizing the framework in different domains.

7 Conclusions and Discussions

In this paper, a video semantic content analysis framework based on ontology combined MPEG-7 is presented. A domain ontology is used to define high level semantic concepts and their relations in context of the examined domain. MPEG-7 low-level feature descriptions expressing in OWL and video content analysis algorithms are integrated into the ontology to enrich video semantic analysis.

In order to create domain ontology for video content analysis, owl is used for ontology description language and Rules in DL are defined to describe how features and algorithms for video analysis should be applied according to different perception content and low-level features, and TDL is used to describe semantic events. A ontology in the sports domain is constructed using Protégé for demonstrating the validity of the proposed framework. A reasoning algorithm based on TDL is proposed for event detection in sports videos. The proposed framework supports flexible and managed execution of various application and domain independent video low-level analysis tasks.

Future work includes the enhancement of the domain ontology with more complex model representations and the definition of semantically more important and complex events in the domain of discourse.

Acknowledgement

This work is supported by the National High Technology Development 863 Program of China (2006AA01Z316), the National Natural Science Foundation of China (60572137) and China Scholarship Council of China Education Ministry.

References

1. Chang, S.-F.: The holy grail of content-based media analysis. IEEE Multimedia 9(2), 6–10 (2002)
2. Yoshitaka, A., Ichikawa, T.: A survey on content-based retrieval for multimedia databases. IEEE Transactions on Knowledge and Data Engineering 11(1), 81–93 (1999)
3. Hanjalic, A., Xu, L.Q.: Affective video content representation and modeling. IEEE Transactions on Multimedia 7(1), 143–154 (2005)
4. Muller-Schneiders, S., Jager, T., Loos, H.S., Niem, W.: Performance evaluation of a real time video surveillance system. In: 2nd Joint IEEE International Workshop on Visual Surveillance and Performance Evaluation of Tracking and Surveillance, October 15-16, 2005, pp. 137–143 (2005)
5. Hua, X.S., Lu, L., Zhang, H.J.: Automatic music video generation based on the temporal pattern analysis. In: 12th annual ACM international conference on Multimedia (October 2004)
6. Resource description framework. Technical report, W3C (February 2004), http://www.w3.org/RDF/
7. Web ontology language (OWL). Technical report, W3C (2004), http://www.w3.org/2004/OWL/
8. Ekin, A., Tekalp, A.M., Mehrotra, R.: Automatic soccer video analysis and summarization. IEEE Transactions on Image Processing 12(7), 796–807 (2003)

9. Yu, X., Xu, C., Leung, H., Tian, Q., Tang, Q., Wan, K.W.: Trajectory-based ball detection and tracking with applications to semantic analysis of broadcast soccer video. In: ACM Multimedia 2003, Berkeley, CA(USA), November 4-6, 2003, vol. 3, pp. 11–20 (2003)

10. Xu, H.X., Chua, T.-S.: Fusion of AV features and external information sources for event detection in team sports video. ACM transactions on Multimedia Computing, Communications and Applications 2(1), 44–67 (2006)

11. Reidsma, D., Kuper, J., Declerck, T., Saggion, H., Cunningham, H.: Cross document ontology based information extraction for multimedia retrieval. In: Supplementary proceedings of the ICCS 2003, Dresden (July 2003)

12. Mezaris, V., Kompatsiaris, I., Boulgouris, N., Strintzis, M.: Real-time compressed-domain spatiotemporal segmentation and ontologies for video indexing and retrieval. IEEE Transactions on Circuits and Systems for Video Technology 14(5), 606–621 (2004)

13. Jaimes, A., Tseng, B., Smith, J.: Modal keywords, ontologies, and reasoning for video understanding. In: Bakker, E.M., Lew, M., Huang, T.S., Sebe, N., Zhou, X.S. (eds.) CIVR 2003. LNCS, vol. 2728, Springer, Heidelberg (2003)

14. Jaimes, A., Smith, J.: Semi-automatic, data-driven construction of multimedia ontologies. In: Proc. of IEEE Int'l Conference on Multimedia & Expo (2003)

15. Bertini, M., Bimbo, A.D., Torniai, C.: Enhanced ontoloies for video annotation and retrieval. In: ACM MIR'2005, Singapore, November 10-11 (2005)

16. Bentitez, A., Chang, S.-F.: Automatic multimedia knowledge discovery, summarization and evaluation. IEEE Transactions on Multimedia (submitted, 2003)

17. Dasiopoulou, S., Papastathis, V.K., Mezaris, V., Kompatsiaris, I., Strintzis, M.G.: An Ontology Framework for Knowledge-Assisted Semantic Video Analysis and Annotation. In: McIlraith, S.A., Plexousakis, D., van Harmelen, F. (eds.) ISWC 2004. LNCS, vol. 3298, Springer, Heidelberg (2004)

18. Kompatsiaris, I., Mezaris, V., Strintzis, M.G.: Multimedia content indexing and retrieval using an object ontology. In: Stamou, G. (ed.) Multimedia Content and Semantic Web Methods, Standards and Tools. Wiley, New York (2004)

19. MPEG-7 Overview (October 2004), http://www.chiariglione.org/mpeg

20. TV-Anytime Forum, http://www.tv-anytime.org/

21. MPEG-21 Multimedia Framework, http://www.cselt.it/mpeg-21_pdtr.zip

22. NewsML, http://www.newsml.org

23. Artale, A., Franconi, E.: A temporal description logic for reasoning about actions and plans. Journal of Artificial Intelligence Research 9, 463–506 (1998)

24. Chen, J.Y., Li, Y.H., Lao, S.Y., et al.: Detection of Scoring Event in Soccer Video for Highlight Generation. Technical Report, National University of Defense Technology (2004)

25. Pan, H., van Beek, P., Sezan, M.I.: Detection of Slow-motion Replay Segments in Sports Video for Highlights Generation. In: Proceedings of IEEE International Conference on Acoustic, Speech and Signal Processing (ICASSP 2001), Salt Lake City, UT, USA (May 2001)

26. Liang, B., Yanli, H., Songyang, L., Jianyun, C., Lingda, W.: Feature Analysis and Extraction for Audio Automatic Classification. In: IEEE SMC 2005, Hawaii USA, October 10-12 (2005)

27. Zhou, W., Dao, S., Jay Kuo, C.-C.: On-line knowledge and rule-based video classification system for video indexing and dissemination. Information Systems 27(8), 559–586 (2002)

28. Lao, S.Y., Smeaton, A.F., Jones, G.J.F., Lee, H.: A Query Description Model Based on Basic Semantic Unit Composite Petri-Nets for Soccer Video Analysis. In: Proceedings of ACM MIR 2004, New York, USA, October 15-16 (2004)

Trajectory Annotation and Retrieval Based on Semantics

Miyoung Cho[1], Chang Choi[1], Junho Choi[2], Hongryoul Yi[1], and Pankoo Kim[3]

[1] Dept. of Computer Science and Engineering, Chosun University
375 Seosuk-dong Dong-Ku Gwangju 501-759 Korea
irune@chosun.ac.kr, enduranceaura@gmail.com,
yihongryoul@hotmail.com
[2] Culture Technology Institute, Chosun University, Korea
spica@chosun.ac.kr
[3] Corresponding author, Dept. of CSE, Chosun University, Korea
pkkim@chosun.ac.kr

Abstract. Recently, the rapid increase of the available amount of multimedia information has revealed an urgent need for developing intelligent methods for understanding and managing information. There are many features such as color, shape, texture and motion for semantic information in video data. Especially, the most important semantic information is based on a trajectory which is the significant factor for event representation of objects in video. In this paper, we focus on semantic representation using topological and directional relations between non-moving and moving objects. In the experiment part, we compared retrieval results using TSR(Tangent Space Representation) with those using rules represented by the proposed model. We extend queries and motion verbs in a specific domain (not general verbs) and apply the proposed method to an automatic annotation or narration system.

1 Introduction

The recent proliferation of multimedia data necessitates the effective and efficient retrieving of multimedia data. This research not only focuses on the retrieving methods of text matching in annotated multimedia data but also on using low-level features of Audio, Video, Image such as color, sound, motion. Especially in the video research field, a variety of compound multimedia features have been exploited.

There are two approaches[2] that relate to the indexing and retrieving of video data. The first approach is by using the visual features of video objects such as color, shape and texture, and auditory features such as audio and music. The other one is by exploiting the spatio-temporal features of objects to represent, index and retrieve the video data. In the former area, there has been a lot of research on some specific video data, such as soccer and billiard video. but it is impossible to generalize the visual and auditory features, for every video differs with each other; In the latter, however, temporal relation, topological relation and directional relation of the moving object in the video are able to acquire and use it for making a definition of semantics for a moving object. Therefore, in this paper, it will specify how to give definitions to the motions

N. Boujemaa, M. Detyniecki, and A. Nürnberger (Eds.): AMR 2007, LNCS 4918, pp. 251–264, 2008.
© Springer-Verlag Berlin Heidelberg 2008

of general moving objects by using the spatio-temporal relation, and match the definition of moving objects and motion verbs in the vocabulary.

To achieve this, first, we build a new model using topological relation and directional relation. And then we match the proposed models with the directional motion verbs proposed by Levin's verbs of Inherently directed motion. Finally, we insert terms using the synonym and antonym relations between concepts in WordNet[10] into our model. We need to measure the similarity between the proposed model and a trajectory of moving object in real video data. Steps for similarity measure are as follows: First, extract the moving object and its trajectory through preprocessing, and then compare the trajectories of moving objects with the proposed model. Because of the different features with each proposed model, finally the rules that have been generated will be applied to the similarity measurement by TSR(Tangent Space Representation). In the experiment, we evaluate semantic-based trajectory retrieval by our proposed method in real data and obtain good results.

2 Related Works

Many researchers have proposed techniques for modeling of video content. Some techniques are based on describing semantic information of objects from a cognitive point of view. Others are to represent semantic event, action, activities by spatio-temporal relationships between objects. There are two approaches listed as follows.

The first approach that uses spatio-temporal relationships for representing video semantics is proposed in [2]. In this approach, visual information is processed and represented by spatio-temporal logic. However, due to the limit of the method used in this approach, the modeling of higher-level concepts, like event and motion, are not addressed. Moreover, no method for the ranking of retrieved video data has been proposed.

The second approach for modeling depends on the semantic classification of video content. For example, the hierarchical abstraction of video expressions representing scenes and events that provides indexing and content-based retrieval mechanisms. A hierarchy consists of 'IS_A' relations and temporal relations which are based on inheritance. For example, we can apply a hierarchy to application for describing the video generated by a monitoring camera. However, they are an annotation-based system and application depending on a specific domain. So, to overcome the limitations of both approaches, we propose a new model for general application to moving objects in video and apply the proposed model to a semantic-based trajectory.

3 Proposed System

The architecture of the proposed trajectory retrieval system based on semantics is shown in the figure 1. We focus on spatio-temporal relations between moving and non-moving objects in particular. The proposed system is organized into 3parts. In the first part, the moving object modeling is used to represent semantic information by trajectory and the second part is the video preprocessing that consists of trajectory extraction and object detection. The final part is the similarity measure between trajectories for semantic-based trajectory retrieval. Specially, we retrieve semantic trajectories using TSR(Tangent Space Representation) and rules.

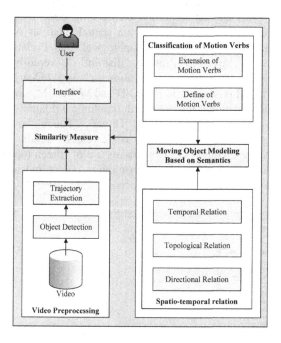

Fig. 1. The architecture of the proposed system

In the next section, we introduce 5 basic elements by topological and directional relations. We define each element as motion verbs using *Levin's verbs of Inherently directed motion*[9] and extend motion verbs through WordNet[10], as a kind of linguistic ontology. Then, we propose a new model for semantic representation of moving objects. In section 5, we describe similarity measure between trajectories. We define the rules of the modified topological relations and show the representation of the proposed directional relations by TSR. In section 6, we apply the proposed method to semantic-based trajectory retrieval. The remaining section concludes this paper.

4 The Modeling for Semantic Annotation

In this section, we propose modeling for semantic representation of a moving object by topological relations, and directional relations. For representation of topological relations, we changed the SMR scheme by Chang and build our model based on topological relation. Further, we describe directional relations based on TSR for measuring similarity among trajectories by object's direction. Specially, in our model, we added the velocity of a moving object however; knowledge of this is assumed, and it is not explained in detail in this paper.

4.1 Topological Relations

The trajectory of a moving object is a presentation of spatio-temporal relationship between moving objects and an important element in video indexing for content-based retrieval. There are many researches on spatial relations of moving objects. Egnehofer and Franzosa[3] proposed eight topological spatial relationships including 'equal', 'inside', 'cover', 'overlap', 'touch', 'disjoint', 'covered-by' and 'contains'. S.Y. Lee and F.J. Hsu[4] have proposed relations such as 2D C-string for the various extensions of the original representations of 2-D and W Ren, M Singh and S Singh[7] proposed to combine directional relations with topological relations by specifying six spatial relationships: 'Left', 'Right', 'Up', 'Down', 'Touch', and 'Front'. Pei-Yi Chen[8] measure velocity similarity by six possible velocity trends.

The SMR scheme by Chang et al.[5][6] makes use of fifteen topological operators to describe the spatial relationships between moving object and non-moving object and also makes a new scheme to identify objects.

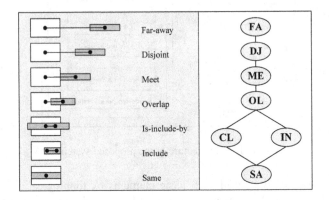

Fig. 2. Positional operators and similarity graph

The figure 2 shows positional operators and the graph that represents semantic distance among topological relations by Chang[5][6]. Modeling of topological relations is accomplished based on a neighborhood graph. However, it is not sufficient to provide a complete representation of the semantic motion based on directional relations by ignoring topological relations and describing the concept or semantics motion. Therefore, we represent the semantics of moving objects through topological relations that we make elements of motion. We also match motion verbs so that they don't have direction features in the 2D based Chang theory.

In this paper, we define *'leave'* and *'go_to'* using inclination and position by combining FA(Far-away) with DJ(Disjoint). Also, we combine CL(Include), IN(Is-include-by) and SA(Same). into *'go_into'*. *'Depart'* and *'approach'* are defined using inclination and position from the definition of ME(Meet).

The figure 3(a) illustrates basic elements of inclination and position. The inclination was classified into inward and outward for representation of moving objects. The figure 3(b) indicates 5 basic topological relations and matching motion verb to each relation. Extensional elements such as *'enter'*, *'go through'* are made through combination with basic elements.

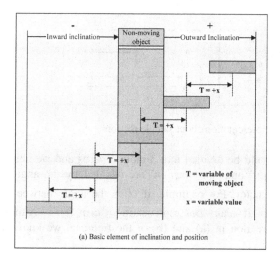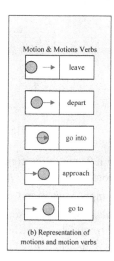

Fig. 3. The definition of basic elements

4.2 Directional Relations

Some motion states can not be distinguished based on the topological relationships that the figure 4 showed us. So, the directional relationship must be considered at the same time.

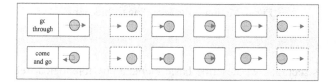

Fig. 4. Difference between *'go through'* and *'come and go'*

There have been some researches about representation of direction in video data. Among them, John Z. Li et al.[13] represented the trajectory of a moving object as eight directions – North(NT), Northwest(NW), Northeast(NE), West(WT), Southwest(SW), East(ET), Southeast(SE) and Southwest(SW). Chang and Jiang[4] proposed the 9DLT scheme to describe spatial relationships between object directions and they are indicated by nine directions from 0 to 9.

In our proposed methods, we use TSR(Tangent Space Representation) for measuring similarity between trajectories by object's direction. In the figure 6, L means a moving length of each moving object and θ is an angle between two motion vectors.

The value of θ is represented in radians. For example, if θ_1 is 45° and the radian of θ_1 is $45\pi/180$, it's radian value is about 0.785.

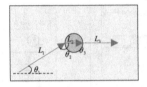 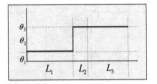

Fig. 5. TSR presentation about sample motion

The left one in the figure 6 could be divided into 3 motion verbs and we obtain 4 directions. '*Turn_left*', '*turn_right*' and '*go_through*' are decided by the angle between input vector and output vector. For example, if θ_1 is the angle between the northwest and the southwest, it can be representing '*turn_left*'. Although '*Go_through*' has a different direction in (a) and (b) of the figure 6, we know that they have the same meaning.

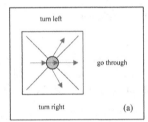 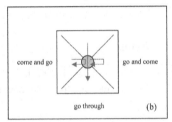

Fig. 6. Motion verbs according to directions

4.3 Modeling

In the previous sections, we describe basic elements by topological relations, directional relations and velocity for semantic representation of moving objects. Especially, we described directional relations based on TSR for measuring and storing the similarity of an object's direction. Our final goal is to provide the basis for describing high-level motion of moving objects. Base on that, we used motion verbs to describe high-level motion which are represented by natural-language terms. Although there are a lot of methods for representing knowledge, we use motion verbs for building motion ontology.

We apply our modeling which combined the topological with directional relations to represent the semantic states for the motion verbs which belong to the 51 classes by Beth Levin[9]. Especially, corresponding motions from interesting objects in semantic level are mapped directly to general concepts and they also become elemental terms so moving objects such as, moving people, car, ball and etc. are mapped to verbs.

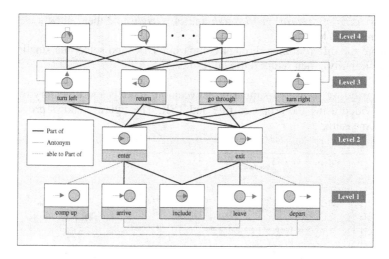

Fig. 7. Hierarchical relation modeling of moving object

The figure 7 shows hierarchical semantic relations[1] for motion verbs, in other words, motion verbs and visual information map from low-level features to the semantic-level. Our model is divided into 3 levels. The level 1 describes basic elements of motion, level 2 is the extension of basic elements and level 3 shows combination of level 2. And, we represent semantic relation between motions and motion verbs for each element. For example, *'go into'* and *'go out'* are subclasses of motion word *'go through'* which was set with 'Part_of ' relation and *'go_to'* can be inserted into *'go_through'*, it also has a relation of antonym between *'go_out'* and *'enter'*. Even if each motion verb is different in directional and spatial relations, the semantic relation is the same. Therefore, we could represent hierarchical semantic relations in our model.

However, it's difficult to distinguish semantics only using topological relations in level 3, which contains trajectories in the same topological relation. That is, we have to consider directional relations. We introduce the proposed trajectory retrieval system based on semantics in the following section. Specifically, we measure trajectory similarity using TSR.

5 Trajectory Retrieval Based on Semantics

In this section, we propose the similarity measure between annotated trajectory by our models and real trajectory for retrieval system based on semantics.

The processing of similarity measure is as follows:

1. Input the query(such as motion verb).
2. Read the trajectory coordinates about moving objects in video from files.
3. Compare trajectory coordinates and Non-moving object with our proposed rule.
4. If trajectory coordinates aren't *'come_up'*, *'arrive'*, *'depart'*, *'leave'*, *'include'*, *'is_include_by'* and 'same' by considered directional relations<?Something missing?>.
5. Calculate angle and length between trajectory coordinates in the previous frame and current frame.

6. Classify *turn_left*, *return*, *go_through* and *turn_right* and then, draw a TSR graph using angle and length.
7. Calculate the different area through comparing TSR, and select the smallest value (good similarity), then return retrieval results.

In this way, we measured similarity between our models and trajectory of moving object in video using the proposed rule and TSR. The figure 8 shows processing of similarity measure.

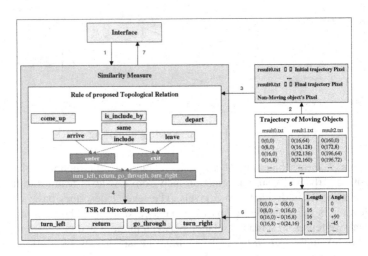

Fig. 8. Processing of similarity measure

5.1 Rule of Proposed Topological Relations

We proposed rule of topological relations for semantic representation of moving objects. If Non-moving object's pixel coordinates is NMP, Moving object's initial pixel coordinates is IP and Moving object's final pixel coordinates is FP, relation between IP and FP is IP, IP1, IP2, ..., FP. Also, IP's left coordinates is IP.left, right one is IP.right, top one is IP.top and bottom one is IP.bottom. The figure 9 shows IP's location about NMP. The abscissa increases from region 1 to region 3, the ordinates increases from region 1 to region 6 in the figure 9.

In the figure 9, we divide area adjacent to NM into 9 regions(Region NM and Region 1 ~ 8) and if there is a moving object in region 1, it has to satisfy ①ⓐ . In this way, the rule is different to IP. '*same*' is where IP, FP and NMP have the same coordinates. And, '*include*' is where IP and FP include region NM. Also '*is_include_by*' is a distribution of all regions of IP and FP. If some IP is the same NMP and IP1 ~ FP don't include region NM, it's a '*leave*' such as that shown in table 1. We also defined rules about '*come_up*', '*arrive*', and '*depart*' and so on.

In the previous section, level 2 ('*enter*', '*exit*') and level 3('*turn_left*','*turn_right*', '*go_thorugh*', '*return*') consist of a combination of level 1 so rules on motion of level 2

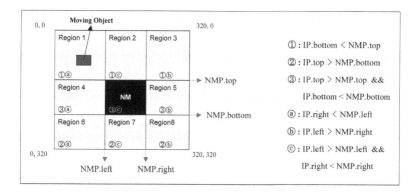

Fig. 9. IP's location about NMP

and level 3 also can represent a combination of level 1. However, we couldn't classify the level 3 only using the proposed rule by topological relations because of directional relations. Therefore, for solving this problem, we used TSR.

Table 1. Rules on '*leave*'

Motion Verb	Rules		
	Common Rules		**Particular Rules**
leave	IP1,left ~ FP.left < NMP.left IP1,right ~ FP.right > NMP.right IP1,top ~ FP.top < NMP.top IP1,bottom ~ FP.bottom < NMP.bottom IP.right >= NMP.left IP.left >= NMP.right		IP.bottom = NMP.top FP.bottom < NMP.top
			IP.top = NMP.bottom FP.top > NMP.bottom
	IP1,left ~ FP.left < NMP.left IP1,right ~ FP.right > NMP.right IP1,top ~ FP.top < NMP.top IP1,bottom ~ FP.bottom < NMP.bottom IP.top =< NMP.bottom IP.bottom >= NMP.top		IP.left = NMP.right FP.left < NMP.right
			IP.right = NMP.left FP.right > NMP.left

5.2 Rule of Proposed Directional Relations

TSR(Tangent Space Representation)[11][12] is a kind of method to measure similarity about a object's shape in two or three dimensions. Actually, polygonal shapes consist of lines and the line also contains points, so we used TSR for measuring similarity between trajectories.

In the figure 10, the left part shows sample motions about '*turn_left*'. Even if, the IP is a difference, they are the same semantic so the right figure shows the same graph about a group of '*turn_left*'. The figure 11(a) shows the real trajectory and defined semantic trajectories of our model. Where, the small rectangles are moving object and big rectangle is a non-moving object. Also, the figure 11(b) illustrates the

TSR about sample trajectory and semantic trajectories(*return, go through* and so on) in the figure 11(a).

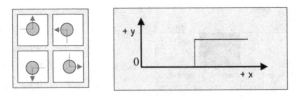

Fig. 10. Sample motions and TSR about '*turn_left*'

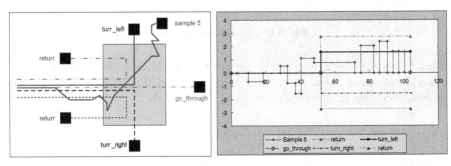

(a) sample trajectories   (b) TSR about trajectories in (a)

Fig. 11. The comparison with trajectories

We get the value after measuring similarity between trajectories(See table 2). If two trajectories are the same, the similarity between those is 0. In other words, similarity is in inverse proportion to measured value. The sample trajectory is the most similar with '*turn left*' in table 3.

Table 2. Similarity measure

	go_through	turn_left	return
Similarity	51.26031	30.4637	97.0059

6 Experiment

We experiment on semantic-based trajectory retrieval with the proposed method in real video data. And we get a sample video database containing nearly 94 video clips which are extracted trajectories from web and local device in the experiment. The Video database contains MMS stream, local device(web camera) and AVI file such as, a person entering a building, CCTV(closed-circuit television) of moving cars on the highway and so on.

6.1 Video Preprocessing

In this sub-section, we briefly mention the video preprocessing to extract trajectory of moving object, as shown in the following figure.

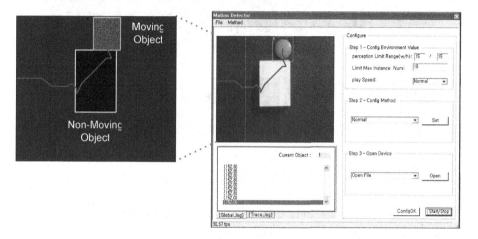

Fig. 12. Moving Object detection and it's trajectory

In the figure 12, the aura rectangle is a moving object and the red line is its trajectory. We can obtain x, y coordinates through object detection. The size of video data is 320×320 pixels. After obtaining trajectories, we simplify the real video data for the efficiency similarity measure. The table 3 is the C# code for the algorithm to extract the trajectory.

Table 3. Algorithm for extracting trajectory

```
1    g.DrawRectangle(pen, rc);
2    rem_ps.X = rc.Left;    // Object's left coordinates
3    rem_ps.Y = rc.Bottom;  // Object's bottom coordinates
4    Pen pen_center = new Pen(Color.Red, 1);  // Rectangle for Object No.
5    g.DrawImage(numbersBitmaps[n], rc.Left, rc.Top, 7, 9);  //Object No.
6    if(rem_psnum == n)  // If there is a moving object
7    { g.DrawLine(pen_center, rem_cps.X, rem_cps.Y,
8    (rc.Right+rem_ps.X)/2, (rc.Top + rem_ps.Y)/2);  } // Trajectory about moving
9 object
10    rem_cps.X=(rc.Right + rem_ps.X)/2 ;  // center of abscissa
11    rem_cps.Y=(rc.Top  + rem_ps.Y)/2;  // center of ordinate
                                    ...
```

First of all, we only retrieve trajectories with the proposed rules (We don't use directional relations). In that case, it is difficult to distinguish 'turn_left', 'go_through', 'return' and 'turn_right' because they have the same topological relations (See figure 13).

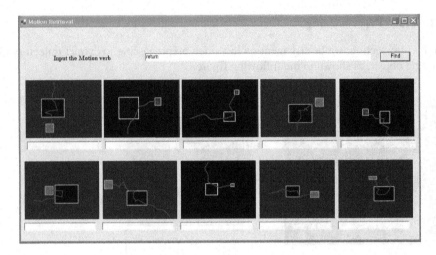

Fig. 13. The retrieval result with the proposed rules

In the case of retrieving only with TSR, we can retrieve *'turn_left'*, *'return'* and *'turn_right'*, and have directional relations. However, as shown in the figure 14, we can't distinguish some trajectories that have different semantics according to topological relations.

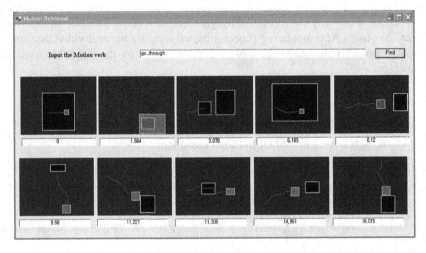

Fig. 14. The retrieval result with TSR

To solve the above problems, we experiment with the combined similarity measure of the proposed rules with TSR (See figure 15).

We evaluate the results of semantic retrieval using 3 methods by precision rate. Our results show that the combined method achieved a precision rate of 92.857% for recognizing semantics of trajectories. We transformed real video data into simple images for the efficient similarity using the coordinates of trajectories.

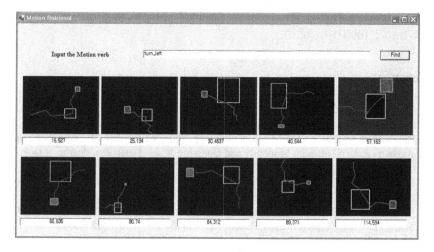

Fig. 15. The retrieval result after combing the proposed rules with TSR

Table 4. Precision rate

Method	Precision rate
The proposed rule	71.428 %
TSR	35.786 %
The proposed rule + TSR	92.857 %

As a result, there are some problems that some trajectories can't be extracted because of complicated trajectories or multi-trajectories. The size of each sample is (320, 320) pixels. It can't recognize smaller objects than that because it uses 8 pixels as the unit of pre-processing to extract trajectories of moving objects. As the main idea for extracting is the difference of color between frames, it's sensitive to illumination. Therefore, non-moving objects are extracted due to moving object and shadow. In future work, it will be solved by an improved object extraction algorithm.

7 Conclusion

We propose a trajectory retrieval system based on semantics, by combining motions with motion verbs to describe semantic relations of moving objects. In the experiment, we compare experiments using proposed rules and TSR, and find an improved result. In the future work, we will extend queries and motion verbs in a specific domain (not general verbs). We will apply the proposed method to an automatic annotation or narration system.

Acknowledgement

"This research was supported by the MIC(Ministry of Information and Communication), Korea, under the ITRC(Information Technology Research Center) support

program supervised by the IITA(Institute of Information Technology Advancement)"
(IITA-2007-C1090-0701-0040).

References

[1] Cho, M., et al.: Comparison between Motion Verbs using Similarity Measure for the Se-
    mantic Representation of Moving Object. In: Sundaram, H., Naphade, M., Smith, J.R.,
    Rui, Y. (eds.) CIVR 2006. LNCS, vol. 4071, pp. 282–290. Springer, Heidelberg (2006)

[2] Aghbari, Z.A.: Studies on Modeling and Querying Video Databases, degree of Doctorate
    of Philosophy, Kyushu University (2001)

[3] Egenhofer, M., Franzosa, R.: Point-set topological spatial relations. International Journal
    of Geographical Information Systems 5(2), 161–174 (1991)

[4] Lee, S.Y., Hsu, F.J.: Spatial reasoning and similarity retrieval of images using 2D C-
    String knowledge representation. Pattern Recognition 25(3), 305–318 (1992)

[5] Chang, J.W., Kim, Y.J., Chang, K.J.: A Spatial Match Representation Scheme for Index-
    ing and Querying in Iconic Image Databases. In: Chang, J.W., Kim, Y.J., Chang, K.J.
    (eds.) ACM International Conference on Information and Knowledge Management, No-
    vember 1997, pp. 169–176 (1997)

[6] Chang, J.-W., Kim, Y.-J.: Spatial-Match Iconic Image Retrieval with Ranking in Multi-
    media Databases. In: Proceedings of Advances in Web-Age Information Management:
    Second International Conference (July 2001)

[7] Ren, W., Singh, M., Singh, S.: Image Retrieval using Spatial Context. In: 9th Interna-
    tional Workshop on Systems, Signals and Image Processing (November 2002)

[8] Chen, P.-Y., Chen, A.L.P.: Video Retrieval Based on Video Motion Tracks of Moving
    Objects. In: Proceedings of SPIE, vol. 5307, pp. 550–558 (2003)

[9] Levin, B.: English Verb Classes and Alternations: A preliminary Investigation. The Uni-
    versity of Chicago Press (1993)

[10] http://wordnet.princeton.edu/

[11] Baek, S., Hwang, M., Cho, M., Choi, C., Kim, P.: Object Retrieval by Query with Sensi-
    bility based on the Kansei-Vocabulary Scale. In: Huang, T.S., Sebe, N., Lew, M., Pav-
    lović, V., Kölsch, M., Galata, A., Kisačanin, B. (eds.) ECCV 2006 Workshop on HCI.
    LNCS, vol. 3979, pp. 109–119. Springer, Heidelberg (2006)

[12] Hwang, M., Baek, S., Kong, H., Shin, J., Kim, W., Kim, S., Kim, P.: Adaptive-Tangent
    Space Representation for Image Retrieval based on Kansei. In: Gelbukh, A., Reyes-
    Garcia, C.A. (eds.) MICAI 2006. LNCS (LNAI), vol. 4293, pp. 828–837. Springer, Hei-
    delberg (2006)

[13] Li, J.Z., Ozsu, M.T., Szafron, D.: Modeling of Moving Objects in a Video Data-base. In:
    Proceedings of the International Conference on Multimedia Computing and Sys-tems, pp.
    336–343 (1997)

Author Index